The Definitive Guide to CentOS

Peter Membrey, Tim Verhoeven,
Ralph Angenendt

Apress®

The Definitive Guide to CentOS

Copyright © 2009 by Peter Membrey, Tim Verhoeven, Ralph Angenendt

ISBN-13 (pbk): 978-1-4302-1930-9

ISBN-13 (electronic): 978-1-4302-1931-6

Lead Editor: Michelle Lowman
Technical Reviewers: Bert de Bruijn, Karanbir Singh
Editorial Board: Clay Andres, Steve Anglin, Mark Beckner, Ewan Buckingham, Tony Campbell,
    Gary Cornell, Jonathan Gennick, Michelle Lowman, Matthew Moodie, Jeffrey Pepper,
    Frank Pohlmann, Ben Renow-Clarke, Dominic Shakeshaft, Matt Wade, Tom Welsh
Project Manager: Beth Christmas
Copy Editor: Kim Wimpsett
Associate Production Director: Kari Brooks-Copony
Production Editor: Candace English
Compositor: Lynn L'Heureux
Proofreader: April Eddy
Indexer: BIM Indexing & Proofreading Services
Artist: April Milne
Cover Designer: Kurt Krames
Manufacturing Director: Tom Debolski

Distributed to the book trade worldwide by Springer-Verlag New York, Inc., 233 Spring Street, 6th Floor, New York, NY 10013. Phone 1-800-SPRINGER, fax 201-348-4505, e-mail orders-ny@springer-sbm.com, or visit http://www.springeronline.com.

For information on translations, please contact Apress directly at 2855 Telegraph Avenue, Suite 600, Berkeley, CA 94705. Phone 510-549-5930, fax 510-549-5939, e-mail info@apress.com, or visit http://www.apress.com.

Apress and friends of ED books may be purchased in bulk for academic, corporate, or promotional use. eBook versions and licenses are also available for most titles. For more information, reference our Special Bulk Sales–eBook Licensing web page at http://www.apress.com/info/bulksales.

The source code for this book is available to readers at http://www.apress.com.

For my dear wife Sarah and xiaobao (little baby): without your unwavering support, none of this would have been possible.
—Peter Membrey

Contents at a Glance

Part 1 ■ ■ ■ Getting Started with CentOS

Part 2 ■ ■ ■ Going into Production

Part 3 ■ ■ ■ Enterprise Features

Contents

Part 1 ■■■ Getting Started with CentOS

Part 2 ▪ ▪ ▪ Going into Production

Part 3 ▪ ▪ ▪ Enterprise Features

Foreword

When I go back in time to when I bought my very first technical book (about Perl 4 programming), I had no idea what it would mean to me. Of course, I had expected to learn about Perl, but indirectly the book opened a whole new world to me. The book introduced me to Unix and taught me valuable things about operating systems in general. It taught me about filesystems and networking, about Perl modules and Perl developers, and about open source and communities.

Not only did it help me to discover all these things, but it also made clear what I didn't know. And although the book didn't go into detail about a lot of topics, the fact that it gave me a framework, a place to put newfound information and relate it to what I already knew, was more important than anything else in that book.

Over the years I realized that the book itself was not that special, except that it allowed me to start doing things with little hassle, learn from them, and build on that. And the book was excellent in building momentum, with me learning and doing in a rapid whirlpool of instant joy and eagerness for more. And although I was far from being a good Perl programmer when I finished the book, it gave me the confidence to explore without the fear of breaking things.

When you apply the examples of this book, *The Definitive Guide to CentOS*, I hope you will get the same satisfaction and build that same confidence to help others with CentOS. By reading this book and trying the examples, you become a member of the CentOS community—or, as we say, the C in CentOS. But what is so special about CentOS? Why CentOS?

Well, if you look at the different Linux distributions that exist today, CentOS has a unique appeal because it doesn't try to consist of the latest and greatest open source software (which is in itself a never-ending story); it focuses instead on being the most reliable and secure environment that is resistant to change over a seven-year lifetime. And apart from resisting change, about every 24 to 30 months a newer CentOS version pops up with newer software that is again tested for stability and goes unchanged for another seven-year time span. It is up to you to decide when to stay or move to another version at any point in time.

Those design characteristics make CentOS (and its commercial twin, Red Hat Enterprise Linux) perfect for environments where you don't want to inflict too much change, like an enterprise data center, but the same applies to, say, your office computer or your personal laptop. With CentOS you minimize the time to maintain the operating system and included software for the longest period possible. And as a benefit, you can discuss your environment with an estimated 10 million users worldwide running the same software as you do.

The CentOS project and its community are there to assist you with any problems you might encounter, and when you think the time is right, we want to help you transform from being a CentOS user to a contributing member.

For this not much is needed, other than the willingness to help others as they have helped you. If you learn something valuable, we welcome you to share it on the CentOS wiki, mailing lists, or forums. Or simply blog about your experience and interact with your peers.

The collective work of writing this book is a milestone for the CentOS community—not only because it is the first book of its kind but mostly because it is the result of a joint effort of the community; Peter Membrey, Ralph Angenendt, Tim Verhoeven, and Bert de Bruijn are contributing members of our community. I am pleased that this book is a good start to learning CentOS and an entry point to the larger worlds of Linux and open source. But most of all, I sincerely hope it does not answer all your questions but instead inspires you to question more.

Dag Wieers

Infrastructure Support and Event Advocacy

CentOS Project

About the Authors

PETER MEMBREY lives in Hong Kong and is actively promoting open source in all its various forms and guises, especially in education. He has had the honor of working for Red Hat and received his first RHCE at the tender age of 17. He is now a Chartered IT Professional and one of the world's first professionally registered ICT Technicians. Currently studying for a master's degree in IT, he hopes to study locally and earn a PhD in the not-too-distant future. He lives with his wife Sarah and is desperately trying (and sadly failing) to come to grips with Cantonese.

TIM VERHOEVEN is a Linux system administrator during the day and a core member of the CentOS Project during his free time. He has been working with Linux for more then ten years and has been involved with the CentOS Project since 2007. He is interested in all things related to enterprise Linux. He lives in Belgium and has an engineering degree in computer science.

RALPH ANGENENDT has been working as a systems and network administrator since 1998. After being introduced to Linux in 1995, Ralph's interest in non-Unix-like operating systems dropped dramatically, so his work environment mostly consists of Linux servers. Besides having a sweet tooth for domesticating mail servers, Ralph has a strong interest in automated system administration. That's the reason why the networks he is responsible for run Cfengine: to ease the pains of administrating growing sites.

Since 2006, Ralph has been a member of the CentOS development team, where he leads the documentation force and does some infrastructure management. You can probably meet him at open source conventions in Europe, largely in Germany and the Benelux countries.

About the Technical Reviewer

BERT DE BRUIJN is a freelance Linux and virtualization specialist who specializes in training and knowledge transfer on VMware and CentOS/Red Hat projects. Bert started his professional IT life on early Linux versions and commercial Unix variants such as SunOS, Solaris, and BSDi. He cofounded a local LUG chapter, helping the community get the best out of free software. Bert prefers to use his experience rather than his RHCE or LPIC-2 certification to show his Linux skills.

Acknowledgments

It's not until you actually try to write a book that you realize just how many people are involved in its creation. It goes without saying that without the support I received from Apress, this book wouldn't be here. I'd therefore like to specifically thank Michelle Lowman and Beth Christmas for their patience and tolerance going well beyond the call of duty—I hope you like the results!

I would also like to thank the CentOS community for everything they have done. Their continued hard work is what makes CentOS such a great operating system, and I really hope that this book will give something back to the community that has given me so much. Thanks to everyone at the project who has been involved in the book's development, including Karanbir Singh, Bert de Bruijn, Tim Verhoeven, Ralph Angenendt, and Dag Wieers.

I am very fortunate to be studying at the University of Liverpool, which is an experience that has completely changed my life. I would like to show my gratitude to Britt Janssen and Ranjay Ghai, who worked solidly for nearly two months on my application and whose hard work made everything possible.

Last but certainly not least, I would like to make a special acknowledgment to two people without whom I would not be where I am today. So, special thanks to Mr. David Uden and Dr. Malcolm Herbert—two people who put their trust in me many years ago and without whom I have no doubt I would be doing something very different today.

Peter Membrey

Thanks to all the people who make CentOS possible. Community, this also means you!

Ralph Angenendt

Introduction

Although CentOS has a huge number of benefits over other operating systems, we cannot escape the fact that it's also free. With virtual machines starting to replace traditional hosted services, people are finding that having their own server is not only much more flexible but also often cheaper.

But running your own server is very different from simply using a hosted service, and this is where *The Definitive Guide to CentOS* comes in. It has been written to help newcomers to the platform get up and running in production as quickly and as painlessly as possible. Each of the chapters has a specific task-oriented goal and explains how to do the majority of tasks that people are looking to do.

Just like CentOS itself, we hope to be able to improve and refine this definitive guide. We would be grateful for any and all feedback with regard to the book and how it could be improved to better suit the needs of new users. Your experiences are hard won, and we would love to hear what you have to say. After all, *The Definitive Guide to CentOS* is here to help, and who better to advise and provide feedback than the very people who have made their first steps with it?

This book will let you hit the ground running, and the CentOS community will ensure that you are able to keep in the race!

Who This Book Is For

The Definitive Guide to CentOS is for anyone who wants to build a production system with the CentOS operating system. Previous Linux administration experience is helpful but not required. We'll show you how to get started and how to build on existing knowledge.

How the Book Is Laid Out

The book is laid out in three parts. The first part explains what CentOS is, where it came from, and where it hopes to be. It also talks in some depth about enterprise Linux and why you should run it on your systems. The first part also covers installation and getting started.

The second part is the largest section and has chapters dedicated to specific topics such as setting up a web server or an e-mail server. These are all task-oriented chapters so that you can immediately start doing what you need to do. Generally speaking, these chapters can be read in any order, although it might make sense to read certain chapters before others, such as reading about DNS before trying to configure subdomains in Apache.

The third part contains more advanced topics that will be of interest to people deploying CentOS in an enterprise environment. The topics will still be of interest to many people, but the concepts are somewhat more advanced than those in the previous part and may require multiple servers and so forth.

The book was written so that you can dip in and take whatever you need from it. You can realistically read it in any order you choose and apply each chapter completely independently from the others. The idea is that it will allow you to quickly get up and running and to focus on the things you need sooner rather than later.

PART 1

Getting Started with CentOS

Part 1 of this book is where you'll start to learn the basics of CentOS. No previous Linux knowledge is assumed, because we'll take things nice and slow. You will learn about CentOS and why it's a fantastic operating system that you can trust with your most important workloads. We'll cover a step-by-step install in Chapter 2 and talk about some of the more advanced options that you can use. Chapter 3 provides a quick overview of how to log in to your new system and move around. It's not a full guide to working with CentOS, but it will get you up and running quickly. Chapter 4 covers updating CentOS and hence is critical to the health of your server.

After you've finished this part, you will be able to talk about CentOS and express why you believe CentOS is a valuable addition to your IT infrastructure. You'll be able to source CentOS and install and configure it. You will also know your way around the system and will know how to update your system.

If you're already somewhat familiar with Linux, then feel free to skip to the chapter that interests you most. However, it would be worth reading through this first chapter if you're not familiar with CentOS.

CHAPTER 1

■■■

Introducing CentOS

The CentOS (short for Community ENTerprise Operating System) Linux distribution is an enterprise-grade, freely available, open source operating system that is derived from the source code of Red Hat Enterprise Linux (RHEL) and developed and maintained by the CentOS Project. The CentOS Project is about more than just a Linux distribution. The project's members are working to provide support, training materials, and, in the future, even certification. Although at its core the project is the CentOS distribution, the CentOS Project encompasses a whole ecosystem of software, developers, and projects. This book focuses on the official CentOS distribution.

Note CentOS is built from the source code that Red Hat makes available at `ftp://mirrors.kernel.org/redhat/redhat/linux/enterprise`. This software has been released under the General Public License (GPL), and the CentOS Project uses this software to build the CentOS distribution. The CentOS Project is not affiliated with, sponsored by, or supported by Red Hat in any way.

CentOS is used around the world by people who need a robust and reliable platform to deploy their applications and services. Although support options are available, CentOS is best suited to those who do not need or want commercial support. When you have commercial support, it usually means that you can pick up the phone and speak to someone or submit a request via a web site. Because you've paid for the service, you can expect your problem to be resolved in a reasonable amount of time. If you already have your own in-house expertise or know people who can help you if you get stuck, you probably don't want to have to pay for support, often at significant expense. But if you prefer to have commercial support available, there are companies that do provide it. A list of companies approved by the CentOS Project is currently being worked on and when complete will be viewable on the CentOS web site (`http://www.centos.org/`).

Before you can really appreciate what CentOS can do for you, you need to explore enterprise Linux (EL) in a bit more depth.

It is common for newcomers to Linux to set up servers using "consumer-grade" Linux distributions such as Fedora and Ubuntu Desktop. Although these distributions make great desktops, they're not the ideal choice for a production server because the software versions change on a regular basis. Enterprise Linux distributions such as CentOS maintain specific software versions over an extended period of time, which helps to ensure that you don't have any nasty surprises (see the "Extended Support" section).

Examples of enterprise Linux are Red Hat Enterprise Linux, SUSE Linux Enterprise Server, Ubuntu LTS, and CentOS. Examples of consumer Linux are Fedora, Ubuntu, OpenSUSE, Gentoo, and Debian.

In this chapter, we'll discuss why you should use enterprise Linux on your servers (and possibly even your workstations) and how CentOS can provide a brilliant, enterprise-grade environment for you to deploy your critical services.

What Is Enterprise Linux?

Enterprise Linux has gained an awful lot of attention recently—for very good reason. Linux has a reputation for being updated and improved at an amazingly fast rate. Conventional wisdom would suggest that this is a good thing. After all, it means you're getting better software, and that can't be a bad thing, can it? Actually, it can, and this is one of the key areas that enterprise Linux looks to resolve.

Imagine for a moment you have developed a popular web site. You are making loads of money, and the customers keep on coming. You hear about a dangerous exploit going around, so you decide to update your server, at which point everything goes wrong. You discover that the new version of the programming language you used to write your application won't work with your application, so you're going to need to make extensive changes to fix it. Not only that, but the database server has been updated as well—only it can't read the old data because the file format has changed in the new version!

An enterprise Linux distribution aims to provide a robust, stable, and reliable platform on which users can deploy their applications. It provides a platform where the previous scenario cannot happen and where you can update as often as you like, safe in the knowledge that your software isn't going to break.

Extended Support

Extended support is probably one of the most important parts of an enterprise Linux distribution, and care must be taken not to confuse it with commercial support. *Commercial support* is the ability to pay someone to provide you with assistance. *Extended support* is where a vendor (in this case the CentOS Project) undertakes the maintenance of a product over an extended period of time. Normally, open source life cycles are very short. For example, the Fedora Project stops releasing updates after about two years. After the two years are up, you have little choice but to upgrade to the next release or live without vital security updates. Assuming that you want to keep your server safe and secure, you will have to upgrade your machine. This may not sound like much of a problem, but Fedora has a six-month release cycle, which means after updating your server for two years, you suddenly have to jump four releases to have a secure server.

There are two big problems with doing this. First, it's unlikely there is a safe and easy upgrade path. Usually (but not always), it's possible to upgrade directly from one release to the next. It's even possible (though riskier) to update to a release two versions ahead. However, trying to jump four versions is asking for trouble, and even if the upgrade seems to work without a hitch, you may find some strange behavior that you can't quite explain.

The second problem is that the software versions on the new release are going to be significantly different from the versions you are currently running. If your server is in production (that is, doing something useful and important), you want it to keep running after the upgrade, and you want as little downtime as possible. It's quite possible, however, that you will find that the new versions of the software you've just upgraded to don't like your old configuration files. This means you'll have to rewrite and test them. Sometimes this isn't a big deal. Other times it can cause many hours of downtime.

Enterprise Linux platforms usually combat these two key issues by releasing new stable versions every couple of years or so. These platforms have significantly longer support periods, ranging on average between five and seven years. This is very important because it gives you plenty of opportunity to update and test new releases.

Low-Risk Security Updates

Enterprise Linux also comes with low-risk security updates. These are updates that are designed to fix a specific issue without making large, sweeping changes to a software application. This is very important in production environments where you need to ensure that your servers are protected against the latest threats and that applying a particular update is not going to adversely affect your machine. Microsoft's Windows Server 2003 had a particularly nasty issue when installing Service Pack 2 (SP2). After installation and the subsequent reboot, Windows would automatically turn on the firewall. This meant that if you were updating the server using Remote Desktop, you'd suddenly find yourself unable to reconnect to the server, and all of the services it was offering would then be blocked. Although this isn't a major issue if the server room is down the hall, if you host in a remote data center, then fixing this problem can be very time-consuming and expensive.

Most updates on enterprise Linux do not require reboots. Generally speaking, a reboot is required only when updating the kernel. This ensures that your server remains up and running without unwanted interruptions. Of course, at some point, you should apply the kernel updates by performing a reboot, but the important difference here is that you will be able to choose when this is done rather than the "all or nothing" options provided by other operating systems.

ABI/API Stability

Application binary interface (ABI) and application programming interface (API) stability is often underrated, but it's especially important for third-party applications. Enterprise Linux guarantees that during a given release, neither the ABI nor the API will change. This means that software that will run on the platform when it is first released will continue to run at the end of its life.

Consumer-grade Linux generally comes with a wealth of software. As long as you use this software, everything will be fine—as one application updates, the supporting applications will also be updated. This breaks down, however, when you are using a custom application that expects a certain library. After an update, if that library version changes, your application will probably break. The vendor may not have an updated package available, and the source code may not be available for you to recompile even if you're comfortable doing that. Basically, it's not a good idea to rely on software that can change at any time.

Freezing the ABI and API ensures that you don't have to worry about this. When security flaws are found in a particular piece of software, rather than simply replacing that software with a new version (the cause of breaking your third-party application), enterprise Linux distributions instead back-port the security fix into the current version. This ensures that your software won't notice the difference, and it also gives you all the security benefits of running the latest version.

There is a downside, however. Because software versions are not updated, various automated security audit solutions get confused and report security issues where there aren't any. For example, it is common for businesses to pay to have their web servers audited. It would not be appropriate or feasible, however, for these tools to actually try to break into the server. Instead, they tend to look at the version numbers of the software you're running. Because enterprise Linux does not update the version numbers, these tools often generate a huge list of security vulnerabilities that apply to that version of the software. Unfortunately, there is no way for these automated tools to know that all the issues they've raised are actually patched already and the threat is effectively imagined. Happily, though, it is fairly easy to check the history of a particular application to ensure that it is indeed immune to the attacks that have been listed.

Regular Updates and Bug Fixes

Enterprise Linux also provides regular updates and bug fixes. These are released on a regular basis and ensure that everything continues to run smoothly. By keeping to a timeline, businesses can plan when to apply updates and schedule downtime or at-risk time if need be. For home users, it might not be a problem to take a machine down in the middle of the day to perform some maintenance. However, for a company that depends on its servers being available, having a release schedule can be very reassuring.

In CentOS, these regular updates are referred to as *point releases* after the way the different versions are named, in other words, "five point two." They are released approximately every six months, and this is where additional functionality or new technologies are introduced to the distribution. Changes are never made in between point releases.

Certification

Enterprise Linux is also certified to run on certain types of hardware, to run certain software applications, and to be used in certain environments. Certification helps give users confidence that the operating system will work as advertised. Many hardware vendors such as Dell and HP ensure that their hardware is certified for popular enterprise Linux distributions. For end users who want to run a particular distribution, it's an easy way to distinguish hardware that is known to work without problems.

Software vendors such as Oracle and IBM certify their products for much the same reasons. Oracle 11*g* is certified for use on both RHEL 4 and RHEL 5. The same is true for IBM's DB2 9.5. Software certifications are important because they show that a particular piece of software not only works but works well enough to pass rigorous testing. If software is certified for your platform, you can be assured that it's going to perform the way you expect.

Because CentOS maintains binary compatibility with Red Hat Enterprise Linux, it is safe to assume that any certified hardware or software will run on CentOS equally well. Unfortunately, the vendor may not see it that way, and even though its products will work perfectly well, the vendor may not be willing to provide support. If your choice of software is at least partly based on the support the vendor will be providing, you should double-check that you're still covered on your chosen platform.

Summary of Enterprise Linux's Benefits

In conclusion, enterprise Linux attempts to provide a platform that is based on stable software, will be updated and supported for an extended period of time, won't change software versions in the middle of a release, and has low-risk security updates. For these reasons, enterprise Linux is far better suited for production servers than consumer-grade solutions.

What Is CentOS?

Because this is a book on CentOS, you're probably wondering how we've managed to get this far through Chapter 1 without actually talking about it. What makes CentOS such a fantastic choice for your next server can only be truly appreciated when you know what enterprise Linux can do for you.

CentOS is rebuilt from another enterprise Linux platform, Red Hat Enterprise Linux. RHEL is free—"free" as in speech but not as in beer. In other words, when Red Hat provides the software to a subscriber, it must also include the source code. The subscriber can alter that source code and use it in any way she sees fit. So although the subscriber has the freedom to use and modify the software, it doesn't necessarily follow that she won't have to pay for it. If she were to improve on the software and wanted to sell her new version, she could do so, but she would also have to include the source code, if requested, and in most cases under the same license. Because of this, free software helps ensure that when software is improved, those benefits are passed on and not held by a single company or person.

In addition, to download RHEL, you need to have an active RHEL subscription, which is not cheap.

Note Software licenses (especially those claiming to be "free" or "open source") can become very confusing very fast. The GPL, for example, requires you to release any modifications to a program under the same license. The Berkeley Software Distribution (BSD) license, on the other hand, makes no such requirement. To add to the confusion, some projects create their own licenses that profess to be free software but aren't recognize as such by the Free Software Foundation. If you're finding this a little overwhelming, you are not alone! For a detailed list and explanation of the various licenses, take a look at the Free Software Foundation's web site at `http://www.fsf.org/licensing/licenses/index_html`.

Because Red Hat Enterprise Linux is based entirely on open source software, Red Hat is obliged to release all of the source code to anyone who has a subscription. Red Hat takes this another step further and makes its source code available to anyone. Although the source code is freely available, Red Hat uses trademark protection laws to prevent people from building their own versions of RHEL and then distributing them. CentOS complies fully with Red Hat's policy on distribution, and the CentOS Project spends considerable time and effort removing all Red Hat logos and trademarks. Once done, the software is rebranded as *CentOS* and then compiled.

CentOS is made available at no charge and is freely downloadable from the CentOS web site. Although the initial packages come from Red Hat, it takes a lot of work to update and maintain CentOS. The CentOS Project consists of volunteers who perform these rebuilds, test updates, and provide support.

Because of their shared heritage, CentOS and RHEL have a lot in common. New versions of RHEL are released every 18–24 months (although usually it's closer to 24 than 18). New CentOS releases tend to trail about a month behind the RHEL release date because the CentOS Project has to do all of the rebuild and testing work. Minor updates are released every six months or so, and these include all the updates from the initial release, additional hardware support, and any new technology or feature enhancements. The 5.3 point release, for example, adds support for encrypted filesystems. Security updates are released throughout the life of the release as and when they're available. Both CentOS and RHEL are supported for seven years from their initial release dates.

Although both operating systems share the same core values, some features are available in one that aren't available in the other. First we'll look at what CentOS can offer over RHEL, and then we'll cover where RHEL scores over CentOS.

The current version of RHEL has two server distributions: Red Hat Enterprise Linux and Red Hat Enterprise Linux Advanced Platform (RHEL AP). RHEL is identical to RHEL AP software-wise and differs only in cost and support options. RHEL, for example, supports only up to two sockets (in other words, physical processors) and allows for four virtual guests. A virtual guest is a Xen-based virtual machine that can run another completely independent RHEL server. A RHEL license will cover both the main operating system and the four RHEL virtual guests, saving a considerable amount in license fees. RHEL AP, on the other hand, has no restrictions on sockets or virtual guests. RHEL AP also ships with "storage virtualization and high availability capabilities" (Red Hat Global File System and Cluster Suite), which RHEL lacks.

There is also a desktop version of RHEL called (somewhat predictably) RHEL-Desktop. This product is aimed more at corporate desktops than for home users and provides a robust platform for people to use on a daily basis.

CentOS, however, provides all of these features in a single product, so there aren't different "flavors" of CentOS. CentOS is built like RHEL AP and does not place any limitations on what hardware configurations are supported. Whereas with RHEL 5.0 Red Hat started using installation numbers to ensure that customers would be able to install only the software that they had purchased support for, happily CentOS does not use installation keys, and some of the more advanced components (such as virtualization and cluster storage) are easily installed by simply selecting the relevant box.

CentOS also boasts a very strong worldwide community of more than 6 million systems installed. Because many of the mirrors used by the CentOS Project are donated by third parties, no exact download numbers are currently available. Many systems are installed from the same disc and many companies set up their own local repositories for updates, so it is thought that there are considerably more CentOS systems out there than estimated.

This community actively maintains and contributes to a wiki and mailing lists and provides support on IRC. The wiki contains vast amounts of useful information about CentOS, including details on the core team members, the purpose behind CentOS, frequently asked questions, and how-tos, among other things. The wiki should probably be your first stop when you look for help with CentOS. Specific mailing lists (you can find a complete list at http://lists.centos.org) provide coverage of a wide variety of topics such as development, promotion, documentation, and announcements.

For real-time support, there are a two channels on the Freenode IRC network that you can join. #CentOS is the main CentOS channel and is where the majority of support takes place. Anything not directly related to this should be discussed in #CentOS-Social, where anything can be discussed. The people in #CentOS will do their best to help you, but remember that they are volunteers; they have their own lives to live and have no obligation to help you. Help them help you by providing well-thought-out questions with lots of information. Generally speaking, the more information you can give about your issue, the greater chance you'll have of getting a reply.

One of the key goals of the CentOS Project is to maintain binary compatibility with RHEL. This isn't too difficult, because CentOS is rebuilt from RHEL's source RPMs. For a lot of users, though, RHEL compatibility is not actually very important if, for example, they are just looking for a solid enterprise system rather than a Red Hat "clone." Of greater interest is using additional software that doesn't ship with RHEL. Red Hat does not support third-party software. This in turn means that companies that need full Red Hat support are restricted to what Red Hat offers.

CentOS has some additional repositories of software available. These provide a great deal of flexibility, and it is up to users to decide which path they want to take. The CentOS Plus repository contains packages that replace the original packages that were rebuilt from RHEL's source code. This breaks binary compatibility, but it does mean you can get your hands on newer software that would otherwise be unavailable. The CentOS Extras repository contains packages that are used in addition to the original packages. Using this repository won't break binary compatibility, because it won't update any of the original packages. However, solutions that depend on these packages won't be able to run on a vanilla RHEL install. To be fair, this is rarely an issue and should not dissuade anyone from using the packages.

Enabling additional repositories affects how your CentOS install will work. The majority of the issues around doing this come down to support and compatibility with RHEL. For most users, these issues aren't relevant, but it is important to understand what the consequences are of using these extra packages.

Of course, there are some downsides when using CentOS over RHEL. CentOS as a community project cannot provide the same levels of support that a commercial entity such as Red Hat can. There are third-party companies that offer CentOS support, and the CentOS community itself does a fantastic job, but even then, it cannot match what Red Hat is offering. On the other hand, a RHEL subscription can cost more than $2,400!

Because CentOS maintains binary compatibility with RHEL, it follows that CentOS must receive the RHEL updates before CentOS updates can be built. This in turn means that there is a slight delay between the time the updates are made available for Red Hat customers and when the updates become available to CentOS users. For the most part, these delays are not significant, and although the CentOS Project has a target window of 72 hours, updates are normally pushed out well within 24 hours. Minor releases lag about four weeks behind the initial Red Hat releases. This is useful only for new installs and doesn't affect the updates received for machines that are already up and running. Unless you need new hardware support, installing a machine with CentOS 5 and doing a full update is equivalent to installing CentOS 5.2 and doing a full update. Obviously, the update from CentOS 5 will take longer, but the end result will be the same.

As a side effect of CentOS being built on RHEL's source code, the CentOS Project cannot directly fix problems within the main distribution. The CentOS Project does have the means to push out important fixes, however, and this was highlighted recently when a performance issue in Perl was fixed in CentOS a few weeks before it was fixed in RHEL. Although the CentOS Project can, of course, submit bugs and supply patches "upstream" to Red Hat, the members have no control over whether the bug will be fixed. This is one of the sacrifices that must be made in order to ensure full binary compatibility.

CentOS doesn't have all the hardware and software certifications that are available on RHEL. Vendors spend considerable amounts of money to have their wares tested and approved. However, although officially CentOS isn't certified because it is built from RHEL sources, anything that runs RHEL can run CentOS equally well. This means that even though vendors may not openly state that their kit is certified for CentOS, if it is certified on RHEL, it will work fine.

In response to the intellectual property (IP) infringement issues raised a few years ago by SCO, Red Hat put into place an indemnification program. This stated that should there be any problems found relating to IP in Red Hat Enterprise Linux, Red Hat would sort out the problem. This means Red Hat will either secure the rights to use the IP or remove the offending code and replace it with fresh code that does not infringe the IP. This gives companies an iron-clad safety net so that they can use RHEL without fear of being targeted for IP infringement. CentOS as a community project does not offer such a guarantee. For most people, this is a nonissue anyway. However, if this protection is important to you or your company, it's a good idea to read up on what protection Red Hat can offer.

Remember that CentOS is an enterprise Linux distribution. This means it is designed for stability and reliability. It does not support the latest and greatest hardware, and it rarely contains bleeding-edge software either. If your hardware is supported and CentOS provides the software you need on a daily basis, you will find CentOS to be the ideal distribution for a desktop machine as well as a server. You will have long-term support, and you won't have to install 100 new packages every other day.

How to Read This Book

This book is divided into three parts. Part 1 covers the very basics, such as getting hold of CentOS, installing it, and then finding your way around it. This is where you should start if you're new to Linux, because these chapters won't make any assumptions about prior Linux knowledge. Part 2 is about taking your new server into production. You don't need to read these chapters in order, and you can go straight to the chapter you need to get started. Part 3 covers how to perform some higher-level tasks with CentOS, normally what you might need in a data center or an enterprise environment. We'll be covering high availability, core builds, and how to package your own RPMs for distribution.

Let's get started!

CHAPTER 2

■ ■ ■

Installing CentOS

CentOS is very easy to install, and for the vast majority of users, the default settings will work very well. At this stage, especially if you're new to Linux, some options might not be obvious, and certain features (such as software RAID) might not be applicable to you. We're also conscious that for many readers CentOS will already be installed and running. So, in this chapter, first we're going to go through a plain-vanilla install without any of the interesting bits. This will get you up and running in the shortest time possible and will allow you to then jump ahead to any of the later chapters that interest you.

Of course, we also want to give a good deal of coverage to the installer itself. Some users will certainly want to use software RAID, disable IPv6, or securely erase their hard disks before they start the install. We'll cover these features after we've done the basic install. This will let you go directly to the topic of interest without having to read through how to install every option that CentOS has to offer.

Note We'll be concentrating on the most current version of CentOS (at the time of writing, Centos 5.2). The install procedure is somewhat similar for older versions of CentOS; however, because this book is for people new to the platform, it's most likely that you'll want CentOS 5. Manuals and installation instructions for older versions are available on the CentOS web site at http://www.centos.org.

Hardware Requirements

CentOS 5 is currently supported only on i386 (32-bit Pentium and AMD) and x86_64 (EM64T and AMD64) hardware. Support is expected in the future for ia64 (Itanium), PPC (IBM Power and pre-Intel Mac), and SPARC (Sun) systems. You can even install CentOS on an IBM s/390 mainframe if you happen to have one handy. You can find an in-depth hardware compatibility list at https://hardware.redhat.com/.

■**Note** Red Hat provides only a 64-bit PPC version of Red Hat Enterprise Linux and doesn't support SPARC hardware, but the CentOS Project is planning to rebuild CentOS so that it runs on 32-bit PPC processors and SPARC hardware. Because there is no direct upstream support for these platforms, these will be variants based on Red Hat Enterprise Linux rather than the 100 percent compatible versions that are based on the platforms that Red Hat supports.

The minimum install requirements for CentOS are surprisingly modest. A text-only install can be completed with as little as 128MB of RAM. Depending on your needs, this could potentially be a perfectly capable production server. The CentOS Project provides a list of tested minimum requirements for an install, but for the majority of production uses, you will want something a bit beefier. The requirements (which you can also find at http://centos.org/product.html) are as follows:

- i386 or x86-64 processor

- 128MB of RAM for text install on i386 (all others are 512MB)

- 1.2GB of disk space

CentOS will install on pretty much any commodity hardware (including virtual environments such as VMware and Virtual Box). However, as an enterprise-grade distribution, CentOS does not have the latest and greatest hardware support, although each point release does add better hardware support, including back-ported drivers. The easiest way to tell whether CentOS is supported is simply to install it or try the LiveCD. However, if you are purchasing hardware specifically for CentOS, please visit the Hardware Certification List and research any hardware choices first.

Getting CentOS

There are few ways to get your hands on the latest CentOS release. Although most people will want to download it from one of the CentOS mirror sites, you can also buy an official CD set or DVD from various vendors. For a list of CentOS-approved vendors, see http://www.centos.org/vendors. These vendors support the CentOS Project by making a donation for every set sold, so please consider buying from these vendors.

To download the images, visit http://www.centos.org/mirrors-list. This page lists North American mirrors by default, but you can select from various regional mirrors if they are closer to you. This page will also show you which servers offer a direct download link for the DVD image. We're assuming you're using the DVD during this install guide, so make sure you pick a mirror that hosts the DVD.

Once you've selected your mirror, you'll need to pick the version of CentOS that you want to install. There will be directories for individual versions, but those without a point in the name always go to the latest version. Currently, 5 goes to 5.2, but when the next point release is released, 5 will then go to 5.3.

You should then go into the isos directory. You'll need to decide which architecture you want to download—either 32-bit or 64-bit. Although a 32-bit release will run without problems on a 64-bit machine, the reverse is not possible. If you're in any doubt, download the 32-bit (i386) version for now.

■**Note** For most purposes it doesn't matter which architecture you install. Generally speaking, the main benefits of the x86-64 version are that it can support large amounts of memory (more than 4GB) and that under certain workloads it has better performance. For most people, however, the i386 version is the still the version of choice (see Figure 2-1).

The easiest install media is without a doubt the DVD image. This contains all the software in the CD set with the added bonus that you don't need to swap CDs during the install.

The CD set is very useful when you don't have access to a DVD-ROM such as on an older server or if you don't have a DVD writer handy to burn the DVD image. In fact, because of the large amount of software that is available as part of the standard CentOS distribution, it can be somewhat difficult to work out which CDs are needed in advance. If you're going to use the CD set, make sure you download and burn all six images just in case.

It's worth noting that you can also download the netinstall image. This is a bare-bones image that contains just enough software to start the install process. The actual installer and package library are then pulled from the network.

The LiveCD provides a full desktop working environment and comes complete with the OpenOffice.org suite, Firefox web browser, Thunderbird mail client, and the Gaim instant messaging client, among others. It's not only a great way to try CentOS as a desktop replacement, but it also makes a great restore and rescue disc (although a dedicated rescue system is currently being developed by the CentOS Project).

The mirrors also include tracker files for BitTorrent. This can provide faster downloads than directly downloading the images from the mirror. As with all torrents, though, the download speed depends on how many other people are sharing the files.

Last but not least, you can download the MD5 and SHA1 hashes. When new images are released, the CentOS Project generates hashes for all the new files. When you download the images, they should have the same hash as the one posted to the web site. We'll cover how to do this on Mac and Windows machines later in this chapter. You should be perfectly safe if you download the images from an official CentOS mirror; however, as a best practice, you should also check that the checksums are valid.

Index of /centos/5/isos/i386

Name	Last modified	Size	Description
◄ Parent Directory		-	
❓ CentOS-5.2-i386-LiveCD.iso	28-Jun-2008 12:19	697M	
❓ CentOS-5.2-i386-bin-1of6.iso	19-Jun-2008 12:13	624M	
❓ CentOS-5.2-i386-bin-1to6.torrent	20-Jun-2008 09:58	299K	
❓ CentOS-5.2-i386-bin-2of6.iso	19-Jun-2008 12:15	636M	
❓ CentOS-5.2-i386-bin-3of6.iso	19-Jun-2008 12:17	634M	
❓ CentOS-5.2-i386-bin-4of6.iso	19-Jun-2008 12:19	636M	
❓ CentOS-5.2-i386-bin-5of6.iso	19-Jun-2008 12:20	637M	
❓ CentOS-5.2-i386-bin-6of6.iso	19-Jun-2008 12:22	652M	
❓ CentOS-5.2-i386-bin-DVD.iso	19-Jun-2008 10:24	3.7G	
❓ CentOS-5.2-i386-bin-DVD.torrent	20-Jun-2008 10:01	300K	
❓ CentOS-5.2-i386-netinstall.iso	19-Jun-2008 08:05	7.7M	
❓ md5sum.livecd	16-Jul-2008 21:21	122	
📄 md5sum.livecd.asc	16-Jul-2008 21:22	358	
📄 md5sum.txt	20-Jun-2008 09:34	505	
📄 md5sum.txt.asc	20-Jun-2008 09:41	741	
❓ sha1sum.livecd	16-Jul-2008 21:23	69	
📄 sha1sum.livecd.asc	16-Jul-2008 21:23	305	
📄 sha1sum.txt	20-Jun-2008 09:35	569	
📄 sha1sum.txt.asc	20-Jun-2008 09:41	805	

Apache Server at linux.mirrors.es.net Port 80

Figure 2-1. *Mirror file listing*

Checking the Checksums

When the CentOS Project releases files for public download, they generate a checksum. Two types of checksum are generated: MD5 and SHA1. MD5 remains the most popular in use on the Internet today, although SHA1 is catching up fast. You should use SHA1 if possible because it is more accurate and hence recommended over MD5. You can verify the checksums on Windows with numerous free tools (such as the one at `http://www.fastsum.com/`). If you're using Mac OS X, you can verify the checksum with the built-in command-line tool `md5` or `sha1`. On Linux you can use `md5sum` or `sha1sum`.

Burning the ISOs

Fortunately, Mac OS X comes with CD-burning tools as standard. If you insert a blank CD or DVD into your drive, it will pop up a dialog box asking you what you want to do with it. From the list, select Disk Utility. If this doesn't come up or you've already set another default, you can find Disk Utility in Applications ➤ Utilities. Once the program is running, click the Burn button (it looks like the radiation symbol). You will then be asked to select which image you want to burn to the disc. Select the CentOS image, and click OK. Mac OS X should now burn the image to the disc for you.

Unfortunately, Windows XP doesn't come with its own built-in tool for burning ISO images. A very popular tool is Nero, which you can download from `http://www.nero.com`. A free trial is available, which should give you plenty of time to burn your CentOS images. You will need to have the .NET 3.0 Framework to run Nero 9, but Nero has thoughtfully provided a direct link from its download page. By default, Nero 9 installs a *lot* of applications. To burn the ISO images, the only component you need to install is Nero Burning ROM.

Once you've downloaded and installed it, start Nero from your Start menu. After it starts, cancel the New Compilation Wizard, and select Burn Image from the Recorder menu. You'll then be asked to select the image you want to burn. Select the CentOS ISO, and then click Open. Nero will then burn the image to disc.

For Linux, my preferred tool of choice is `cdrecord`. This tool is available packaged for most distributions and can be easily installed through your platform's own installer. Normally `cdrecord` is very smart and works out the correct settings for your DVD writer. To use `cdrecord`, you can run the following command:

```
cdrecord <ISO filename>
```

Here's an example:

```
cdrecord CentOS-5.2-386-bin-DVD.iso
```

cdrecord should then find your DVD writer and burn the image. Although various graphical tools are available on Linux (such as K3b), cdrecord is really easy to use and can be run without having to install any extra dependencies.

Performing a Super-Quick CentOS Install

For our super-quick CentOS install, we'll assume that you're installing from the DVD image. This doesn't make any real difference apart from the disc swapping during the actual install stage.

First you need to boot from DVD. Depending on your machine, this may already be the default. If not, on newer machines, an option is often displayed during the memory check stage (POST) to boot from a different device. Click this button, and select the option for the DVD drive. This might be displayed as "removable media," or it might actually list your DVD drive by name. BIOSs tend to vary on how they display device names, but it should be fairly obvious from what is offered. If your hardware is a bit older, you may need to go into the BIOS itself and change the boot order. If you do have to change the boot order, it's a good idea to change it back once you're done. There's usually a section in the BIOS on boot order or boot priority. Because each BIOS is different, we can't provide exact instructions here, but a quick look at the manual (assuming you didn't toss it, of course) or Google should help you out.

Once you have booted from the DVD, you'll get a nice CentOS screen displaying the two basic install options: graphical or text (see Figure 2-2). Generally speaking, you want to do the graphical-based install because it is considerably easier to work with and has some options that aren't available in a text install. Having said that, a text install is quite useful if you have a machine with limited amounts of RAM or there are issues with your graphics card. Because we're just stepping through a quick install to start with, simply press Enter to start the default option (which happens to be the graphical installer). If you want to use the text-based installer, you can start it by typing linux text instead.

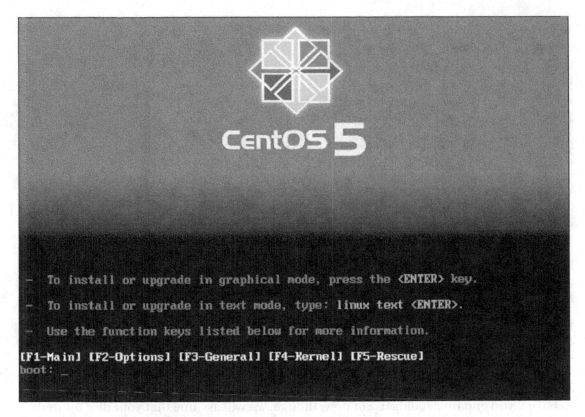

Figure 2-2. *CentOS boot screen*

After a short wait, you'll see the media check screen (see Figure 2-3). The idea here is that you can feed CentOS all of your discs, and it will check to make sure that the check-sums match. This is mainly to ensure that your media isn't going to fail halfway through an install and leave you with a broken machine. This is not a big deal on a test server, but it can be rather upsetting if you've just traveled 100 miles to the data center to do an urgent install only to find that you're not going to be able to, especially if you find out halfway through because the installer tells you that your disc has errors!

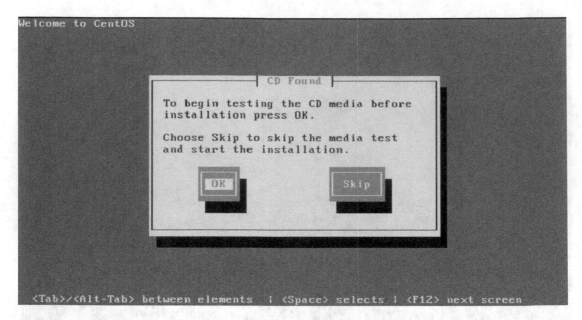

Figure 2-3. *Media check*

Generally speaking, your disc is likely to be fine, especially if you've just used it to install another machine. Most of the time this option is skipped, but it is a handy feature to have if you end up needing it. For now, though, we will assume that your disc burned correctly, and we'll skip the media check by pressing Tab and then Enter. If you are feeling masochistic and have some time on your hands, feel free to just press Enter.

The next screen you should see (after the graphical installer has started) is a rather empty welcome screen (see Figure 2-4). You have only two options on this page; you can either read the release notes or click Next and continue with the install. In CentOS, the release notes are only pointers to the full release notes available on the CentOS wiki at http://wiki.centos.org. Because we're on the fast track, just hit Next.

The next screen will ask you which language you want to use to install CentOS (see Figure 2-5). The language selected here will then be used throughout the rest of the installer. This doesn't mean you have to use this language after CentOS is actually installed, however. You will be able to select a range of languages later in the install process. For now, we'll stick with English. Because there's nothing else to be done on this page, select Next.

Figure 2-4. *Graphical installer start screen*

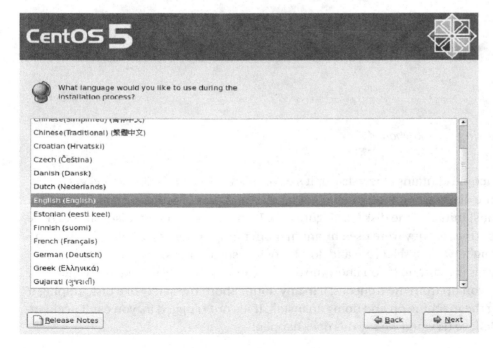

Figure 2-5. *Selecting your language*

You'll now be asked which keymap you want to use (see Figure 2-6). We prefer to select the United Kingdom keymap regardless of the actual keyboard we're using because we touch type and get easily confused when characters aren't where our fingers expect them to be. If you're not sure which keyboard you're using, then sticking with the default is probably a safe bet. Once you've selected your keyboard, click Next.

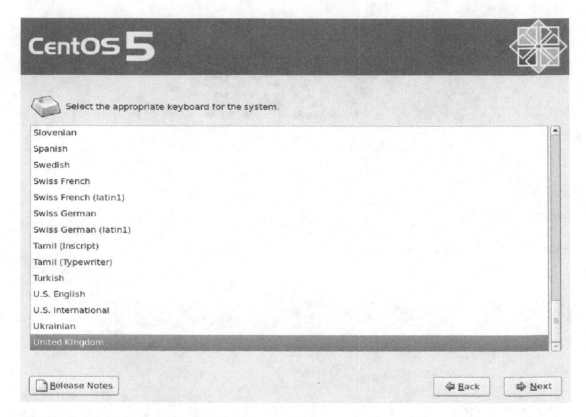

Figure 2-6. *Selecting your keyboard*

If your machine contains a new disk or it's a completely fresh install, you will get a warning that the disk partition table could not be read and that in order to create partitions the installer must initialize the disk (see Figure 2-7). If you think that your disks should have partition tables (that is, they were used by another operating system or another Linux distribution), you might want to select No and do a bit of investigation, especially if the data on any of the disks is important. If you know the disks are new or freshly erased, then click Yes. Here's a hard-won tip from the trenches: if in any doubt about the safety of a disk, unplug it before turning the machine on and doing an install. If it's not plugged in, you can't accidentally wipe it. Believe us when we say this does happen!

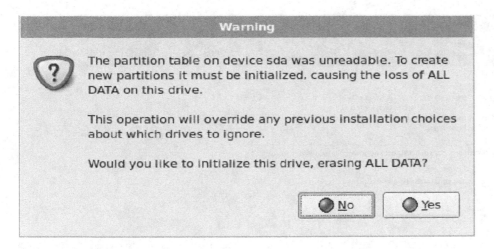

Figure 2-7. *Initialization warning*

Assuming you clicked Yes (or you weren't asked the question because the disk was already initialized), you will now be given some choices for partitioning the disks (see Figure 2-8). From the first drop-down menu, you can select how you'd like the installer to set up the disks. The default is to remove any Linux partitions and create the default layout. This is what you want if your machine is a fresh install. However, if you had a Linux distribution installed previously, you probably don't want to blitz your data partitions. If you do have important data on the disk or you don't want to remove the Linux partitions, you will need to do a custom layout. We'll cover more details about using this option later in this chapter.

You can also tell the installer to remove all partitions and create the default layout. This is the same as the default except that it will also remove any Windows partitions. If you're replacing a server and want to remove everything, this is a good bet. It's also possible to use the free space on a disk to create the default layout, or if all else fails, you can select a custom layout.

As with the previous warning about uninitialized disks, you will need to be careful about what you're wiping. The standard options are all fairly safe for setting up a dedicated server, but if you're in any doubt, now is the time to check, because recovering data after accidentally wiping the disk is practically impossible. If in doubt, unplug any disks that contain data you want to keep.

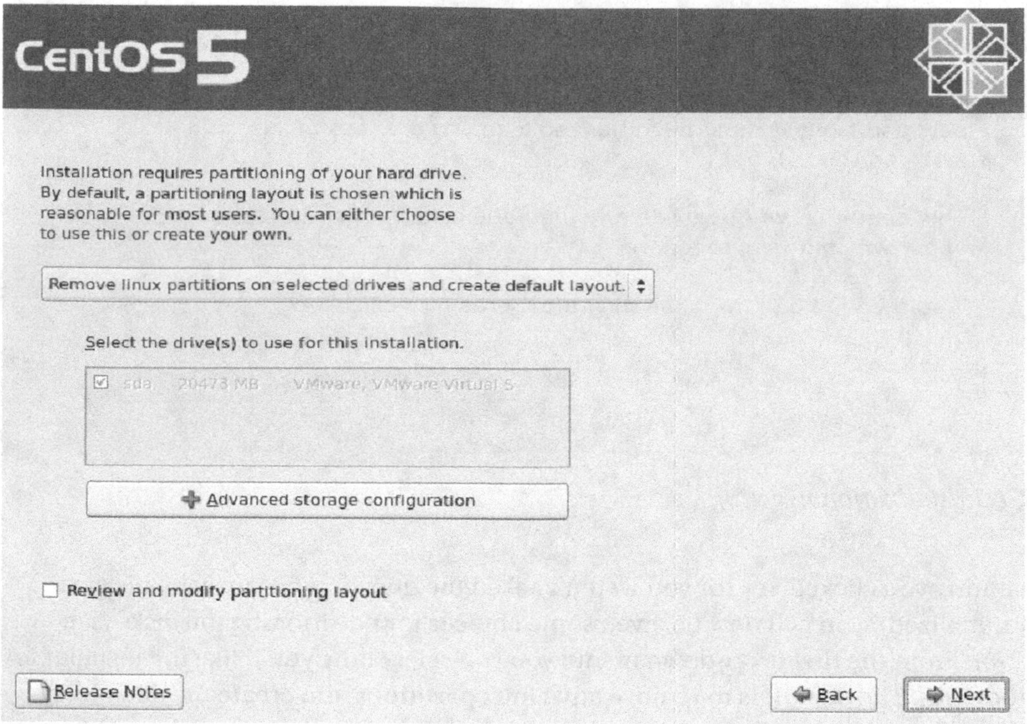

Figure 2-8. *Selecting the partitioning scheme*

You can also tell the installer which disks you want to work with. They will be shown in the order that the kernel detected them. To make things clearer, it will also tell you the size of the disk and the manufacturer. For the most part, this will help you decide which disks you need to work with. You should select only the disks that you want the install to perform the partitioning tasks on. In other words, make sure you unselect your data disks! You can also select the option "Review and modify partitioning layout" to see what exactly the installer has in mind for your disks. We talk about this again later in the "Custom Partition Layout" section when we cover the Custom Layout option.

▪**Note** Sometimes hardware information is not reported correctly. This can happen when using hardware RAID or when the hard disks are not reporting SMART data. If you can't figure out which disks are which and there is important data on them, get hold of someone who knows for sure. You don't want to accidentally erase irreplaceable data.

The default layout is ideal for most servers. If you should be using a different layout, chances are you would already know about it. By default the installer will create two partitions on the disk (we're assuming a one-disk install here). One partition (/boot) will be around 100MB, while another partition for Logical Volume Manager (LVM) will take up the remainder of the space.

LVM is a great piece of software that allows you to separate the underlying physical partitions and disks from the logical partitions that you format and use in Linux. As usual, we look at this in a lot more depth later in the book, but for now just know that it lets you create logical partitions from a combination of physical disks. This in turn means you can create logical partitions that span more than one disk, which can greatly simplify how you set up and use your disks. It's also a great way of handling disks from a storage area network (SAN) or providing storage space to Xen virtual machines. For now, though, let's just accept that LVM is a good thing.

Because you haven't selected "Review and modify partitioning layout," the next screen you see will ask you to configure your network settings (see Figure 2-9). You should see a list of network cards and an Edit option next to them. By default all the settings are set to DHCP. For most home networks and corporate environments, a DHCP server will be able to provide a working address. However, best practice states that you should configure IP addresses of servers manually. This ensures that should DHCP fail, you will still be able to contact your server. For our quick install, we'll be leaving the IP address set to DHCP here, but we'll cover how to set the IP address manually later in the "Setting IP Manually" section.

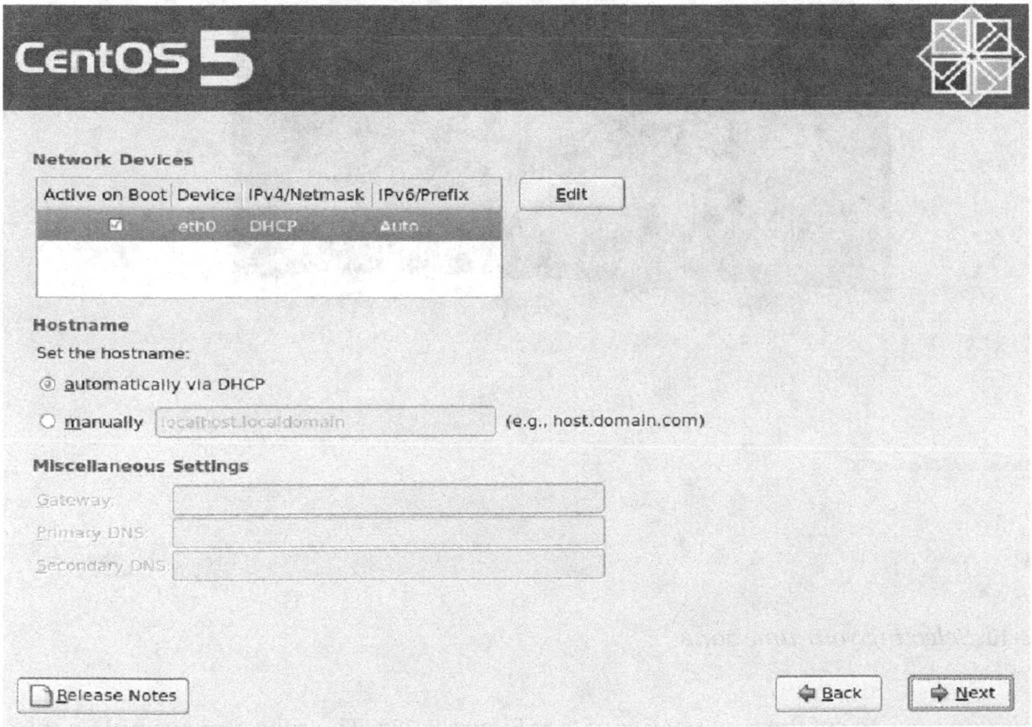

Figure 2-9. *Network settings*

One thing that is certainly worth changing is the hostname. When using DHCP, the default is to request the hostname from the DHCP server. This usually results in being assigned a rather cryptic name at best or *localhost* at worst. Either way, it won't prevent you from shutting down the wrong machine because you thought you were connected to the test box instead of the production server. Select Manually, enter the hostname of your choice, and then click Next.

The next screen (Figure 2-10) lets you set the time zone for your server. You can move the red box over the map of Earth and highlight the country you're in. It will then zoom in, and you can pick your location from the options it provides. If this seems a bit difficult, you can also select the time zone from the drop-down menu under the map. Once you get used to it, the map is actually a very quick way of setting the time zone. By default the option "System clock uses UTC" is selected. This means that the hardware clock will track UTC time, and the system will apply the time zone difference. This is generally standard practice for servers. Once you've selected a time zone that you're happy with, click Next.

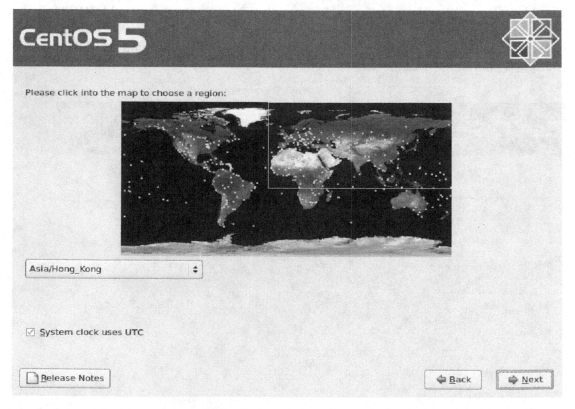

Figure 2-10. *Selecting your time zone*

Now you have to set the root password (see Figure 2-11). The root user account is the most powerful account on a Linux system. This password should be made as complex and as long as possible while preserving your sanity. Ideally, use a mixture of uppercase and lowercase letters, numbers, and punctuation. Once you've entered the password twice, click Next to continue.

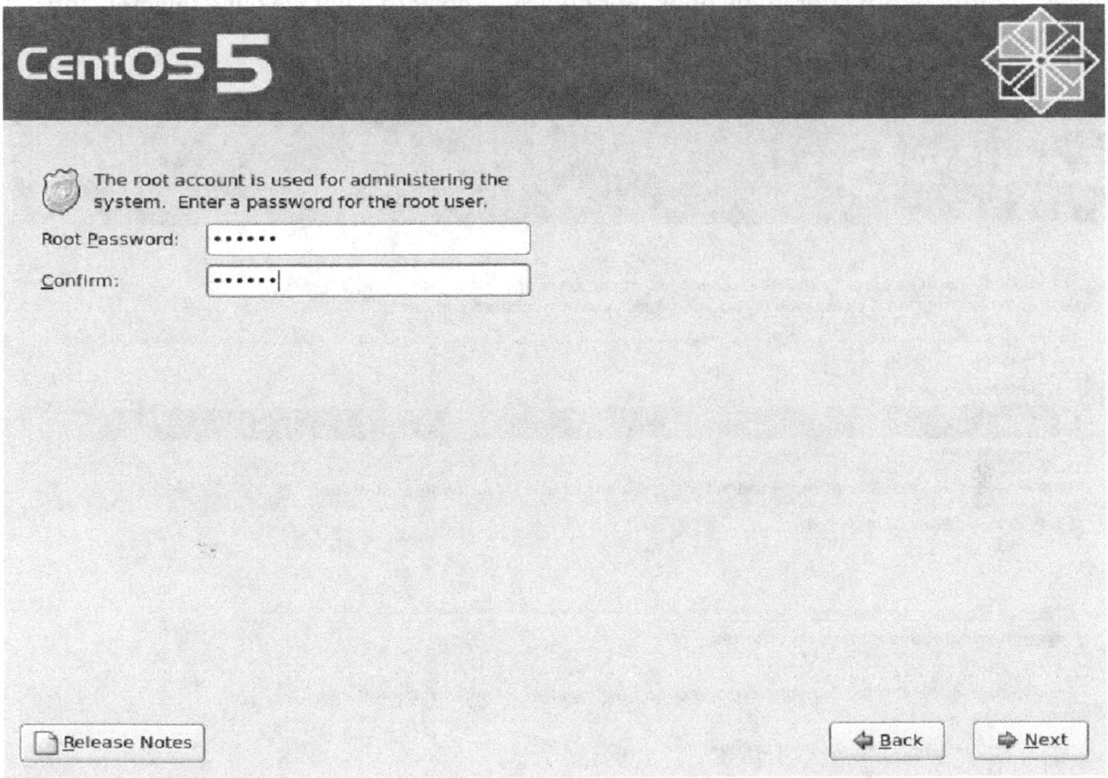

Figure 2-11. *Choosing a root password*

The next page is where things get more interesting (see Figure 2-12). From here you can pick the type of machine you're installing. Each of these options automatically selects a set of packages for installation. Most are fairly straightforward. For example, Desktop – Gnome installs a desktop environment using Gnome, and Desktop – KDE installs a similar environment but with KDE instead.

For this book we're going to select the Desktop – Gnome, Server, and Virtualization options. You can add any other packages that you want after the install is complete using the Yum package manager (see Chapter 4). You also have the option of adding the CentOS Extras repository for installation (although this will require a working Internet connection). The base CentOS distribution includes only the software that has been rebuilt from the RHEL source RPMs (SRPMs) released by Red Hat. (SRPMs are packages of source code with the instructions on how to build the software into a usable form.) Because one of the key goals of the CentOS Project is to maintain complete compatibility with RHEL, the project builds its software from the same blueprints as Red Hat. There is a lot of software that Red Hat does not distribute that would be very useful (and in some cases, essential) to have installed. The CentOS Extras repository provides additional software to the software packages released by Red Hat. We will cover the different repositories in more depth later in the book. For now, let's go with what we have selected and click Next.

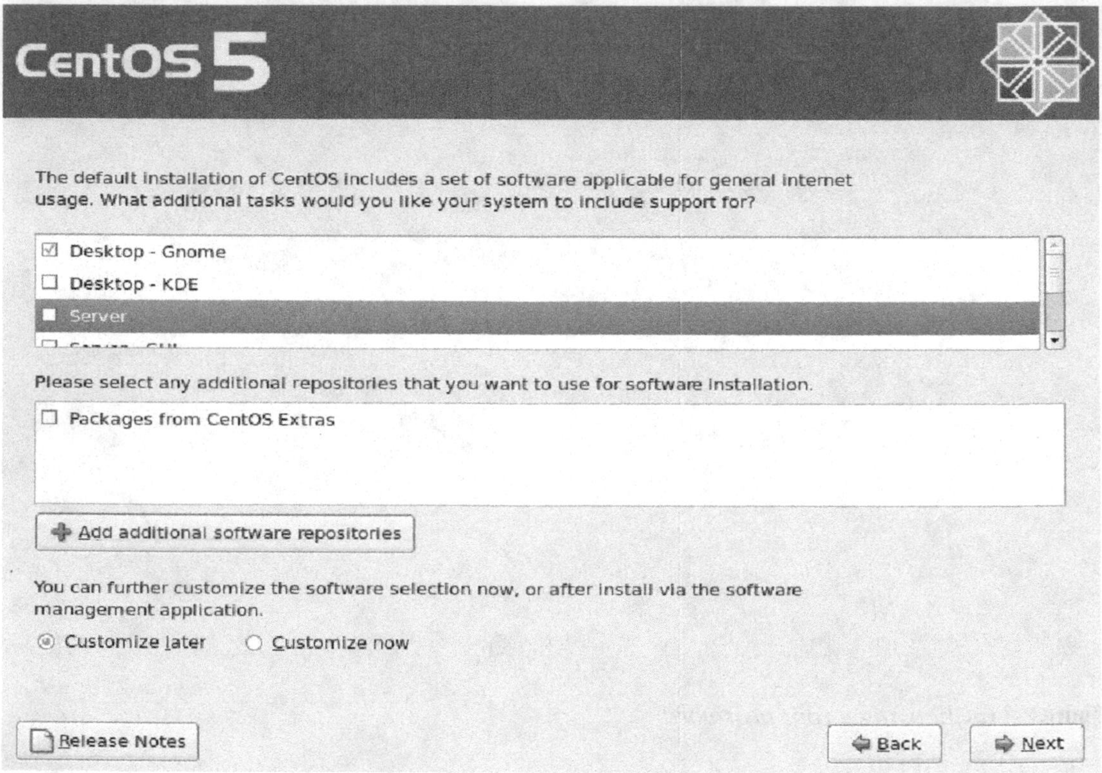

Figure 2-12. *Selecting base packages for your CentOS install*

If everything is going well, you should now be presented with a confirmation screen telling you that you're ready to install CentOS. Click Next to start the install and go and grab a coffee, or if you're feeling sufficiently paranoid, you can keep a very close eye on the install process.

When the install has completed, you will see a screen telling you that everything went as planned and that you should remove the CD and reboot the system (see Figure 2-13). Congratulations! CentOS is now installed on your machine!

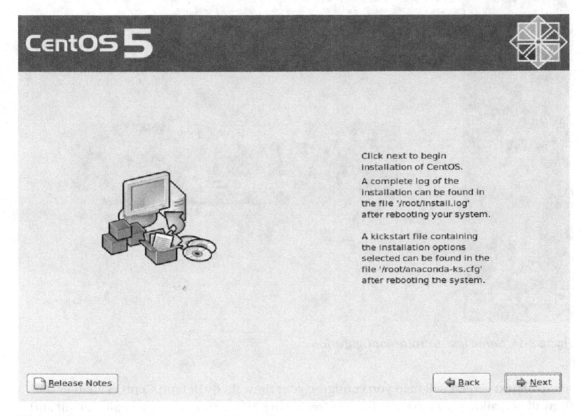

Figure 2-13. *Clicking Next to install CentOS*

Reboot the machine, and it should start booting into CentOS (but don't forget to take out the DVD first, or else you'll start the install process again). This can take a couple of minutes, and you'll see a lot of text being printed on the screen. This is actually great for debugging and seeing what your system is doing, but for now you can safely ignore it.

When the machine starts up for the first time, it will take you to the "first boot" configuration screen. The first screen you'll see explains that there are a few more settings that need to be tweaked before the system is ready for use (see Figure 2-14). Click Forward to move to the next screen.

Figure 2-14. *Some last-minute configuration*

The next screen will help you configure your firewall. By default CentOS enables the firewall and allows SSH to pass through (see Figure 2-15). This is a pretty safe default and is ideal for an initial setup. You can disable the firewall if you really want, but there really isn't a good reason to do this. Instead of disabling the firewall, simply select the services that you want other people to access from the list. If the service you want to allow isn't in the list, click the Other Ports drop-down arrow. From here you can allow access based on port number and protocol. Once you're happy with the settings, click Forward.

■**Note** Not knowing what port a service runs on is not an excuse to turn off the firewall. Doing so can accidentally make you vulnerable to malicious attacks that the firewall would otherwise have prevented. Instead of turning off the firewall, check the services documentation and Google for port listings. Although this takes a bit more effort, it will ensure you have a well-protected server.

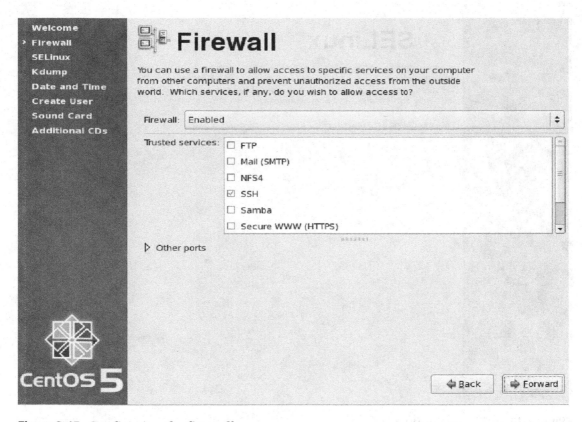

Figure 2-15. *Configuring the firewall*

SELinux is simple in theory, but in practice it can be something of a challenge. On Linux there are really just two access levels—either you're root or you're not. This has historically meant starting services initially as root so that you could access certain resources, although root access is usually dropped almost immediately afterward. This meant that if an attacker could compromise a service while it still had higher privileges, the attacker could also gain root access. SELinux provides mandatory access control (MAC), which greatly restricts what an application can do. It can also be used to grant privileges. For example, the Apache web server could be given permission to bind to port 80 (a privilege normally requiring root access). This then would permit Apache to work properly without ever needing higher access. An additional side effect is that if an attacker were to exploit a service, they would be heavily restricted as to what files or system calls they could make. All in all, SELinux is a good thing (see Figure 2-16).

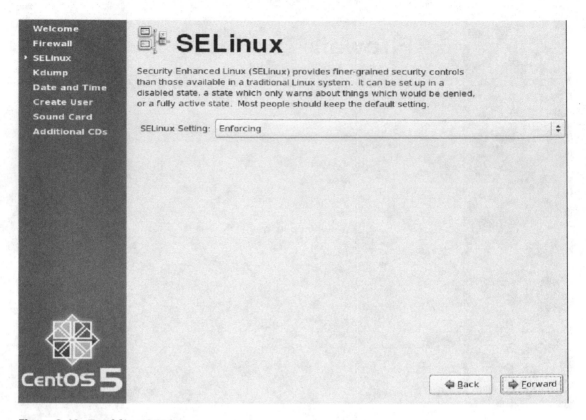

Figure 2-16. *Enabling SELinux*

However, there is a downside. SELinux has a nasty habit of blocking behavior that was commonplace and hence expected previously. It is possible, for example, to set up Apache to display the contents of a directory via the Web but for seemingly random files not to be shown in the list, even though they can be seen in the directory listing on the server. Some applications simply don't work with SELinux out of the box. Many consultants and sysadmins just disable SELinux as a standard installation procedure.

If possible, it is much better to leave SELinux on and then adapt the system to work with it. For most software provided with CentOS, everything will work as expected, and SELinux won't cause any trouble whatsoever. However, if you start seeing something a bit weird, it might be worth checking the system audit logs to see whether SELinux has done something. For now, unless you have a good reason, leave SELinux set to Enforcing and click Forward.

Kdump (see Figure 2-17) is a way for your system to record far more in-depth information after a system crash than is normally possible. The only real downside with turning it on is how much memory Kdump will take away from your system. It isn't used much currently, and with the CentOS kernel being heavily tested for robustness, kernel crashes aren't often seen. However, you can of course enable Kdump if you start to have problems with your system and you do want to collect more information. For now, though, we aren't going to enable it, so just click Forward.

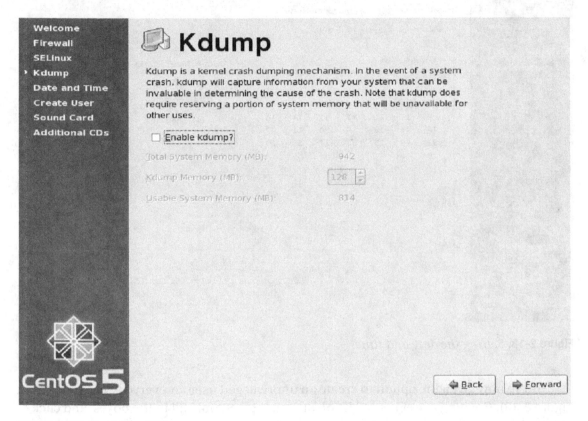

Figure 2-17. *Enabling Kdump*

The next screen (Figure 2-18) lets you set up your system date and time. With all going well, it should already have the correct time set. If not, simply set the correct time. If you want your system clock to keep in sync with Network Time Protocol (NTP) servers on the Internet rather than having to be updated by hand, click the Network Time Protocol tab and select the Enable Network Time Protocol box. By default CentOS lists Internet NTP servers that should work for most people. If you have your own NTP servers (such as a Windows domain controller), then feel free to remove these servers and replace them with your own server details. When you have set your clock the way you want it, click Forward.

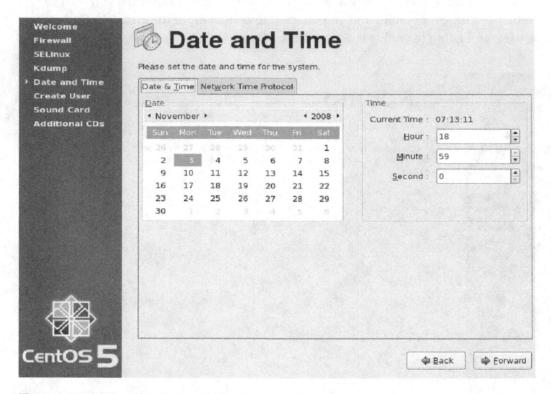

Figure 2-18. *Setting the date and time*

You're now given the option to create an unprivileged user for everyday use (see Figure 2-19). Creating a user is straightforward enough. Simply fill in the boxes, and click Forward.

Now you can test your sound card (if you have one installed, of course), as shown in Figure 2-20. CentOS generally does a good job of detecting and setting up the sound card automatically. If you click the Play button, you should hear the sound file being played. If you're planning on using this machine as a production server, chances are you aren't all that interested in its ability to play music. Either way, once you're satisfied that all is as it should be, click Forward.

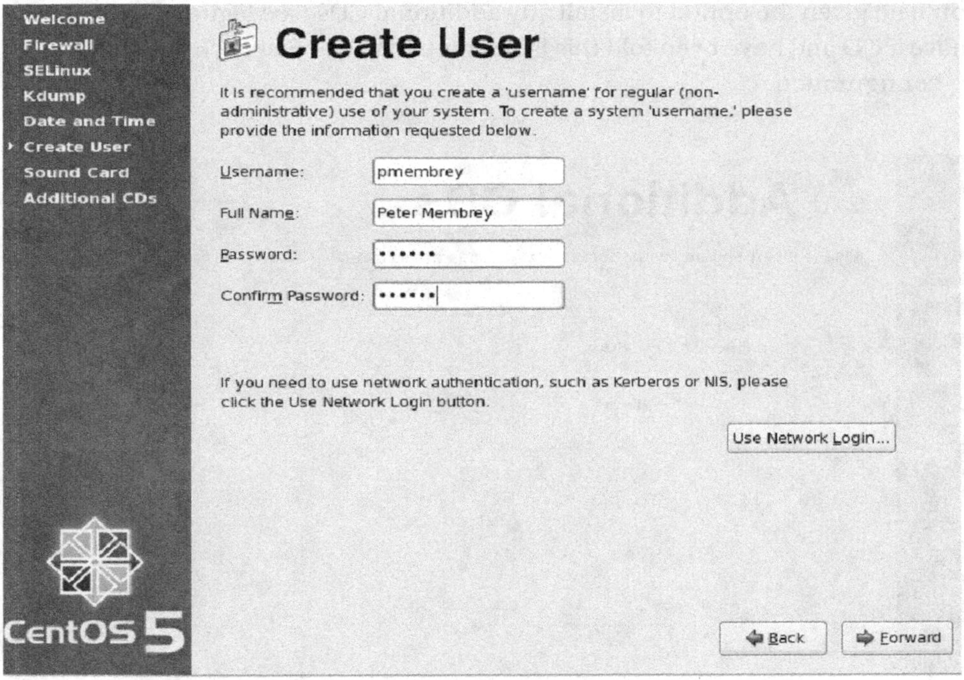

Figure 2-19. *Creating an unprivileged user*

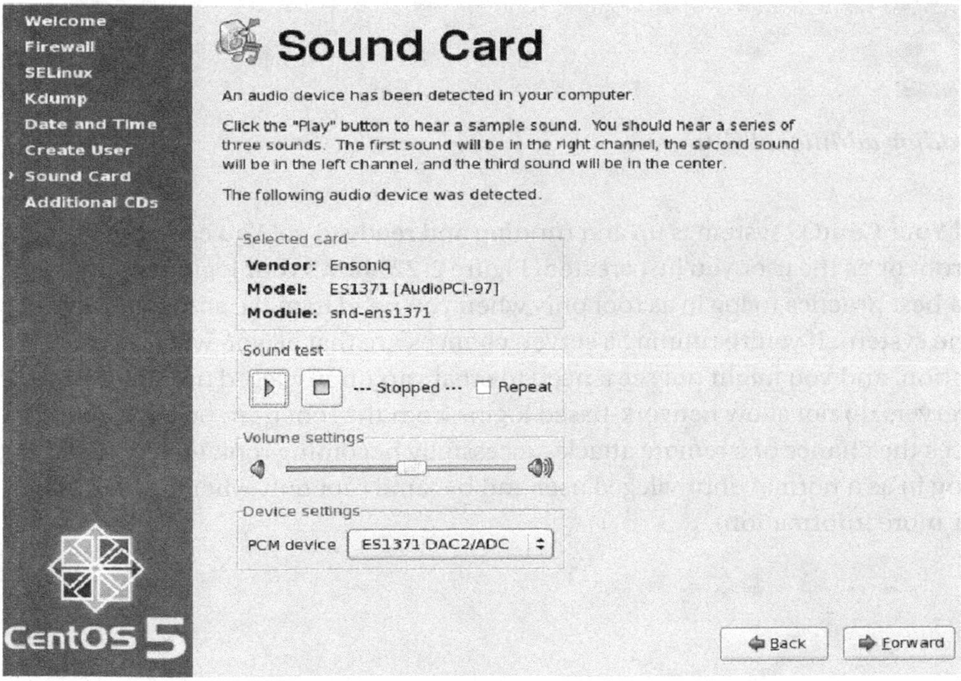

Figure 2-20. *From here you can test your sound card.*

Lastly you'll be given the option to install any additional CDs (see Figure 2-21). Unless you have a CD and have been told this is the time to use it, just click Finish to complete the configuration.

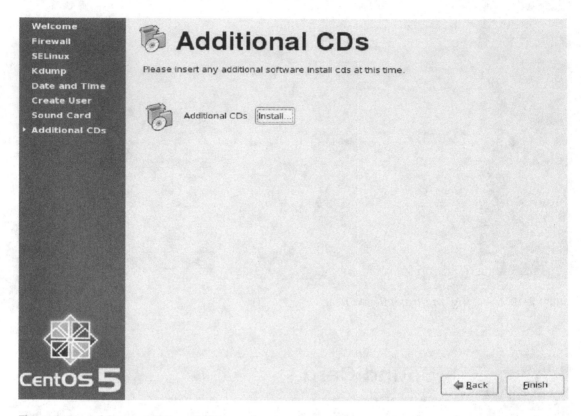

Figure 2-21. *Adding additional CDs*

That's it! Your CentOS system is up and running and ready to go! You can now log on either as root or as the user you just created. Figure 2-22 shows your login screen. It is considered best practice to log in as root only when you need to make administrative changes to the system. If you're running a server, chances are that all you will ever do is administration, and you might not see a need to create an unprivileged user. However, many servers do not allow network-based logins from the root user, because this greatly reduces the chance of a remote attack successfully becoming root. Ideally then, you should log in as a normal unprivileged user and become root only when needed (see Chapter 3 for more information).

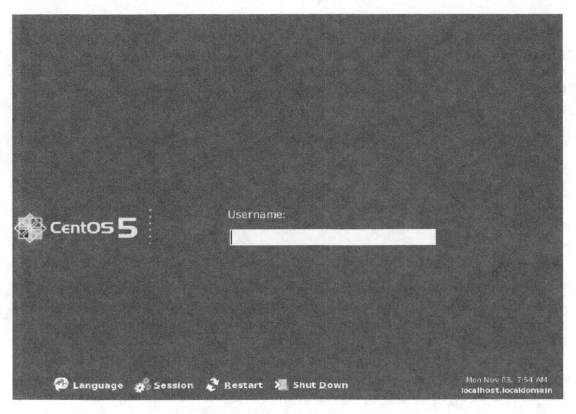

Figure 2-22. *Logging in to your new CentOS server*

Setting Other Installation Options

Now that we've shown how to do a basic installation, the following sections cover some other features you can set during installation.

Securely Erasing Your Disks

CentOS makes it very easy to securely erase your disks before installation. You can remove the old data in a few ways. The simplest and least effective (as in easiest to recover) is to zero the disk. This literally means writing zeros onto the disk, replacing whatever content was there before. This can take quite a long time even on fast machines, but it is the fastest way to erase a disk. This option is useful if you want to wipe a disk with a reasonable certainty that the data can't be recovered.

First, start the installer as normal. When you get to the installer's first graphical screen, press Ctrl+Alt+F2. This will switch to a text-based console. It's very important that you identify your disk before attempting to erase the data, because even zeroing the disk is almost impossible to recover from. If you're not sure which disk is the correct one, jump ahead in the installer first and check from the list of disks. For this example, we will assume your disk is /dev/sda.

The command to zero /dev/sda is as follows:

```
cat /dev/zero > /dev/sda
```

It is also possible to use the same technique to wipe a partition rather than a disk. For example, to wipe the first partition on sda (that is, /dev/sda1), you can use the following command:

```
cat /dev/zero > /dev/sda1
```

As mentioned, this processing can take considerable time to complete; depending on the size of the disk, the time required could be measured in minutes and hours rather than seconds. If you cancel the command before it completes, part of the disk will not have been erased.

A similar technique to zeroing the disk involves writing random characters to the disk. The theory is that it would be harder to recover data from a disk where the end result is unknown. To do this (again wiping /dev/sda), you can use the following command:

```
cat /dev/urandom > /dev/sda
```

This will take considerably longer than simply zeroing the disk. It is worth noting that most people prefer to zero the disk after they have written random data over it.

These methods are effective for the vast majority of people and are relatively painless to do. If you need something a bit more industrial in strength, CentOS ships with the shred tool. This tool follows best practices in erasing disks and hence takes considerably longer than either of the other two methods. In this case, by "longer" we mean it can take days!

shred has a couple of options, but the ones most used are as follows:

-n: Sets the number of passes including zeroing if selected

-z: Zeroes the disk

-v: Prints out continuous status reports

Currently, doing seven passes conforms to the US Department of Defense 5220-22 M standard for erasing magnetic media. A 35-pass conforms to a similar standard issued by the German government. For example, to shred a disk seven times followed by zeroing the partition, you would use this:

```
shred -vzn 8 /dev/sda
```

Note that the total number of passes includes the zeroing; so if you want to make seven passes in addition to zeroing the disk, you need to specify eight passes in total. It is always advisable to use -v so that you have a rough idea what shred is up to. The erasure process is very time-consuming and can take days on a slow or large disk.

When all is said and done, these techniques will make the data practically irre-coverable by anyone. Having said that, there are certain techniques (such as magnetic aura scanning) and certain issues (RAID devices not overwriting the exact same blocks, journaling filesystems recording data, and so on) that may prevent secure erasure even if the command completes successfully. If the contents of the drive are really that sensi-tive, your safest bet is to physically destroy the disk. With terabyte disks being available at reasonable prices, there is little point worrying about erasing a disk when it would be cheaper and safer to simply destroy and replace it.

Creating a Custom Partition Layout

Sometimes the default options offered by the CentOS installer will need to be tweaked. For those occasions, choosing Custom Layout from the menu will give you the ability to create and delete partitions as well as set up LVM and software RAID. A bare-bones parti-tion table should have a swap partition and a root partition. Technically, a swap partition isn't needed, but even if the server has a lot of RAM, having a swap partition can still come in handy. Although most systems can boot from a large root partition, this wasn't always the case, so you will often see recommendations for creating a small (around 100MB) boot partition at the beginning of the disk. By default CentOS creates a boot par-tition because it uses LVM for the root partition and it's not considered best practice to boot directly from LVM.

Note As long as these basic requirements are met, you can create whatever partition scheme tickles your fancy. We prefer to have a large root partition and then add specific partitions for data rather than having lots of little partitions for the system itself.

Note If possible, you should probably use LVM. This will allow you to easily expand partitions in the future and be able to respond rapidly and easily (and potentially without any downtime) to demands for more disk space. Although it's possible to resize standard partitions, the benefits of LVM (such as partitions being able to span multiple disks) really make it a must-have for all new systems.

Using Software RAID

Software RAID seems to be one of those technologies that some people swear by and others swear at. Sometimes using hardware RAID is simply not possible, and getting a commodity server with two identical disks is fairly common and not all that expensive. If you want redundancy but you don't want the cost of buying a hardware RAID controller and aren't planning to run with very high CPU loads, then software RAID is for you!

There are different types of software RAID. Each unique type is called a RAID *level*. The three levels you will see the most often are RAID 0, RAID 1, and RAID 5.

RAID 0 is also referred to as *striping*. This level effectively sticks the disks together to create one large disk. The total size of the new disk is the sum of all the other disks' sizes. This gives you a large disk, but it does not protect you from disk failure. In fact, if a single disk fails, the whole array will be useless. LVM provides the ability to span disks with its logical partitions. Use LVM over RAID 0 if possible.

RAID 1 is also known as *mirroring*. This is where you have two disks of the same size and each is an identical copy of the other. The total size of the new disk is the same as the size of the smallest disk. This level provides redundancy because if a single disk were to fail, there is a complete copy on the second disk. It is possible to add more disks to the array as "hot spares" that can be used to automatically replace a failed disk. CentOS will automatically copy the data from the remaining good disk on to the hot spare, upgrading it to one of the actual mirrored disks. You can then remove the failed disk (and ideally add a new hot spare) when it is convenient.

RAID 5 is the most common RAID level when several disks are involved. RAID 0 provides no redundancy, and RAID 1 takes considerable amounts of space. RAID 5 provides a compromise by allowing full redundancy but not requiring as much space. RAID 5 requires at least three disks, however. Although this is supported in CentOS, it's not as commonly used. If you need RAID 5 (or RAID 6, which is similar), it is normally considered best practice to invest in a hardware RAID controller.

CentOS supports software RAID out of the box, and you can enable it at install time. This is a great way to ensure that your data is well protected. Of course, no amount of RAID replaces the need for backups.

Before you can create a RAID device, you must first create some RAID partitions. These can be created on any disks that CentOS can see. However, although you can create two RAID partitions on a single disk and then create a RAID device from them, this serves no real purpose because if the disk were to fail, both partitions would be lost.

You can create a RAID partition in one of two ways. You can select the RAID option from the menu, or you can do it by selecting New from the menu and then selecting Software RAID from the File System Type menu. Once you have at least two RAID partitions available, you'll then be able to access the Create a RAID Device option. Make sure that this is selected, and click OK.

Depending on the number of RAID partitions you have created, you will have a number of options at this point. First you need to select what type of filesystem you want to create. Usually it's a good idea to create a physical LVM partition because you can then create as many partitions as you need and they will all be backed by the RAID device. It's quite common if two disks are involved to create a small (say 200MB) RAID 1 device for /boot (formatted to ext3), then create another RAID 1 device using up the remainder of the disk space, and finally create an LVM volume group. In this volume group, you would then create a swap partition (say 2GB) and dedicate the remaining space to root (/). This ensures that either hard disk can be booted from and both have complete copies of the root partition.

Setting IP Manually

To configure an individual network card, select it from the list, and click the Edit button. Figure 2-23 shows where you will set your IP. From the pop-up window, you'll be able to enable both IPv4 and IPv6. If you aren't planning on using IPv6, then it's a good idea to disable it. IPv6 can cause some interesting and hard-to-find problems (such as delays in resolving an IP address). If you want to disable IPv6, you can do it here by deselecting the IPv6 box. By default, IPv4 is set to be configured from DHCP. Select Manual configuration, and enter your IP address and gateway. Once you're happy that you've set the details correctly, click OK.

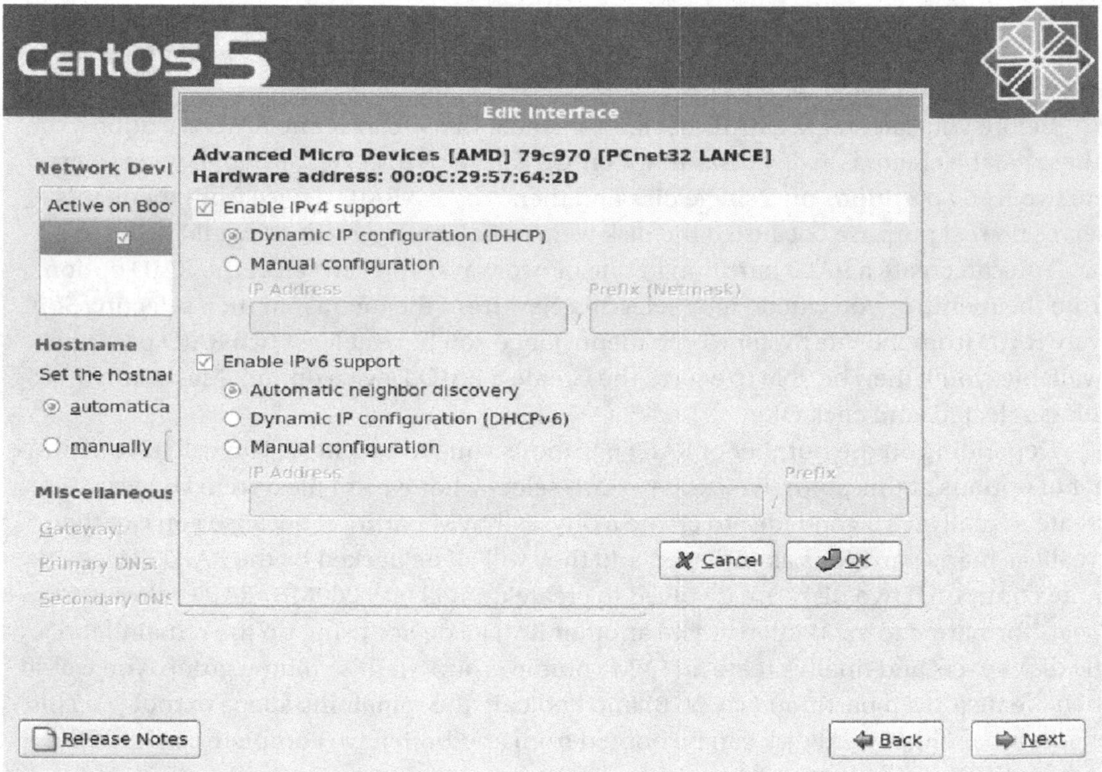

Figure 2-23. *Setting the IP address manually*

If there are no network cards set for DHCP, you will have to set the hostname and associated details manually. Choose a hostname, and enter your gateway IP address along with your primary and secondary DNS servers. When you're happy, click Next, and continue with the install.

Summary

You now know a lot more about CentOS than when you started this chapter. You know where to find the various releases, how to check them for authenticity, and how to burn the images to disc.

You have also walked through the entire install process from start to finish and should have a pretty good idea of the steps involved, what they do, and how you might install the system differently next time.

We also touched on some more advanced topics that weren't part of our basic install such as software RAID and how to securely erase data from your hard disk.

Many of you will be surprised at how easy this process is. After all, Linux is supposed to be much harder than Windows! Yet, it wasn't so bad, was it? As we proceed through the rest of the book, you will come to see that although the CentOS way of doing things is rather different from what you might be used to, it's not as bad as some people make out.

In the next chapter, we'll touch on some basic skills and information you need to find your way around your newly installed system. It will give you the grounding you need when you explore later chapters. If you're desperate to install your web server or you really want to have a play with DNS, feel free to skip ahead to those chapters. We have tried to make them as "stand-alone" as possible. However, if you do find yourself a bit out of your depth, refer to Chapter 3, because it might just point you in the right direction.

CHAPTER 3

■ ■ ■

Getting Started with CentOS

CentOS is a very powerful operating system, and it can be overwhelming at first if you have never used Linux before. This chapter hopes to dispel the myth that "Linux is hard" and give you a firm grounding to tackle the rest of the book. If you're coming to CentOS from another Linux distribution, then you're probably going to want to skip this chapter because it focuses on some Linux fundamentals that you're most likely to have already mastered.

We will cover the basic filesystem layout and what each directory contains or what it does. We won't go into much depth at this stage because this chapter is really meant to give you an overview only. You will come across all of these topics again in later chapters when we talk about how specific services use these directories.

Once you have an idea of how the filesystem is laid out, we'll then cover some essential commands for moving around and creating, editing, and deleting files. We'll also cover file permissions and ownership along with the commands needed to manipulate them. Before that, though, we'll discuss how you can actually get to the command line in the first place and how to use bash.

CentOS Filesystem Layout

CentOS, like all Linux systems, has a single root for all of its filesystems. Although this is standard on Unix systems, users coming from a Windows background are more used to seeing C: and D:. Each of these is a separate root and represents a physical or logical device.

Under Linux, however, individual device type/location isn't important. Instead, the file layout provides a homogenous view over all the content independent from where that content comes. In theory, this means that working with files on a Linux system is simplified because the files look the same regardless of where they are. For example, files on a CD-ROM look the same as files on a hard disk or network share.

Sometimes this transparency can actually make things more difficult because the line between separate filesystem roots is often blurred without directory names that clearly label the device and the data within it. Although at first the Unix way of handling files may be a little more confusing, it does give a great deal of flexibility. For example, say you have a web application that runs on a particular server and serves files from its local disk in /var/www/html/files. Now your application becomes very popular, and you need to store a lot more files than will currently fit on your disk. Your application may be hard-coded and require that these files be in this location. There are various ways to solve this problem, but most of them involve adding storage (whether network or local) and attaching it under /var/www/html/files. You can achieve something similar in Windows using mapped drives, but it isn't as elegant or as flexible as the Unix method. We'll be looking at mounting filesystems a little later in the chapter.

There are times, however, when you do need to see exactly what device is attached where. You can find this out quite easily with the mount command, which will list all the filesystems and where they are mounted (called the *mount point*). We will look at this command in more depth at the end of this chapter.

Relative and Absolute Paths

Knowing the difference between relative and absolute paths is important and fortunately very easy to understand. A *path* is the route you need to take to get from your current location to another. The end result could be a file or another directory. There are two ways to specify a path. You can specify the path based on your current location (a *relative* path) or from the root directory (an *absolute* path).

The problem with a relative path is that it is dependent on your current location. This isn't a problem if you're working on a machine and moving between a few directories, but it's not much use if you e-mail it to another user. If you need to be explicit about which file you are talking about or you want to provide the path to a third party, it is far better to use an absolute path.

Filesystem Layout

Now that you've had a quick overview of how filesystems work in CentOS, it's time to take a look at how the filesystem is actually laid out.

/

This is the root directory, and all other directories and files exist underneath it. It is often confused with the root home area (/root/), which we'll look at next. It also contains all the key directories for the system.

/root

This directory is the root home area. This is where all of root's personal configuration and files go. It is often confused with the root directory (/) itself. When asked the location of a particular file, people will often say, "I put it in root." Generally they are referring to the root home area, although if you can't find the file there, the next place to check before complaining would be in the /root directory.

/etc

/etc is arguably the most important directory on your system. The /etc directory contains all the configuration and settings files for your server applications. Sadly, despite its importance, it is constantly overlooked when preparing backups. New users often safely back up all of their applications that they could easily replace but forget to back up the unique configuration files. Generally speaking, however, this mistake is made only once. Make sure you don't learn this the hard way, and ensure that /etc is first on your backup list!

/proc

/proc is a virtual filesystem used by the kernel to communicate with userland tools. It gives you everything you need to know about your running system such as details on the CPU (/proc/cpuinfo), memory usage (/proc/meminfo), and much more. Tools such as top use the contents of this directory. It is read-only; after all, the /proc filesystem is only a virtual representation of the status of the machine. It is a great place for extracting raw information either when the provided command-line tools don't go into enough depth or when you need a different output layout. The filesystem isn't actually stored anywhere, so it doesn't take up any disk space.

/var

/var (short for variable) is traditionally where data that is created during the running of a machine would go. It's the default location now for web content (/var/www/html/) and mail spools (/var/spool/mail/) as well as all of the system log files (/var/log/). This directory also has a nasty habit of getting full very quickly. Many people consider this to be a sufficient reason for implementing /var on its own partition. Doing so ensures that even if /var is completely filled, the rest of the system is unaffected. With the size of today's disks and with proper maintenance and monitoring, the chances of this happening today are considerably less. Having said that, partitioning is much easier now that Logical Volume Management (LVM) allows dynamic creation and resizing. At the end of the day, like a lot of other setup and configuration options, it comes down to the sysadmin's individual tastes.

/boot

/boot contains all the files needed to successfully boot CentOS. This includes the configuration files for GRUB (the boot loader) and the kernel itself. It is very common (and in fact the default in CentOS) to create a small (approximately 100MB) partition at the beginning of the disk to hold this data. This has been standard practice for many years, firstly because older BIOSs could boot only within the first 1024 cylinders of a disk (preventing users from booting from a large disk with one partition) and then because LVM became the standard and BIOSs can't boot from these partitions (yet) either. Generally speaking, there isn't anything you'd want to tweak or change in this directory, and, for security reasons, many admins actually unmount it once the system has booted. Because changes here can prevent the machine from booting, don't make any changes unless you really know what you're doing!

/bin and /sbin

/bin is the home for most user programs, and /sbin is the home for administration tools and privileged binaries. By default, /sbin is put only into the root user's path, which means when a normal user tries to run a command in /sbin (such as ifconfig), they will get "command not found." The user does have permission to run this command, however, and giving the full path (/sbin/ifconfig) will work.

/dev

This is the location of all the device files on a Linux system. On newer systems (including CentOS), device files are created as and when they're needed. Older distributions still create all the device files regardless of whether the system has or supports a particular type of hardware. All hardware is accessed via a file in this directory. Some files point directly to a piece of hardware (such as /dev/hdc pointing to a CD-ROM drive), and others are symlinks (shortcuts) such as /dev/cdrom that actually point to /dev/hdc. The shortcuts are there for convenience and are often used instead of the hard links.

■**Note** /dev/cdrom is system specific. On one of our machines, we have an IDE CD-ROM connected as the secondary master, which is why it has been assigned to /dev/hdc. Depending on your system, /dev/cdrom might point to something else entirely. This is OK and is one of the benefits of using shortcuts. If an application looks for /dev/cdrom, it will find the CD-ROM regardless of how it's attached.

/home

This directory holds the home directories of users. On smaller systems (and some larger systems), the home directories are created directly under /home such as /home/pmembrey. On servers with thousands of users, however, it is quite common to see subdirectories created based on a naming scheme such as /home/pm/pmembrey. Although convention dictates that home directories should be stored here, that is not a requirement. Indeed, home directories can be anywhere on a system.

/lib

/lib contains system libraries. There's rarely anything that needs changing in here, and most changes are made through installing software packages. Sometimes it becomes necessary to manually create some symlinks in here, but this practice is generally something that should be avoided if possible.

/lost+found

This directory can be found in the root of any ext2 or ext3 filesystem. It is used during disk checking (fsck) to store files that have become detached or missing from the filesystem because of filesystem damage. Files that end up here are often still intact, and data can be recovered. It's not an easy process, and it is often far easier to restore files from a known good backup. However, it's nice to have just in case, but it's really more useful as a way to determine you're looking at the root of an ext filesystem.

/media

In order to access data stored on removable storage, the devices have to be mounted first. On newer Linux systems, /media is the location of choice. Inserting a USB key, for example, will cause the system to attempt to mount it in /media under a recognizable name (usually the name stored on the device). /media has mostly replaced /mnt as the mounting directory of choice, although it is still considered the correct place to mount remote filesystems such as NFS or a Windows file share.

/mnt

On older systems, removable media was generally mounted under the /mnt directory. Now that /media handles this, /mnt is really used only for infrequently mounted filesystems such as mounting a directory from a Windows server. Some sysadmins still prefer to mount permanent filesystems here, but while this is largely down to personal choice and is still fairly common, it doesn't take advantage of the unified file structure available on Unix-based machines.

/usr

This directory contains the vast majority of user software and is often the largest directory on a machine. Although it's good to know where your software actually resides, because the default path includes /usr/bin (and /usr/sbin for root), most software "just works" wherever you are located on the system.

/opt

/opt is most often used for large third-party applications. It's not uncommon to find /opt empty on some systems and jam-packed on others. For example, by default, Oracle will attempt to install itself in /opt. This directory doesn't get all that much use on CentOS systems, and on most of our servers it is still empty. Do not worry if you never have the need to use this directory.

/srv

/srv is used for storing files that are used in providing a service. Most services don't make use of this directory and instead place such files somewhere under /var/. Like /opt and /mnt, /srv is provided by default but doesn't actually have to be used for anything. If you do decide to use /srv, you will need to be aware that the default setup and most documentation will presume that the files are in their default locations. Although separating the actual content from other related files is not a bad idea (some would say it was essential), moving away from the standard defaults may at first make things a bit more challenging than they need to be. Once you are more comfortable with CentOS, do feel free to use this directory.

/sys

This directory is for storing information about the system. The data stored here is written to hard disk, so it can survive a reboot. This directory doesn't seem to be used very often, and you may never need to refer to the information stored there. Having said that, you need to use it only once to appreciate why it exists.

/tmp

This directory is used for the creation of temporary files. Anything can be created here, and most applications that need temporary information stored will put that data in

/tmp. /tmp isn't emptied automatically, although many sysadmins do wipe /tmp every time the system is rebooted. It is also used as a temporary dumping ground for files, especially when there's no other logical location to store them. Again, it is not safe to leave files here because anything in /tmp is assumed to be replaceable. If in doubt, save it in your home directory.

For more information on the way the filesystem is laid out, take a look at the Linux Standard Base (LSB) at http://en.wikipedia.org/wiki/Linux_Standard_Base. This is part of a combined community effort to make the various distributions as similar as possible. This should make it easier for software developers, administrators, and users to work with different Linux platforms and easily apply skills learned from one to another.

Getting Your Hands on a Command Prompt

Before we can discuss how to use bash or work with your new server, we need to first gain access to the command line. This is normally referred to as a *command prompt* on a Windows machine but is normally simply called a *shell* on Unix machines. The command line is where most administrators (and some users) spend the vast majority of their time. Although a wealth of graphics- and web-based tools exist (some good, some not so), editing configuration files directly is generally considered to be the best way to administer a machine.

There are a few ways of getting your hands on a bash prompt. Both Gnome and KDE provide applications (Terminal and Konsole, respectively) that will give you access to the command line. If you are having trouble with your graphics card or you haven't installed the X graphical system, you can access a text-based login prompt by pressing Ctrl+Alt+F1 all the way through to F6. You will still need to provide login details to gain access.

The most common way you'll probably be accessing your new server is via SSH. SSH (which stands for Secure SHell) is a suite of tools that provides secure access to machines across an untrusted network. Before SSH, the standard way to connect to a server was to use telnet. Unfortunately, telnet sends everything on to the network "in the clear," so it was often possible for attackers to be able to steal passwords directly from the network. On top of this, there was no way to tell whether the server you were logging into was actually the server you thought it was.

Getting an SSH Client

For Linux and the Apple Mac, SSH is a standard part of their operating systems. On Linux, wherever you can get a shell prompt, simply typing ssh will give you access to the program. The same is true for OS X (which has a very strong BSD background). You will need to run the Terminal program, which can be found in Applications ➤ Utilities. This tool gives you a very similar command line that you would expect to see on CentOS. Indeed, they both run bash!

If you're running Windows, you won't have an SSH client as standard. Fortunately, there is a really good client called PuTTY that's open source and freely available for download. You can download PuTTY from its web site at http://www.chiark.greenend.org.uk/~sgtatham/putty/download.html.

PuTTY is a pretty simple tool that can be downloaded as a stand-alone executable as well as part of an installer. The stand-alone executable is particularly handy for placing on USB sticks when you need to connect to your server from someone else's machine.

Using SSH

SSH provides basic authentication for your server using fingerprints. Each server has a unique fingerprint that can be used to identify it. When you first connect to a new hostname or IP address, your SSH client will prompt you that it hasn't seen this machine before and will ask whether the fingerprint is correct. To be honest, very few people actually know what the fingerprint on their server is supposed to be. It's a fairly safe bet that if the first four characters and last four characters match, then the server is in fact the server you think it is.

Should this fingerprint change in the future, you will be warned that the fingerprint doesn't match, and SSH will refuse to connect. The most common reason for this is reinstalling the server and hence generating new sets of SSH keys. If you have a good reason to suspect the keys have changed, then this is nothing to worry about, and you can update SSH to use the new fingerprint.

You're Logged In; Now What?

Of course, once you're logged into your new CentOS server, you now need to know how to move around and perform basic tasks. This chapter cannot hope to tell you everything there is to know about bash because entire books have been written about it. Instead, we're going to help you feel more at home without pretty windows and a mouse. Chances are this is where you will spend the majority of your time on a Linux system, so you'll need to get used to it as quickly as possible.

First, the Prompt

Because you'll be spending a lot of time at "the prompt," we'll talk about what that means. The following is an example of a prompt:

```
[pmembrey@doublehelix ~]$
```

This is the standard user prompt on CentOS. It is possible to change the prompt and customize it to suit your preferences. Most users tend to leave it alone because the default tends to be a good all-around prompt.

The first part of the prompt is `pmembrey` followed by the at (@) sign. This shows the current user. The next part, `doublehelix`, identifies the hostname of the machine to which you're connected. Together, these two pieces of information uniquely identify who and where you are. This is very important, especially if you're working on more than one machine. When you have ten different windows open to ten different servers, it can become a challenge keeping track of everything!

The next part of the prompt tells you where you are in the filesystem. The tilde (~) is a special Unix convention meaning home directory. In this example, the prompt is showing that we're in the home directory.

The last part of the prompt is either a dollar sign ($) or a number (or hash) sign (#). This denotes whether the current user has root privileges. Generally speaking, you will only ever see the hash sign when you are logged in as root. All other users show the dollar sign. Seeing the hash sign is a useful reminder that you should be careful what you type because you have unlimited access to the system.

Important Commands

If you haven't used a Linux distribution before, you will find certain commands extremely useful. The most important ones are described in the following sections.

pwd

The `pwd` command does nothing more than show you which directory you're currently in, but the usefulness of this information is rarely understated. For example, you can use this command to make sure you're editing the right file. There will be many times when you'll be working on files with identical names stored in different directories. `pwd` will ensure you don't accidentally change the wrong one!

```
[pmembrey@doublehelix ~]$ pwd
/home/pmembrey
[pmembrey@doublehelix ~]$
```

You can see that we're in the home directory (`/home/pmembrey`). That's pretty much all there is to `pwd`, but it really comes into its own when you're using a lot of relative paths because it's very easy to get lost.

ls

This is another command that you will use on a very regular basis. ls will show you a
directory listing. It will also show various features such as symlinks and directories in
color. This really helps when you're looking through a long directory listing to help you
find what you're looking for more easily.

```
[pmembrey@doublehelix ~]$ ls
test1  test2  test3  test4  test5
[pmembrey@doublehelix ~]$
```

You can also use the –l option to provide far more information. This includes information on file ownership and permissions as well as how big the file is. This shows the
amount of space used in bytes, which is not generally all that useful (unless you're writing scripts that parse the output), and you can use the –h option to display the file sizes
in "human-readable" format. This will show much space is used in kilobytes, megabytes,
gigabytes, and so on. Of course, you can combine more than one option so that –lh shows
a listing with human-readable size.

```
[pmembrey@doublehelix ~]$ ls -lh
total 20K
drwxrwxr-x 2 pmembrey pmembrey 4.0K Nov 10 13:47 test1
drwxrwxr-x 2 pmembrey pmembrey 4.0K Nov 10 13:47 test2
drwxrwxr-x 2 pmembrey pmembrey 4.0K Nov 10 13:47 test3
drwxrwxr-x 2 pmembrey pmembrey 4.0K Nov 10 13:47 test4
drwxrwxr-x 2 pmembrey pmembrey 4.0K Nov 10 13:47 test5
[pmembrey@doublehelix ~]$
```

We're going to take a quick detour here and talk briefly about file permissions and
ownership. The first thing you'll notice is that long line of letters at the beginning of each
row. Ignoring the first letter for a moment, we have three sets of three letters—one each
for user, group, and other (or world). Each set is rwx (or read-write and execute). In our
last example, all of the files are read-write and executable by the user pmembrey (the username is in the third column), the same for the group pmembrey (the group is in the fourth
column), and lastly only read and executable for everyone else. The w is missing, leaving a
hyphen or minus in its place. This means that that particular permission is not available.

The first character tells you what kind of file you're viewing. A normal file is simply a
hyphen, but a directory is shown with a d. As you can see, in our example, all the entries
are directories. Symlinks (shortcuts in Windows) are shown with an l.

The fifth column tells you the size of the file. As far as directories are concerned, it shows the amount of space taken up by the directory record, not by the contents of the directory. This is why you will see directories being 4.0K the vast majority of the time.

The sixth column is the time the file was last modified, and the seventh column is the name of the file itself.

We'll revisit file permissions throughout the book as they apply to each of the tasks that we're working on. For now, though, just be aware that CentOS provides security mechanisms for the files and that there is a way to view them.

Lastly, the option -a will show you all the hidden files in a given directory. By convention, any file that starts with a period or dot is considered a hidden file. There's nothing mysterious about these files, and they can be seen easily—it just helps to keep various directories clean and tidy because they are directories that you'll seldom use. They generally contain configuration information such as your command history (.bash_history) or your SSH configuration (the .ssh directory). Here's the same command as earlier but with the full -lha:

```
[pmembrey@doublehelix ~]$ ls -lha
total 44K
drwx------  7 pmembrey pmembrey 4.0K Nov 10 13:47 .
drwxr-xr-x 14 root     root     4.0K Nov  9 15:37 ..
-rw-------  1 pmembrey pmembrey   81 Nov  9 16:47 .bash_history
-rw-r--r--  1 pmembrey pmembrey   33 Nov  9 15:37 .bash_logout
-rw-r--r--  1 pmembrey pmembrey  176 Nov  9 15:37 .bash_profile
-rw-r--r--  1 pmembrey pmembrey  124 Nov  9 15:37 .bashrc
drwxrwxr-x  2 pmembrey pmembrey 4.0K Nov 10 13:47 test1
drwxrwxr-x  2 pmembrey pmembrey 4.0K Nov 10 13:47 test2
drwxrwxr-x  2 pmembrey pmembrey 4.0K Nov 10 13:47 test3
drwxrwxr-x  2 pmembrey pmembrey 4.0K Nov 10 13:47 test4
drwxrwxr-x  2 pmembrey pmembrey 4.0K Nov 10 13:47 test5
[pmembrey@doublehelix ~]$
```

Here you can see two directories that are simply a dot and two dots. We explain these special directories when we talk about cd later in this chapter. The other four files are used by bash. We will look at these files later in the book.

■**Note** When presenting options in this way, they can be given in any order. We've always used -lha, but -lah, -hal, -alh, and -ahl are all equally valid.

---

mkdir

Once you can look at which directories you have, you'll need mkdir to create new ones. mkdir is short for "make directory," and it pretty much does what it says on the tin. To create a directory, simply pass it the name of the directory to create. Here's an example:

```
[pmembrey@doublehelix ~]$ mkdir mydir
[pmembrey@doublehelix ~]$
```

If the directory was created successfully, you won't receive any confirmation; you will just be taken back to the command prompt. If there is a problem, you will get an error, and the directory won't be created. For example, use this if the directory already exists:

```
[pmembrey@doublehelix ~]$ mkdir mydir
mkdir: cannot create directory 'mydir': File exists
[pmembrey@doublehelix ~]$
```

It does have a very useful option in -p. This option will attempt to create the directory but won't complain if a directory doesn't exist and will create it if need be. For example, if you want to create lots/and/lots/of/directories and you use the previous command, you get the following:

```
[pmembrey@doublehelix ~]$ mkdir lots/and/lots/of/directories
mkdir: cannot create directory 'lots/and/lots/of/directories': No such file or
directory
[pmembrey@doublehelix ~]$
```

Now, if you run the same command but this time add -p, you instead get this:

```
[pmembrey@doublehelix ~]$ mkdir -p lots/and/lots/of/directories
[pmembrey@doublehelix ~]$ ls lots/and/lots/of/directories/
[pmembrey@doublehelix ~]$
```

The previous code also shows a quick ls to do a directory listing of our newly created directory. As you can see, no errors were returned by the creation or listing attempts, so you know that the directories have been safely created. However, you should always check to make sure. You can also use the tree command to create a more graphical representation:

```
[pmembrey@doublehelix ~]$ tree lots
lots
'-- and
    '-- lots
        '-- of
            '-- directories
```

```
4 directories, 0 files
[pmembrey@doublehelix ~]$
```

cd

Of course, once you can see and create directories, you'll need to be able to move between them. cd, which is short for "change directory," lets you do just that. If you don't provide a directory to change to, it will take you back to your home directory. This is actually quite a handy shortcut, and you'll probably find that you use it all the time. When you do specify a path, you can specify either a relative or an absolute path—both will work fine.

Two special directory entries that you need to know about (and are common also in Windows) are the single dot (.) and the double dot (..). The single dot refers to the current directory. It would be very unusual to change to this directory unless you did it by accident. Far more useful is this command: cd ... The two dots (..) have a similar function, but they refer to the parent directory, that is, the one that your current directory sits in. This is very useful for copying files or moving things around. You will most probably use it to jump back a directory with cd ... However, unlike Windows, cd.. is not a valid command (unless you create an alias), so you need to have a space between the command and the path. For example:

```
[pmembrey@doublehelix ~]$ pwd
/home/pmembrey
[pmembrey@doublehelix ~]$ cd ..
[pmembrey@doublehelix home]$ pwd
/home
[pmembrey@doublehelix home]$
```

Although you could just use cd pmembrey to go back to your home directory, you can also just type cd by itself. This will always take you back to your home directory:

```
[pmembrey@doublehelix home]$ pwd
/home
[pmembrey@doublehelix home]$ cd
[pmembrey@doublehelix ~]$ pwd
/home/pmembrey
[pmembrey@doublehelix ~]$
```

Lastly, a useful bash feature to remember is cd -. This will take you back to the last directory you were in. This is very handy if you entered cd by itself and want to go back where you were.

rmdir

This command lets you remove a directory. It will remove a directory only when it is completely empty. This prevents you from deleting directories with content in them.

```
[pmembrey@doublehelix ~]$ rmdir test1
[pmembrey@doublehelix ~]$
```

If you try to delete a directory (such as the directories that were created earlier in this chapter), you will get an error message:

```
[pmembrey@doublehelix ~]$ rmdir lots
rmdir: lots: Directory not empty
[pmembrey@doublehelix ~]$
```

We'll look at the rm command next, which can do just that: delete a directory with contents. To remove a chain of empty directories, you can use the option -p, which works a lot like the mkdir option. If any of the directories aren't empty, however, rmdir will fail. This is a built-in safety feature.

```
[pmembrey@doublehelix ~]$ rmdir -p lots/and/lots/of/directories/
[pmembrey@doublehelix ~]$ cd lots
-bash: cd: lots: No such file or directory
[pmembrey@doublehelix ~]$
```

rm

rm is by far the most dangerous command on any Linux system. rm with the correct (or incorrect depending on how you look at it) options can destroy a server with just a single command. Remember, Linux assumes you know what you're doing when you work on the command line, so if you tell it to remove every file on your system, it will do its best to accommodate you. Recovering files that rm has removed is extremely difficult and problematic. This is another great reason for ensuring you have good backups!

By default, root on CentOS systems has aliases that help to prevent destroying your data. Although they do a good job, they can be overridden (by starting the command with a backslash), or their protection doesn't kick in until damage has already been done. When used with the -r option, rm will attempt to remove any files and directories in the path that you specify. It will prompt for confirmation in certain circumstances such as the file being read-only. The option -f, however, effectively tells rm to ignore confirmations and errors and just keep on going. Combining the two gives you rm -rf, which is probably the most dreaded command in a sysadmin's arsenal. Like nuclear weapons, this is one command that should be used with extreme caution and even then only after checking that everything is typed in as it should be.

For example, say you want to vaporize your current directory. You could enter a command like this:

```
rm -rf ./
```

which as expected removes the current directory. However, if a typo was made and there was a space between the dot and the slash:

```
rm -rf . /
```

the command would erase the current directory and continue to erase everything under the root (/) directory! This includes all your device files and configuration files. True, it won't be able to remove everything, but it will certainly be more than enough to sink your battleship. It cannot be stressed enough—be very, very careful where you point this command!

touch

This command has two purposes. First, it will update the last modified time on a given file. This is useful if you want to update a cache or simply make a program reload a configuration file. Second, if the file doesn't exist, touch will create it. This makes it a fantastic tool for just creating a file when you aren't concerned about the contents:

```
[pmembrey@doublehelix ~]$ touch test
[pmembrey@doublehelix ~]$ ls -lha test
-rw-rw-r-- 1 pmembrey pmembrey 0 Nov 10 16:02 test
[pmembrey@doublehelix ~]$ touch test
[pmembrey@doublehelix ~]$ ls -lha test
-rw-rw-r-- 1 pmembrey pmembrey 0 Nov 10 16:03 test
[pmembrey@doublehelix ~]$
```

You can see that initially it created a file called test. The initial timestamp is 16:02. A minute or so later we used touch on the file again and took another look. You can see that the timestamp now reads 16:03.

nano

nano is a fantastic little text editor. You will no doubt find people who tell you that vi or emacs is the only way to edit your files, but there is a lot to be said for simple and basic tools. nano is simple; it opens, edits, and saves files. It doesn't do color coding, but if you just want to save a couple of lines or quickly edit a config file, nano will do the job brilliantly.

A useful option to remember, though, with the `nano` command is -w. This tells nano that you don't want to wrap the text on to different lines. In config files especially, ending the line early is likely to stop the application from working properly or to reject the config file altogether. -w will ensure that one line is actually one line, and nano won't try to format the text for you.

cat

`cat` is a handy utility for taking the contents of a file and printing it to the screen. This is really useful if you want to see the contents of a file but don't need to edit or adjust it. For example, you can see the content of /etc/hosts with this:

```
[pmembrey@doublehelix ~]$ cat /etc/hosts
# Do not remove the following line, or various programs
# that require network functionality will fail.
127.0.0.1        localhost.localdomain      localhost
::1              localhost6.localdomain6    localhost6
[pmembrey@doublehelix ~]$
```

Summary

In this chapter, we touched on a few important ideas to get you started with CentOS. You are able to get to a command prompt either locally on the machine itself or over the network via SSH. You know how to move around the filesystem, create and delete files and directories, and edit them in the nano text editor.

This background will help you as you move on to the next chapter and learn how to use Yum to search, install, update, and generally manage your software packages.

CHAPTER 4

■■■

Using Yum

One of the most important things that you will need to do now that you are running your own server is ensure that you keep it up-to-date. On many operating systems, applying updates can be a rather "exciting" process and—usually—one to be avoided like the plague. This is because updates have a nasty habit of not just fixing bugs but also introducing a complete set of new ones.

With CentOS, though, you can rest assured that applying updates is safe and isn't going to cause any major problems. This is because during a given release, all bug fixes are back-ported into the currently running version. This means that the version of, say, Apache running on a CentOS machine will be the same on the last day as it is on the first, even though hundreds of updates might have been made since then. Each package is also rigorously tested to ensure that new bugs aren't created and, more important, that old bugs aren't reintroduced.

Yum is a powerful update manager that makes finding, installing, and updating packages simple and straightforward. Under CentOS, for example, running `yum update` will be enough to completely update the server out of the box. Yum provides powerful tools for working with multiple software repositories and provides a collection of powerful commands to search the repositories for the software you want to find. Yum provides automatic dependency resolution (making sure everything installs and keeps working) and provides mechanisms to verify the authenticity of the packages its finds. Yum is not just for updates!

What Are RPMs?

CentOS uses the RPM software packaging system. An RPM file contains not only the software files but also in-depth information about the software, such as what it's called, when it was released, what changes have been made, and what other packages it depends on to work. Every piece of software in the CentOS distribution comes in RPM packages. When you installed CentOS, you selected the type of system you wanted to build. This gave the installer a list of packages that it needed to install and, from the dependency information, all the packages that those packages were dependent on. This helps ensure that whenever a new piece of software is installed, it is all but guaranteed to work as expected.

There are many RPM-based Linux distributions such as Red Hat Enterprise Linux, Fedora, Mandriva, and Yellow Dog Linux. Because of this widespread usage, people have come up with various different tools and systems to handle installing and updating RPM packages. One of the best solutions is Yum (which stands for Yellow dog Updater, Modified).

Yum is a management tool for RPM-based Linux distributions and was originally developed by Seth Vidal (who now works for Red Hat) and a collection of volunteers at Duke University. Yum is now the standard update tool on most RPM-based platforms (although SUSE uses YaST) and has several benefits over its competition such as automatically syncing repository information.

What Are Yum Repositories?

RPMs are generally stored in *repositories*. These repositories store not only the RPM files but also significant amounts of metadata and the means to find the RPMs that you're looking for. When you want to install or update a package, Yum will look in these repositories to find the relevant software. If the RPMs are simply stored on a local disk, it is not overly difficult to search through them—but if you have access only to a remote web site, you don't want to have to guess at a file name. Even if you did get the name right, you would have to download that file and then inspect it to see whether you needed any others.

Repository metadata solves this problem by providing all of this information in a collection of files referred to as *repomd*. Yum uses this information to work out which RPMs it needs, and then it can proceed to download those files.

CentOS Repositories

CentOS has quite a large number of official repositories. This is to ensure that administrators can maintain their servers in a known state. By using the default repositories, only packages that are updated upstream are made available. This ensures binary compatibility with Red Hat Enterprise Linux.

For some people, this may be very important, especially if they are running software that is certified for Red Hat Enterprise Linux. But what if you just want the CentOS core but want to be able to use software that isn't available upstream? What if you want to try a newer version of a piece of software? Chances are you will find what you're looking for in one of the CentOS repositories, but if not, you can always add a third-party repository.

Official CentOS Repositories

The following are the official CentOS repositories.

[base]

This repository contains the RPM packages as they are supplied on the related ISO images. This repository is enabled by default, although the contents of this repository don't update after a given release.

[updates]

This repository, which is also enabled by default, is where all the security, bug fix, and enhancement updates for the [base] repositories are placed. All of the other repositories contain their own updates.

[addons]

This repository (enabled by default) does not contain packages that are released upstream. Instead, it contains additional packages that are needed to build software from the source RPMs (SRPMs). Using this repository doesn't cause CentOS to lose binary compatibility with upstream versions and should remain enabled.

[contrib]

This repository is not enabled by default and contains additional software packages that have been contributed by the CentOS community. The important distinction with this repository is that none of the software will conflict with software in the base distribution. This means that it is generally safe to use these packages and that they won't break binary compatibility with upstream versions. However, they are not tested by the CentOS developers and may not necessarily follow upstream versions of the software all that closely.

[centosplus]

This repository is similar to the [contrib] repository in that it contains contributed software. Like [contrib], these packages are contributed by CentOS users, but packages are also supplied by CentOS developers. The major difference, though, is that the software that this repository provides may very well replace or upgrade packages that are included in the base distribution. This means that use of this repository could break binary compatibility with upstream versions.

Before using this repository, you should be fully aware of what this means to you. If you have no interest in maintaining compatibility with upstream versions or your project desperately needs the software included in [centosplus], then by all means feel free to use it. If you are more conservative and would rather keep your system as close to upstream versions as possible, you'd be better off not enabling this repository.

[extras]

This repository is enabled by default and contains packages that add functionality to the distribution. It's written by the CentOS developers and has undergone reasonable testing. Software versions should track upstream versions fairly closely, and these packages will never conflict or interfere with [base] packages.

[testing]

The testing repository contains packages that are currently being tested and debugged. Unless you have a specific reason for doing so, this repository should not be enabled on a production server.

Third-Party Repositories

Now that you've seen the official repository list, you should also be aware that there are many third-party repositories that you can use. These are not approved by the CentOS Project but often contain many useful packages. For more information on third-party repositories and how to use them, check out the CentOS wiki at http://wiki.centos.org/AdditionalResources/Repositories.

Getting Started with Yum

Because it's integrated into CentOS, Yum is pretty much ready to use out of the box. The only thing that doesn't come preinstalled with CentOS is the CentOS public signing key. Every official package released by the CentOS Project is cryptographically signed with a PGP key. This ensures that Yum installs only authentic packages.

Installing the key is very straightforward, and you will be prompted to accept it as soon as you attempt to do an update or an install. If the key hasn't already been installed, you will see a message similar to this:

```
warning: rpmts_HdrFromFdno: Header V3 DSA signature: NOKEY, key ID e8562897
Importing GPG key 0xE8562897 "CentOS-5 Key (CentOS 5 Official Signing Key)
<centos-5-key@centos.org>" from http://mirror.centos.org/centos/RPM-GPG-KEY-CentOS-5
Is this ok [y/N]:
```

Just say y to this, and Yum will carry on with the task that you've given it. This happens only the first time Yum tries to access the CentOS repositories and shouldn't happen again. When using a new repository, however, you will most likely have to accept and install its public key when you first try to access the repository.

Updating Your Server

As we mentioned earlier, installing updates for CentOS is generally painless and safe. It is almost always the case that not installing an update is far riskier than leaving the machine unpatched.

It is also worth remembering at this point that CentOS updates itself incrementally. This means that if you install CentOS from the original ISO images and do a full update, it will be exactly the same as installing from the latest ISO images and doing a full update. Obviously, it will take considerably longer to update the first machine, but ultimately the machines will end up in the same state.

If you have been provided with a CentOS server (perhaps from a hosting company), it is possible that the host will have already updated your server to the latest release. If, on the other hand, you've installed the server yourself, you will want to run a full update as soon as the machine first boots.

Generally speaking, it is best to update your server on a regular basis and update all the packages that have new versions available. Although you can be more specific in what you update, apart from saving bandwidth there is no real benefit to being specific.

To update your server, enter this command:

```
yum update
```

If your server has already been updated to the latest release, you will see something like this:

```
[root@doublehelix ~]# yum update
Loading "fastestmirror" plugin
Loading mirror speeds from cached hostfile
 * base: mirror.bytemark.co.uk
 * updates: mirror.bytemark.co.uk
```

```
 * addons: mirror.bytemark.co.uk
 * extras: mirror.bytemark.co.uk
Setting up Update Process
No Packages marked for Update
[root@doublehelix ~]#
```

Otherwise, you'll see something like this:

```
[root@doublehelix ~]# yum update
Loading "fastestmirror" plugin
Loading mirror speeds from cached hostfile
 * base: mirror.bytemark.co.uk
 * updates: mirror.bytemark.co.uk
 * addons: mirror.bytemark.co.uk
 * extras: mirror.bytemark.co.uk
Setting up Update Process
Resolving Dependencies
--> Running transaction check
---> Package ruby-libs.i386 0:1.8.5-5.el5_2.6 set to be updated
---> Package ruby-rdoc.i386 0:1.8.5-5.el5_2.6 set to be updated
---> Package ruby-devel.i386 0:1.8.5-5.el5_2.6 set to be updated
---> Package ruby.i386 0:1.8.5-5.el5_2.6 set to be updated
---> Package ruby-irb.i386 0:1.8.5-5.el5_2.6 set to be updated
--> Finished Dependency Resolution
Dependencies Resolved


================================================================================
 Package            Arch         Version           Repository        Size
================================================================================
Updating:
ruby                i386         1.8.5-5.el5_2.6   updates           280 k
ruby-devel          i386         1.8.5-5.el5_2.6   updates           555 k
ruby-irb            i386         1.8.5-5.el5_2.6   updates            69 k
ruby-libs           i386         1.8.5-5.el5_2.6   updates           1.6 M
ruby-rdoc           i386         1.8.5-5.el5_2.6   updates           136 k
```

```
Transaction Summary
===========================================================================
Install       0 Package(s)
Update        5 Package(s)
Remove        0 Package(s)

Total download size: 4 M
Is this ok [y/N]:
```

If you press y, Yum will proceed to download and install the available updates. That's really all there is to it!

One thing to remember, though, is that if software is in use when it gets updated, the new version won't be used until that application is restarted. Because kernel updates affect the core of the operating system, a reboot is required to activate them. Although it's not essential to do so, you really should also reboot your server if you've installed any glibc updates.

Installing a Package

Installing a package with Yum is also very easy. All you need to do is specify the name of the package that you want to install. For example, if you want to install php, you use yum install php. This gives the following output:

```
[root@localhost ~]# yum install php
Setting up Install Process
Parsing package install arguments
Resolving Dependencies
--> Running transaction check
---> Package php.i386 0:5.1.6-20.el5_2.1 set to be updated
--> Processing Dependency: php-cli = 5.1.6-20.el5_2.1 for package: php
--> Processing Dependency: php-common = 5.1.6-20.el5_2.1 for package: php
--> Running transaction check
---> Package php-cli.i386 0:5.1.6-20.el5_2.1 set to be updated
---> Package php-common.i386 0:5.1.6-20.el5_2.1 set to be updated
--> Finished Dependency Resolution
```

Dependencies Resolved

Once dependencies are resolved, you'll see all the necessary packages being installed, along with a warning about the size of the packages:

```
================================================================================
 Package              Arch        Version          Repository       Size
================================================================================
Installing:
 php                  i386        5.1.6-20.el5_2.1  updates          1.1 M
Installing for dependencies:
 php-cli              i386        5.1.6-20.el5_2.1  updates          2.1 M
 php-common           i386        5.1.6-20.el5_2.1  updates          154 k

Transaction Summary
================================================================================
Install      3 Package(s)
Update       0 Package(s)
Remove       0 Package(s)

Total download size: 3.4 M
Is this ok [y/N]:
```

As before, if you continue, Yum will install and set up php for you. If the package is already installed, Yum is smart enough not to try to install it a second time. However, if the package does need to be upgraded, then Yum will take care of that for you.

Yum also takes care of any dependencies that the software package might have. In our example with php, the php package depends on both php-cli and php-common. Yum has therefore arranged for these packages to be added to the install list.

Installing a Group of Packages

Yum also has the ability to install groups of packages. This is really useful because many tasks require a collection of different software that may on first glance not look at all related. One thing to remember is that Yum will install only those packages that are marked as mandatory. This is normally fine because it usually installs all of the key packages, but if you find it didn't install what you're looking for, you can still install any missing packages individually. To find out what groups are available (and also which ones you have already installed), you use the following:

```
yum grouplist
```

This will generate a list similar to the following:

```
[root@localhost ~]# yum grouplist
Setting up Group Process
Installed Groups:
    Administration Tools
    Graphical Internet
Available Groups:
    Tomboy
    Cluster Storage
    Engineering and Scientific
    MySQL Database
    Development Libraries
    Beagle
    GNOME Software Development
    .....
    X Software Development
    Virtualization
Done
[root@localhost ~]#
```

You will certainly see more than this because we have removed a large chunk of the groups so that the list wouldn't take up half the book! One of the groups that most people tend to end up installing is Virtualization. This group contains all the packages you need such as the Xen kernel, support libraries, and administration tools.

To install a group, you use the groupinstall command:

```
yum groupinstall Virtualization
```

If the group you want to install has a space in the name, enclose it in quotes:

```
yum groupinstall "Yum Utilities"
```

As with installing packages, Yum will present you with a list of packages that it needs to download and install in order to fulfill your request.

Updating Individual Packages

Updating a package is a cross between updating the whole system and installing a single package. To do this, run the following command:

```
yum update php
```

In this case, Yum will update the php package and any packages on which it depends. If you already have a running web server using PHP, the new version will not be used until you restart the web server.

Updating a Package Group

It is possible to update all the packages within a given group. Like updating individual packages, it is usually better to update the entire system rather than just a handful of packages. To update a group, run this:

```
yum groupupdate Virtualization
```

This will update all the packages in the Virtualization group.

Removing a Package with Yum

Although Yum is mostly used for installing and updating software, it can also be used to remove it. This is especially helpful when removing package groups (which we'll look at in a moment). To remove a package, run the following command:

```
yum remove php
```

Note that this will remove the php package from the system. However, when we initially installed php, Yum also installed php-cli and php-common. These will not be removed by this command, but other packages that might depend on the php package will be. It is always best to very carefully check what Yum is proposing to do, especially when you are removing packages.

Removing a Package Group

This command follows the same pattern as the other group commands. To uninstall the Virtualization group, for example, you can use the following command:

```
yum groupremove Virtualization
```

This will remove all the packages within this package group.

Searching for Packages

Yum has a sophisticated search facility that will allow you to find pretty much any package across your repositories. The key to actually finding a specific package, though, requires a more in-depth knowledge on how RPM packages are named—specifically, how the version numbers work.

RPM Package Names

RPM packages are named in the following way:

```
package_name-version- release.architecture.rpm
```

package_name is the name of the package. For example, you saw how to install the php package earlier. version is the version of the software that the package contains. release is the CentOS release number. Most packages are version locked, whereas the release changes as patches are added. architecture is what type of hardware the package is compiled to run on.

For the vast majority of people, the architectures of interest are i386 (32-bit Pentiums and Athlons), x86_64 (64-bit Pentiums and Athlons), and noarch, which is compatible with all platforms. This usually implies that there are no precompiled files. Collections of Python scripts usually come in a noarch package, for example.

Generally, if you're working with Yum and the standard repositories, you won't need to do much with either architecture or version because Yum will make the correct choices for you. However, knowing how the packages are put together will let you search for specific versions and give you the option of manually locating and installing a file.

Doing a Simple Search

A simple search will look for packages based on the package name. To search for the php package, you can do the following:

```
yum list php
```

This would show the following output:

```
[root@localhost ~]# yum list php
Available Packages
php.i386                            5.1.6-20.el5_2.1       updates
[root@localhost ~]#
```

This tells you the package name and architecture (php.i386), the current version (5.1.6), the release (20.el5_2.1), and which repository the package is in (updates). Now that you've found the package, you can install it the same way as before.

Using Wildcards

Sometimes you aren't going to know which specific package you want, or you might want to see a list of all related packages. You can use an asterisk (*) to perform a wildcard search. For example, if you search for php*, you get the following output:

```
[root@localhost ~]# yum list "php*"

Installed Packages
php.i386                          5.1.6-20.el5_2.1        installed
php-cli.i386                      5.1.6-20.el5_2.1        installed
php-common.i386                   5.1.6-20.el5_2.1        installed
php-gd.i386                       5.1.6-20.el5_2.1        installed
php-mbstring.i386                 5.1.6-20.el5_2.1        installed
php-mcrypt.i386                   5.1.6-15.el5.centos.1   installed
php-mysql.i386                    5.1.6-20.el5_2.1        installed
php-pdo.i386                      5.1.6-20.el5_2.1        installed
php-pecl-Fileinfo.i386            1.0.4-3.el5.centos      installed
php-pgsql.i386                    5.1.6-20.el5_2.1        installed
Available Packages
php.i386                          5.1.6-23.2.el5_3        updates
php-bcmath.i386                   5.1.6-23.2.el5_3        updates
php-cli.i386                      5.1.6-23.2.el5_3        updates
php-common.i386                   5.1.6-23.2.el5_3        updates
...
[root@localhost ~]#
```

■**Note** You can see here that the php package is installed (5.1.6-20.el5_2.1) and an update is available (5.1.6-20.el5_3).

A More Useful Search

Using list is helpful only when you already know the package name that you want to find. Generally, you'll have a rough idea what it is you need but might not be able to put your finger on the name. You can get a list of all the packages by using yum list—but if you want to find a specific package, you will want to do a search.

To do a search that will look at the name, description, and summaries of all packages in the repositories, you can use the search command. For example, you can do a search for everything with php in it with this command:

```
yum search php
```

Currently this returns 87 potential hits. The list shows the package name with a description next to it so that you can tell whether any of the packages are the one that you want to find. Another way to perform the search is to use the `provides` command. When using this, Yum will look to find any packages that provide the search item (for example, a library package), and it will also look at the individual file list. However, doing so requires the use of indexes that are considerably larger than those for a simple search. That said, with a reasonably fast Internet connection, the delay is not really noticeable.

To do a search for any packages that provide php, you can use the following command:

```
yum provides php*
```

Adding a Custom Repository

Dag Wieers helps run a third-party software repository, and we'll be using this repository as the example in this section, because many people find his packages useful and would rather have easy access via Yum than have to download and install the RPM packages manually.

Setting It Up with RPM

Dag makes it very easy to set up and use his repository by providing all the configuration as an RPM file. The `rpm` command-line tool can accept any valid URL that points to an RPM package, which means it's possible to install the RPM directly from Dag's web site without downloading it first. Installing this RPM file adds the correct `.repo` files for Yum and configures the repository without any further intervention.

For example, the command listed on Dag's web site is as follows (for i386):

```
rpm -Uhv \
http://apt.sw.be/redhat/el5/en/i386/rpmforge/RPMS/
    rpmforge-release-0.3.6-1.el5.rf.i386.rpm
```

Running this command downloads and installs the RPM file from the web site. This RPM contains the public keys for the signers, the repo configuration files, and the documentation, among other things. Using RPM to distribute the information makes sense because it's easy to update and manage future releases.

How to Do It Without an RPM

If you don't have an RPM file, you will need to do a few extra steps to set up a new repository. Most repositories make two files available—a `.repo` file containing all the information about the repository and the public key that was used to sign the packages to verify their authenticity. Both are required in order to get a repository up and running.

Another excellent CentOS repository is provided by Karanbir Singh. Actually, he updates and maintains two repositories at http://centos.karan.org. These repositories contain packages that are available on similar platforms but aren't available for CentOS without being rebuilt. One contains packages from Fedora Extras, and the other contains miscellaneous packages that Karanbir has built. One thing to keep in mind is that packages from the Extras repository will not update or conflict with the [base] repository. The Misc Packages repository, on the other hand, does contain packages that do. As mentioned on his web site, if you choose to use the Misc Packages repository, you also need to enable the Fedora Extras repository because there are numerous dependencies that are resolved in there.

As with some of the official CentOS repositories, you need to be aware that some packages will replace the base packages. It is important that you understand the consequences of using third-party repositories before proceeding any further.

If you would still like to benefit from Karanbir's work, you will need to tell Yum where to find the two repositories. The easiest way to do this is with wget—a handy command-line utility that can download files from web sites and FTP servers.

What you want to do is download the two .repo files available on the web site and store them in /etc/yum.repos.d/. To do this, you can use the following commands (as root):

```
cd /etc/yum.repos.d/
wget http://centos.karan.org/kbsingh-CentOS-Extras.repo
wget http://centos.karan.org/kbsingh-CentOS-Misc.repo
```

This will download the files and store them in the current directory. The only thing you need to do now to complete the setup process is to install the RPM signing key. This is also available from Karanbir's web site, and fortunately, RPM can work with a URL as well as a local file. To install his PGP key, you can run the following command:

```
rpm --import http://centos.karan.org/RPM-GPG-KEY-karan.org.txt
```

To test that this is working properly, try running yum update. On one of our servers, after you have run the previous commands, the output starts with this:

```
[root@localhost ~]# yum update
kbs-CentOS-Extras        100% |==========================|  951 B    00:00
primary.xml.gz           100% |==========================|  157 B    00:00
kbs-CentOS-Misc          100% |==========================|  951 B    00:00
primary.xml.gz           100% |==========================|  157 B    00:00
Setting up Update Process
```

Here you can see that it knows about the new repositories and it has downloaded the repository information for processing. You can return a list of enabled repositories by running the command yum repolist. If you run yum repolist all, you will see the repositories on your system, even if they haven't been enabled. You can now make use of any of the RPMs in the new repositories, using the same commands discussed earlier.

Yumex

CentOS comes with a tool called Yumex that provides a useful graphical interface to the yum command. If you want to give Yumex a try, you'll first need to install it. It's available in the standard CentOS repositories and can be installed with yum install yumex.

Because Yumex is a graphical tool, you will need to log in to the graphical interface on your server. You'll find Yumex (which stands for Yum Extender) in System Tools under the Applications menu. When you first start Yumex, it will show you Package view (Figure 4-1).

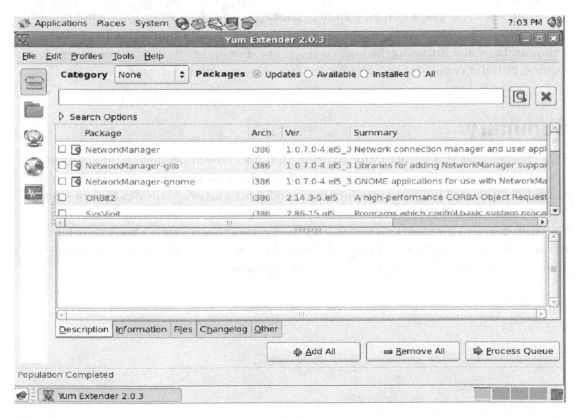

Figure 4-1. *Starting Yumex*

As you can see, Yumex lists the packages that need to be updated. You can select packages individually or click Add All to select all the packages. Clicking Process Queue will attempt to update the packages that you have selected.

You can view the available packages, the installed packages, or all the packages by selecting the respective radio button. The search feature will allow you to find specific packages that you want to install.

Selecting a package will show its description in the bottom window. By selecting the different tabs, you will be able to see all the information about that specific package.

The buttons down the left side provide access to additional features. The first button selects Package view, which is what is selected by default. The next button selects Group view and shows packages based on their groups for easy selection. The next button selects Queue view and lets you see an overview of what will happen once you process the queue itself. The fourth button, Repos, shows you all the repositories that are available on the machine. You can also enable and disable repositories from this screen. Lastly is Console view, which shows the raw output from all of the Yum-related commands that Yumex has executed.

Yumex is a really nice tool for handling packages, especially when you're not quite sure which package you want to find. It's often much friendlier than trying to use the command line and browsing through reams of text. For more information on using Yumex, visit the Yum Extender web site at `http://www.yum-extender.org/`.

Summary

This chapter gave you a quick guide to using Yum. You now know how to update your system and install, update, and remove specific packages and package groups. You also know how to search for packages and how to add third-party repositories to your system both by using an RPM file and by manually updating your configuration.

Yum is one of the tools that you will use on a regular basis, but it's not overly hard to use or understand. Now that you've learned the basics, you can learn more about the advanced features by running `man yum` or running `yum help`.

PART 2

Going into Production

Certain services are required in any production environment. These include web services, mail, name resolution, DHCP, file sharing, and more. The chapters in this part will show you how to configure and run these essential network services on your CentOS server.

CHAPTER 5

■ ■ ■

Using Apache

When you hear the word *Internet*, what's the first thing that pops into your head? If you said "web sites," you wouldn't be alone! Indeed, most people think that the World Wide Web and the Internet are the same thing. Perhaps it is no surprise then that one of the most common reasons for setting up a Linux server is to run a web site of some kind. People have all sorts of different reasons for putting content on the Internet. Sometimes they want to share their photos with friends and family, they might want to set up a home page for their business, or perhaps they want to start their own blog.

Whatever the reasons, before you can host your own stuff, you need a web server. In this chapter, we'll go through how to install the web server, and once everything is installed, we'll show how to do some initial configuration such as setting the web server to start when the server boots and updating the firewall to allow people to connect from the outside. Then we'll show where all the configuration files are and do some basic configuration such as setting the server name and contact details. We'll also be setting up SSL (see the "Using SSL" section a bit later in the chapter) and demonstrating how to use virtual hosts (see the "Setting Up Virtual Hosts" section).

■Note DNS is very important for making your web site available to the masses. It's also critical for providing virtual hosting. This (and more) is covered in depth in Chapter 7.

After that, we'll move on to some of the more interesting tasks you're likely to want to do. We'll look at password protecting a directory (a firm favorite), using caching to improve the performance of your web site, finding where the logs are kept and what to look out for, setting up virtual hosts, and more!

How Does the Server Work?

You are no doubt very familiar with using a web browser, searching the Internet, and viewing web pages. But do you really know what's going on in the background? Do you know how these pages actually get to you? Before you can view a web page or download a file, you need to provide your browser with a uniform resource locator (URL). A URL contains a number of distinct parts that affect how a page is requested. For example, let's dissect the following:

```
http://www.apress.com/book/catalog
```

The first part, `http://`, specifies which protocol will be used to access the page. These days, you are likely to see only two protocols: HTTP and HTTPS. Occasionally you will see others, such as FTP or application-specific protocols such as IRC and Skype. From a web site point of view, though, we're interested in only the first two. We will look at HTTP in more depth in a moment. HTTPS is really just a special case of HTTP. The only real difference is that the connection is secure. We look at setting up a secure server a little later too.

The second part is the hostname or address of the server that you are requesting the page from (from our example, `www.apress.com`). Generally, you will use a hostname rather than an IP address because it's easier for the user, and on the server side it has some additional benefits such as a basic form of load balancing. One of the important things to remember is that a single web server can handle many different web sites. For example, a web server could provide completely different web sites for both `www.apress.com` and `www.example.com`. Just as important to remember is that `www.example.com` and `www2.example.com` can point to completely different IP addresses and as such can be hosted on completely different servers. You will see this technique a lot where companies host the static parts of their web sites (such as graphics and JavaScript files) on different machines than the ones that run the main web site. eBay, for example, uses the `ebaystatic.com` domain to host its static files and serves the dynamic part of its site from the `ebay.com` domain.

The third bit tells the web server which file or resource you want to access (from our example, `/book/catalog/`). Not so long ago, this path would usually map quite closely to specific files or scripts sitting on the server's hard disk. These days, most web sites hide the implementation details and try to present cleaner URLs.

When the web server receives the request, it will look at the whole URL that has been requested. This is how it can tell the difference between the various sites that it hosts. This technique is called *virtual hosting* and is covered in depth later in the chapter.

So, when you enter a URL and press Enter, your browser will look up the port for the protocol you have requested. Unless you have specified a different port (for example, `http://www.example.com:1234/downloads/`), by default HTTP will connect to port 80,

CHAPTER 5 ■ USING APACHE

and HTTPS will connect to port 443. If you have provided an IP address rather than a hostname, the browser will immediately try to open a connection. If you provided a hostname, the browser will ask the operating system to resolve it to an IP address before trying to connect.

Once the connection has been established, the browser will send a GET request. A GET request looks like this:

```
GET http://www.apress.com/book/catalog/
```

With every reply, the server includes a status code to indicate whether something went wrong. These are defined in the HTTP protocol (RFC 2616). You might have come across some of these:

200 OK: Not usually seen by end users because this means that the file requested was found and is being returned.

404 Not Found: Very common and usually caused by someone moving a file that someone else had linked to.

401 Unauthorized: You usually see this after entering an invalid username and password. Technically, though, it is this status code that makes your browser ask you to authenticate in the first place. We look at this a bit later in the ".htaccess" section.

500 Internal Error: Something blew up on the server, usually seen only with web applications rather than static web sites.

When your browser has downloaded the file requested, if it is X/HTML, it will then repeat the whole process for all the files that the document refers to, such as graphics, Cascading Style Sheets, and JavaScript. Depending on the web site, there can be more than 50 individual requests needed to build a single page. Fortunately, most browsers will cache these files, which tend to be reused on other pages. This greatly improves performance and saves on bandwidth.

A Brief Introduction to SSL

Secure Sockets Layer (SSL) is a technology that provides a secure way to communicate over a potentially insecure network such as the Internet. Although it's most commonly associated with secure web sites (such as those used for online banking), it is also equally useful for securing other services such as e-mail. SSL provides two very important security features. First, it provides an encrypted connection so that the data you send and receive cannot be read by anyone else. The client and server send each other a list of encryption standards that they both support. They then choose the highest level that's supported by both. The second feature is the ability to identify the remote server. This is done using certificates. The server presents its certificate to the client when it first connects. The client has a database of certificate authorities (CAs) that it trusts, and it looks to see whether one of these authorities signed the server's certificate. If it has been signed, if it hasn't expired, and if the hostname matches, the client will show the web page without prompting. If the certificate cannot be verified for some reason, a warning will be displayed to the user.

There are some issues relating to using SSL with a web server (often referred to as HTTPS), and we'll cover these in more depth in the "Using SSL" section later in the chapter. Although SSL sounds rather complicated, it's surprisingly easy to set up. If you're going to be sending or receiving any personal or potentially confidential information, using SSL would be a good idea.

Why Run Your Own Server?

Now, because this is a chapter on setting up and running a web server, you might be thinking that the question in the heading is somewhat redundant. If you've already set your heart on running a shiny new web server, feel free to skip to the next section. If you're still not sure if it's for you, read on.

Running your own web server gives you a lot of flexibility because you control exactly how everything is configured. You can decide where to put your files and whether you want to run PHP, but most important, you can add web sites to your heart's content. You may have only one site in mind at the moment, but you'd be surprised how others tend to crop up, especially when your friends find out you can give them some space for only a modest charge.

Flexibility is the biggest benefit of having your own web server. Most shared hosting companies restrict what you can host. They may not allow files over a certain size. They may have older versions of the software that don't have all the features you need. They might restrict how long your scripts can run for or how much memory they can use. To be fair, these are all valid precautions when running a system that many individuals have access to; after all, one user should not be able to monopolize all the resources.

Actually, if too many people hear about your newfound skills, you might find yourself implementing some of the same restrictions on your own server!

What It Involves

Running your server isn't all fun and games, though. There is a serious aspect to it as well. It becomes your responsibility to make sure that you keep your web server up-to-date with the latest security patches. You also need to ensure that all of the web-based applications that you're running (for example, Gallery or SquirrelMail) are also kept up-to-date, much for the same reasons.

Fortunately, updating any software that's been installed as part of CentOS is very easy to do and will be done during the normal update process. You'll also need to be on the lookout for any funny business, so you'll need to keep an eye on the logs. If you're allowing other people to upload their own content, this becomes even more important because you not only need to make sure that they're not serving anything unsuitable but also that their data is kept secure. To be honest, we're not talking about a great deal of work here. As long as you keep an eye on things and run regular updates, it's unlikely that you'll have any trouble.

When to Let Someone Else Do It

Now that you've seen what's involved, you might be wondering whether you really want to run your own web server after all. Even if you are going to, there are good reasons why a future web site might be best hosted elsewhere. For example, if you are hosting on a machine at home or at work, you might not have a very fast Internet connection. If you're going to be serving large files such as streaming video, it may be best to see whether you can host at least that aspect on a system that has more bandwidth available.

You may also have a friend who you just know is going to hassle you with questions, so it might be worth pointing them to a commercial provider that will get paid to answer all of their questions. Normally when we talk about hosting with a third party, hosting is on a shared server. This is where you are provided with the details on where to upload your content, and the provider handles the technical side of things. If you need something a bit more special, though, you can lease a dedicated server. This is a real machine that sits in a data center somewhere.

As the name suggests, it is dedicated for your use, and you can install whatever software you like. For all intents and purposes, it's the same as the PC sitting under your desk. As you'd expect, though, these services are a bit on the pricey side and generally have minimum contract terms and other less than exciting restrictions. If you need the flexibility of a dedicated server but don't want to overcommit yourself, you could look at a virtual private server.

What Is a Virtual Private Server (VPS)?

A *virtual private server* (VPS) is a fully functional Linux server. However, they could more accurately be described as server instances because there can be numerous VPSs on a single physical server. A VPS usually means that you won't have dedicated hardware and will in fact be sharing with other users. This is why they are offered at a much lower cost. You have full root access, and you can install whatever software you like and use it in the same way as you would a real server.

The difference is that your server is most likely sharing real hardware with other virtual private servers. Linux servers are well known for their ability to handle heavy workloads without consuming much in the way of resources. A VPS puts this to good use by allowing a collection of servers to share the same hardware. This means that for a given amount of hardware, considerably more servers can be provided. It also means that VPSs are significantly cheaper than real dedicated servers, and for most people, a VPS will be more than sufficient for their needs. If not, it is very easy to upgrade your VPS with some extra memory or hard disk space. If you do decide to get a VPS, make sure you find a reputable provider. Lots of providers use weird and wonderful techniques to get the maximum number of Linux instances running on one machine as they can. This means you pay very little for the service, but you don't really have a true dedicated Linux server. When you start trying to install software or need to access certain devices, you'll come across all sorts of strange and arcane error messages.

If you're just starting out with running your own server, a VPS could be for you. It's much cheaper than a real dedicated server, and there is usually plenty of room for expansion. It will also save you from having to keep a machine permanently connected at home. Most VPS are hosted in high-quality data centers and so have very fast Internet connections. Many of our friends use a VPS combined with a server at home so that they can have the best of both worlds!

Picking a Web Server

Picking the right web server software can be either very complicated or very straightforward depending on what you're looking to achieve. For the vast majority of people, the choice of web server isn't particularly important. Although it spoils the surprise a little (and you've probably already guessed anyway), we'll be going with the Apache web server in this chapter. It's one of the most popular web servers on the planet, has tons of features, and has a great user community with lots of support, tutorials, examples, and too many books to count. Because it's the most commonly used web server, you'll be in a much better position to get help and support.

If you really need something a bit lighter on its toes (for example, if you have limited memory) or just want to try something a bit different, by all means take a look around. nginx seems to be the current favorite especially for deploying Ruby on Rails applications, but lighttpd still commands far more web share. At the end of the day, the choice is yours, but if you're new to the game and would like to ease your way into it before trying something a bit more exotic, then we strongly suggest starting your web-serving career with Apache.

Installing Apache

If you followed the install guide in Chapter 2, you'll already have Apache installed. The easiest way to check this is to use the `service` command:

```
service httpd status
```

Because you haven't started Apache yet, you should receive the following message:

```
httpd is stopped
```

If Apache isn't installed, you will get an error message:

```
httpd: unrecognized service
```

Installing Apache is very straightforward and can be done with a single command:

```
yum install httpd
```

If you haven't updated your system before, you will be prompted to accept the CentOS signing key (see Chapter 4). Otherwise, after the package has been installed, you will be taken back to the command line.

Configuring the Firewall

Now you need to update your firewall because there's not much point in going to all that effort to set up a web server if no one is going to be able to see your lovingly crafted web pages. We'll use the `setup` tool that comes with CentOS because it already has the options in there to easily enable both HTTP and HTTPS.

So, from the command line, run the following:

```
setup
```

This will open up a text-based menu system that you'll be able to use to configure a number of key system services such as the network configuration and the time zone (Figure 5-1).

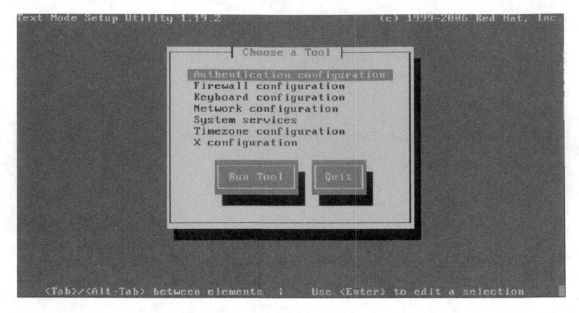

Figure 5-1. *Setup tool, configuring essential system services*

Use the arrow keys to select Firewall configuration, press Tab, and then press Enter. This will bring you to the Firewall Configuration screen where you can also configure SELinux. Press the Tab key four times to highlight Customize, and press Enter (Figure 5-2).

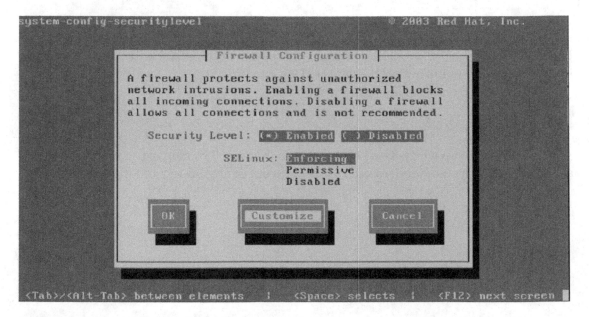

Figure 5-2. *Customizing the firewall*

You should see a section labeled Allow incoming. SSH will have an asterisk next to it (Figure 5-3). Press Tab three times, and press the spacebar.

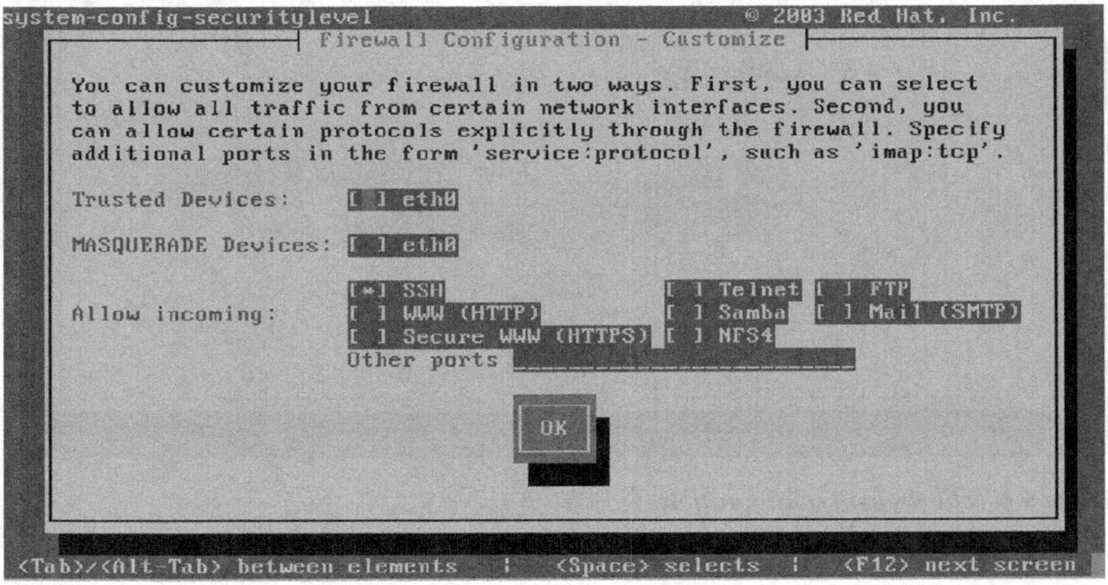

Figure 5-3. *Current firewall configuration*

This will add an asterisk next to WWW (HTTP). Press Tab and then the spacebar to highlight Secure WWW (HTTPS) (Figure 5-4). If you don't want to support secure web traffic at this stage, then there's no need to select it from the list. You can come back here at any time to enable it in the future.

Finally, press Tab to highlight the OK button, and press Enter. This will take you back to the previous page. Press Tab four times to select the OK button. After pressing Enter, there will be a slight delay as the firewall rules are applied. Depending on whether any rules were loaded previously, you may see some text relating to Netfilter. Don't worry about this; you'll be taken back to the main menu as soon as the rules have been updated.

On the last page, press Tab once to select Quit, and press Enter. You should then be returned to the command line. Congratulations, your firewall has now been configured to allow other people to connect to your web server.

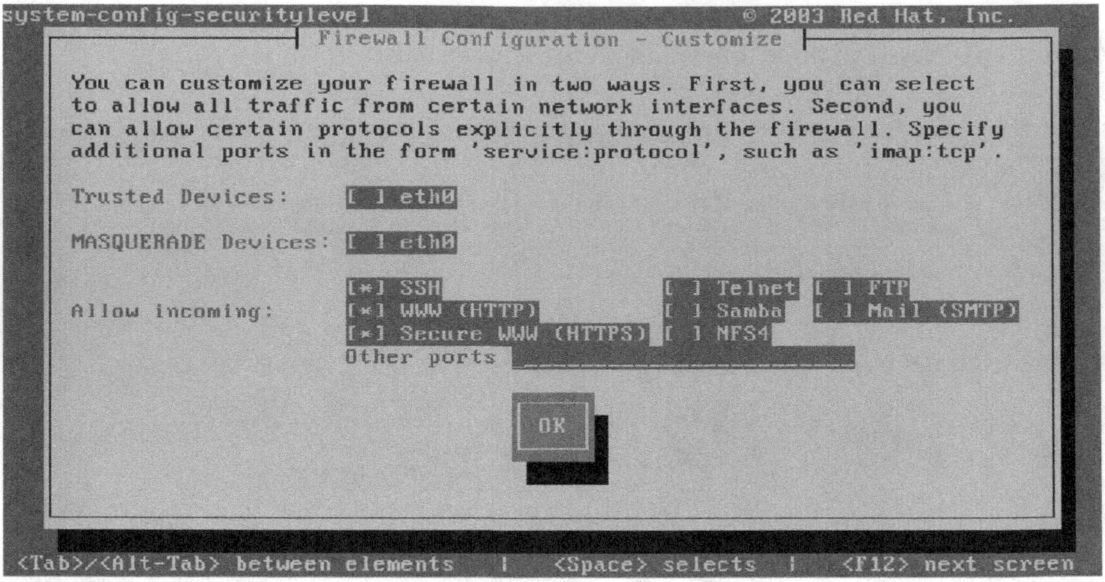

Figure 5-4. *New firewall configuration*

Making Sure Apache Starts Each Time the Server Reboots

Believe it or not, this last step is often missed completely. If that happens, it's usually noticed only after a reboot and people are already on the phone complaining that the web site appears to be down. Don't let this happen to you, and make sure that you configure Apache to start at the same time your server does.

Fortunately, this is really easy to do. Just run the following command:

```
chkconfig httpd on
```

That's all there is to it! You can verify that Apache is going to start by using chkconfig's -list option:

```
chkconfig --list httpd
```

This should return something like this:

```
[root@centos ~]# chkconfig --list httpd
httpd              0:off    1:off    2:on    3:on    4:on    5:on    6:off
[root@centos ~]#
```

CentOS servers start in either run level 3 or run level 5. As you can see, we've configured the system so that Apache is started in both those run levels. You could get more specific if you wanted and specify precisely which run levels that you want to start Apache in, but that's rarely done.

You can also update which services should start when the server reboots using the same configuration tool that you used to configure the firewall. Some of the services in there might be required for your system to start up properly, so disable only those services that you are sure won't cause any problems. Disabling Apache, for example, would be fine, but disabling network would be a bad idea, especially if your machine is in a remote location.

Starting Up and Testing Apache

You will no doubt be delighted to know that at long last you're able to start up your web server!

Although Apache has been configured to start each time the system does, CentOS won't start the service now. You can manually start the service by using this:

```
service httpd start
```

All going well, the output should look like this:

```
[root@centos ~]# service httpd start
Starting httpd: httpd:                       [  OK  ]
```

You can use the same command you used at the beginning of the installation section to check whether Apache is running. This time you should see something like this:

```
[root@centos ~]# service httpd status
httpd (pid 25082 25081 25080 25079 25078 25077 25076 25075 25073) is running...
[root@centos ~]#
```

Apache creates a number of processes to handle the incoming web requests. Under Linux, each process is given a unique number to identify it. This is called the *process ID* (PID). The status command is showing you that Apache is running and giving you a list of the processes that have been created. Generally speaking, you won't do much with this information, but it's useful if you ever have to do any debugging.

When you started Apache, you may have received a warning, although it seemed to have started anyway. The warning you may have seen is as follows:

```
Could not reliably determine the server's fully qualified domain name,
using 127.0.0.1 for ServerName
```

All this means is that Apache wasn't sure which name to use to identify itself. Most of the time it's possible to work it out based on the network configuration, but on a fresh install, this information may not be readily available. We will actually set this manually in the Apache config file in the next section. Once it has been set manually, Apache will no longer raise it as an issue. Apache will run perfectly happily even if you keep getting this error message, so although it's good form to ensure that ServerName is set correctly, it won't cause you any trouble.

Now it's time to take a look at your new web site! The best way to really appreciate your handiwork is to start up a browser on another machine and punch in the IP address of your CentOS server. You should see something like Figure 5-5.

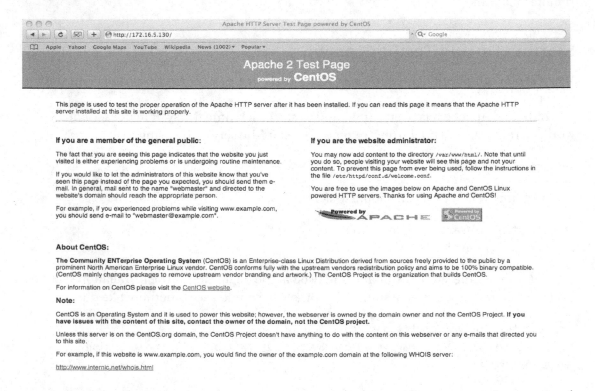

Figure 5-5. *Web site as seen by a Mac*

You should also be able to use HTTPS to access the same page, only this time the link will be secured with SSL. At this stage, you will receive a warning that the certificate is not valid. Don't worry, this is normal. The certificate you're using currently is one that was created during the install process. It is perfectly fine for internal use, and if only a few people are going to use the secure site, there's probably no need to change it. Having said that, you're likely to give a panic attack or at least second thoughts to anyone who visits your site. In the "Using SSL" section, we'll cover how to generate your own self-signed certificate as well as how to generate a certificate-signing request so that you can order a trusted certificate from a third-party certificate authority.

If you don't have another computer handy, you can still check that Apache is up and running from the command line. `links` is a fully featured command-line web browser. It doesn't display graphics or any of the advanced features you've come to expect from the browser on your desktop, but it's an invaluable tool for testing web sites or doing some basic browsing. It's certainly a useful command to know. To try your site with `links`, run the following command:

```
links http://localhost
```

This should give you something like Figure 5-6.

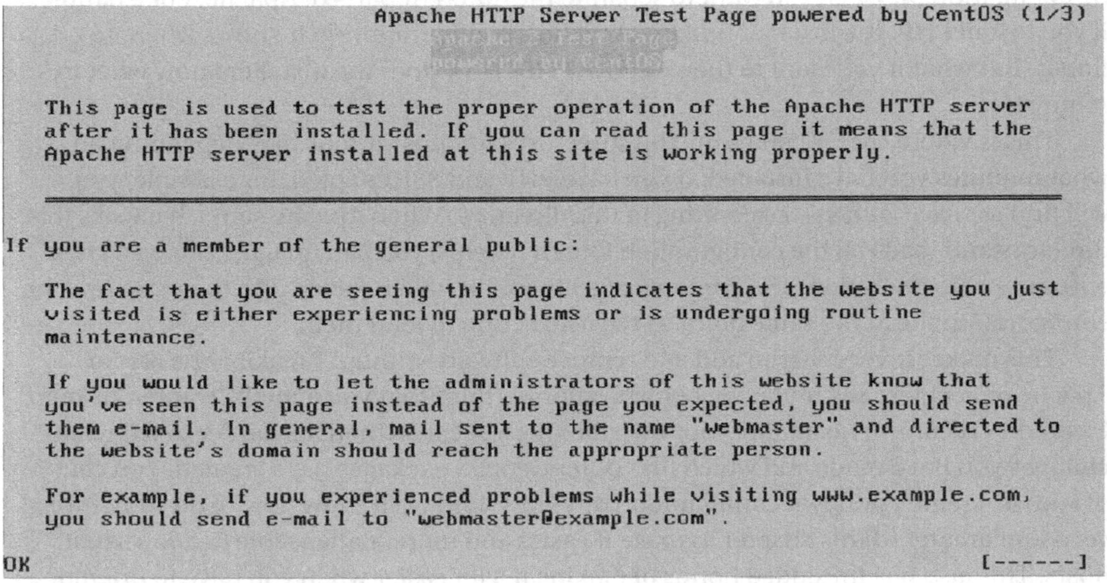

```
                    Apache HTTP Server Test Page powered by CentOS (1/3)



   This page is used to test the proper operation of the Apache HTTP server
   after it has been installed. If you can read this page it means that the
   Apache HTTP server installed at this site is working properly.
   ──────────────────────────────────────────────────────────────────────────
If you are a member of the general public:

   The fact that you are seeing this page indicates that the website you just
   visited is either experiencing problems or is undergoing routine
   maintenance.

   If you would like to let the administrators of this website know that
   you've seen this page instead of the page you expected, you should send
   them e-mail. In general, mail sent to the name "webmaster" and directed to
   the website's domain should reach the appropriate person.

   For example, if you experienced problems while visiting www.example.com,
   you should send e-mail to "webmaster@example.com".

OK                                                                    [------]
```

Figure 5-6. *Web site as seen in* `links`

To get out of `links`, press Q, and then press Enter. You'll be taken back to the command line.

Well, that didn't take long, and you have a nice new Apache server up and running.

Configuring Apache

Now that Apache is up and running, you can start to configure it. Most people don't make a lot of changes to the defaults. Apache comes out of the box configured in such a way that it serves the needs of most people. The main things that people alter are configuring the SSL settings so that they can use a new certificate, creating virtual hosts so they can host multiple web sites, and changing access control so that they can use `.htaccess` files to password protect directories. We will be looking at all three of these topics as well as a few other useful options that you can set to get the best out of Apache.

Where Is Everything?

You can find all the configuration files relating to Apache in `/etc/httpd/`. Right now you're really interested only in the contents of the `conf` and `conf.d` directories.

`conf` contains only one file of interest, and that's `httpd.conf`. This file contains all the core Apache configuration settings. On other distributions or when building for source, it isn't uncommon for Apache's entire configuration to be stored in this file. This becomes a problem, though, when you want to separate the different parts of Apache. For example, if you install PHP, the installer updates Apache's configuration so it knows where to find it. But what if you want to then remove PHP? How does the installer know what to remove?

This is where `conf.d` comes in. This directory contains various files depending on what modules you have installed. If you have PHP and SSL enabled, for example, you will find `php.conf` and `ssl.conf` sitting in this directory. When Apache starts, it checks this directory and loads all the configuration files. If it helps, you can imagine this as a large cut-and-paste operation. The contents of all these files are injected into the main Apache configuration file at the same point as the instruction to load them.

This makes it very easy to add and remove software without breaking the rest of Apache or accidentally removing configuration settings that you actually wanted to keep. I wouldn't recommend adding your own files here because then it's harder to tell what changes you have made and which files other CentOS packages have created. You can, of course, create your own configuration directory, and we'll show how to do something very similar later in this chapter to make it easier and more manageable to add virtual hosts. This also has the added bonus of making it a lot easier when you have to upgrade your system later.

Getting Started

First, let's start with the basics in `httpd.conf`. Really, there isn't much to change here, and it won't be until you actually come up against a problem that you'll want to delve in and try tweaking some of these options. In this section, we'll look at setting `ServerName` and `ServerAdmin`.

The `httpd.conf` file is fully commented and provides a lot of useful information about each of the options. To edit this file, we'll use the basic text editor nano. So, to get started, run this command:

```
nano /etc/httpd/conf/httpd.conf
```

■**Tip** nano automatically uses line wrapping, which can break configuration files. You can prevent this from happening by using `nano -w`.

To save you from scrolling through the file by hand (at just less than a thousand lines, it can take quite a bit of patience), we will show how to use nano's search functionality. Hold down the Ctrl key, and press W. You should then see a search prompt. Type in the following, and then press Enter:

```
ServerAdmin
```

Configuring ServerAdmin

This will take you to the first place that word appears in the document. In this case, it's the first word in one of the comments telling you about the option and what it means. `ServerAdmin` is the e-mail address that should be shown on error messages and other content that is generated by the server. As you can see, it defaults to `root@localhost`, which isn't really ideal. Feel free to replace this with your own e-mail address. That way, people will know who to contact if they are having trouble accessing a resource on your web site.

Configuring ServerName

Next we'll modify `ServerName`. There's no need to search for this one because it's situated directly below `ServerAdmin`. This is the cause of the error message you looked at earlier. In theory, you can set `ServerName` to anything you like, but it makes much more sense to point it at something that truly represents what the server is called.

Saving the Configuration File

Saving a file in nano is straightforward. You can see the menu at the bottom of the screen. The ^ character refers to the Ctrl key. So, to exit nano, you need to press Ctrl+X. If you have made any changes to the file, then nano will ask you whether you want to save changes. After you've confirmed that you want to save, it will ask you to choose the file name. By default this will be the same as the file that you opened originally (in our case `/etc/httpd/conf/httpd.conf`). To accept the default, just press Enter, and you'll be taken back to the command line.

Testing Your New Configuration File

It's possible to restart Apache without testing your configuration, but we don't advise it. Sometimes even a small change that shouldn't affect anything suddenly causes Apache to go on strike, which is not really what you were hoping for while making that quick change over the lunch break.

One way to help protect you against these little mishaps is to check the config file before restarting Apache. You can do this with the service command. Consider this example:

```
[root@centos ~]# service httpd configtest
httpd: Could not reliably determine the server's fully qualified domain name,
using 127.0.0.1 for ServerName
Syntax OK
[root@centos ~]#
```

Now, to show you what it looks like, we've uncommented the last line of the config file. This means that we've closed a tag without first opening it. This is a very common reason for Apache to refuse to start; however, more often, people tend to forget to close a tag rather than forget to open it. In this case, the output from the configtest command looks like this:

```
[root@centos ~]# service httpd configtest
httpd: Syntax error on line 991 of /etc/httpd/conf/httpd.conf: </VirtualHost>
without matching <VirtualHost> section
[root@centos ~]#
```

You now have a very good idea of what went wrong. You know at which line the error occurred (991), and you have a helpful description of what Apache believes to be the problem. Although this is usually a very good guide and will generally point you in the right direction, it's also possible that the error Apache sees is caused by an unrelated problem further up in the config file itself. If you suddenly see a complaint about the virtual host configuration but you've been working on something completely different, take a look at the area you were working on rather than trusting Apache's guidance completely.

A quick way of moving to a specific line number in nano is to press Ctrl+W exactly as if you were going to do a search, and then press Ctrl+T. You will then be able to enter the line number that you want to go to.

Restarting Apache

When you're confident that your Apache config file is good to go, you can restart Apache. Again, we do this with the service command:

```
[root@centos ~]# service httpd restart
Stopping httpd:                                    [  OK  ]
Starting httpd:                                    [  OK  ]
[root@centos ~]#
```

.htaccess

Apache also has the rather useful ability to allow its main configuration to be overridden on a directory-by-directory basis. There are two ways to achieve this functionality. You can enable support for .htaccess files, or you can add the configuration directly into the main config file itself. Generally speaking, it's more secure and better practice to enable these settings in the main config file. That way, all the information is in one place rather than scattered around the filesystem. Using .htaccess files isn't exactly insecure, especially if you're the only person who is making changes to the server. In fact, they are very convenient because a lot of open source applications (such as Drupal) come with an .htaccess file that modifies Apache's settings so that the application works nicely out of the box.

Enabling .htaccess

For security reasons, Apache ships with .htaccess disabled. This prevents an administrator from accidentally giving users or software the ability to make changes. Enabling .htaccess file support is quite easy, though.

First, open the Apache config file in nano, and do a search for AllowOverride. The first section you'll come across is the one where .htaccess is specifically disabled. If you search a couple more times, it will take you to the line inside the configuration area for /var/www/html. If you want to enable .htaccess support, you can do so by changing AllowOverride None to AllowOverride All. Once you've saved your changes and restarted Apache, you'll be able to use .htaccess files.

How to Password Protect a Directory

Password protecting a directory involves two distinct steps. First, you need to create an .htaccess file in the directory that you want to protect. Then you must create a password file so that Apache knows who can and can't log in.

We'll make use of what you've already set up to show how to secure the default directory. To do this, create an .htaccess file in /var/www/html/. Use your trusted nano to create the file (make sure you don't forget the dot before htaccess):

```
nano /var/www/html/.htaccess
```

Configuring Password Protection

One of the key things that many people miss is that if they don't put a restriction on it, once a user has authenticated, the user can actually download the .htaccess file from the server. This is probably not what you want because if the password is somewhere in that directory, the user will be able to download that too. So, the first thing you need to put in your .htaccess file is the following:

```
<Files .htaccess>
order allow,deny
deny from all
</Files>
<Files .htpasswd>
order allow,deny
deny from all
</Files>
```

This will prevent anyone from downloading either the .htaccess or .htpasswd file. It is better to ensure that your .htpasswd file is stored outside of any area that may accidentally become available for download. Many people create their .htpasswd files in /etc/httpd. If you do this, then there's no need for the second Files statement. You should leave the first one in place, however.

Next you can specify that you want to protect this directory. Add this after the Files statement:

```
AuthUserFile /etc/httpd/htpasswd
AuthName "Secret Secure Area"S
AuthType Basic

require valid-user
```

Here's what each directive means:

- AuthUserFile points to the .htpasswd file that contains the login details for our users. We'll create this in a moment.

- AuthName is the text to display when the login windows pops up. You can name it anything you like, although if you want to put spaces in the name, you'll need to remember to put them inside quotation marks.

- AuthType is usually set to Basic. There are other options, but they are rarely used. Basic is just the exchange of a username and password. Because you want to use password authentication here, this is the best choice.

- `require valid-user` tells Apache that any valid user in the `.htpasswd` file should be allowed to access the site. You can specify a particular username by using `require user <username>`. For example, to allow access only to the admin user, you can use `require user admin`.

If you save this file and restart Apache, you should find that when you go to your web server, you get a login prompt. Of course, this page is now too secure because you haven't added any users yet, so no one can actually log in!

Creating User Accounts

To create a user account, you can use the `htpasswd` command. The command is very straightforward and looks like this:

```
[root@doublehelix ~]# htpasswd -c /etc/httpd/htpasswd admin
New password:
Re-type new password:
Adding password for user admin
[root@doublehelix ~]#
```

The `-c` option tells `htpasswd` to create the file if it doesn't already exist. After you've added your first user, you don't need to use this option again. The next argument is the file you want to create or update. In this example, we've used the same path that we specified in our `.htaccess` file. The last argument is the username that you want to be created. After you press Enter, you will be prompted for the password to use for this account and then again to confirm it.

That's it! Now you should be able to log in to your new secure web site with your new account!

Improving Performance

Web site performance is a topic where entire books can (and have) been written. In this section, we'll look at some of the easier ways that you can get a performance boost from your web server.

Compressing files lets you trade CPU time for network bandwidth. Because text compresses extremely well, this is usually a big win, especially when combined with some form of caching.

We'll also look at some settings that you can fine-tune, why you might want to fine-tune them, and how to make sure that your performance-enhancing changes don't end up slowing your whole machine down!

Compression

One of the fastest and easiest ways to get a real performance boost out of your server is to enable compression. Of course, like most things, there is a trade-off taking place. In this case, we are going to use more processing power to handle each request because Apache must take the file and compress it. Once compressed, the file will be much smaller and hence will take considerably less time to be sent over the network to the client. Because even basic computers can very quickly extract compressed content, overall you should find that your web site feels far snappier.

There is a really nice tool here: `http://www.gidnetwork.com/tools/gzip-test.php`.

You can put in any URL, and it will tell you whether compression is being used and, if not, how different levels of compression would have improved the performance of the site.

Enabling Compression in Apache

Enabling compression in Apache takes just a single line. This can be added in numerous places, but for now, we'll add it to the end of the main config file.

So, open the config file as before with this:

```
nano /etc/httpd/conf/httpd.conf
```

and move to the end of the file. The quickest way to do this is to hold down Ctrl+V until you reach the end. Once you're at the end, append this line of text (for formatting reasons, it appears as two lines here, but it should be one line in your configuration file):

```
AddOutputFilterByType DEFLATE text/html text/plain text/xml text/css
application/javascript application/x-javascript
```

Save the file as before, and restart Apache. You should now find that you are providing compressed content to the world! Currently you have only told Apache to compress the text files that you will most commonly use on your web site by specifying their MIME types. To find a list of possible MIME types that you can compress, take a look (using nano) in `/etc/mime.types`.

Why You Don't Compress Everything

There are two reasons why you shouldn't compress every file that Apache sends out. The first reason is that most image and music files such as JPEG, PNG, or MP3 are already highly compressed. This means that even though Apache will spend time compressing them, it won't make much difference in the file size and hence won't help the file to be sent any faster.

The second issue is that although all the key browsers such as Firefox, Safari, Opera, and Internet Explorer support compressed text, sometimes they don't handle other compressed formats very well. This is mainly a problem in Internet Explorer. Internet Explorer looks at the content type of a given file and based on that decides which application to open it with. For example, a file with a content type of application/pdf would for most people be opened with Adobe's Acrobat Reader. Unfortunately, in this case, Internet Explorer passes the compressed file data to Acrobat Reader rather than decompressing it first. Because it is not expecting compressed content, Acrobat Reader will fail to open the file properly. Currently, this works fine in the other three browsers. It is expected that once this particular issue is ironed out, most web servers will start compressing all of their compressible content.

Improving Server Performance

There are six key configuration options that relate to performance. These options control how many Apache processes are created, when they're created, and when they are to be destroyed.

You can find these settings around a tenth of the way through the config file. Although this might change in a future revision, the options currently start on line 101.

The first option is StartServers. This is the number of processes that Apache will initially create when the server is first started. By default, it will create eight processes initially. If you are running a busy web site, it may be a good idea to increase this number, but make sure you read the next section on what to look out for.

The second option is MinSpareServers. This is the minimum number of processes that should be kept around to service new requests. Apache will always have at least this number of processes running. By default this is set to 5, so if the server isn't particularly busy, Apache could end up shutting down some of the spare processes.

The third option, MaxSpareServers, is the opposite of the last option. This is the maximum number of processes that Apache can have waiting around. The default for this option is 20. If there are more than 20 idle servers, Apache will close them down.

The fourth and fifth options are somewhat related and should generally be set to the same value. ServerLimit and MaxClients are both by default set to 256. MaxClients is the number of incoming requests that Apache will serve at any given time. If your web site receives more than 256 requests at any one time, the additional requests will be queued until a slot becomes available. ServerLimit is the hard limit for the number of additional processes that can be created during the lifetime of the running server.

You must be very careful with these two options. Setting them to too high a value can sometimes cause Apache to fail to start or make your server unstable. Likewise, there is no benefit to setting ServerLimit to be any higher than MaxClients. Doing so just takes additional resources from the system, which neither Apache or other applications on your server can take advantage of.

Things to Watch Out For

In the previous section, we talked about the most common performance-related configuration options that Apache offers. The important thing to remember is that there is no secret recipe of options to give you optimum performance. For example, if you set MaxSpareServers too high, you'll find that although there are plenty of processes running, Apache ends up spending more time switching between them than actually getting work done. If MinSpareServers is set too low, you may find that if your web site has an uneven load (busy and quiet times), Apache may spend too much time creating and destroying server processes. Again, this takes time away from actually serving requests. For most average workloads, the Apache defaults are perfectly acceptable. If you want to try to improve performance, make small changes, and retest often. Lastly, for most people, far greater performance benefits can be gained by designing the web site for performance. For example, separating out CSS and JavaScript from your HTML files will allow them to be cached, and hence there will be less load placed on your server.

Log Files

Apache keeps extensive log files in /var/log/httpd/. With a default install, three logs are kept. The first is the access_log. This contains detailed information (such as remote IP address, the time and date of the request, and what was requested) of all requests received by Apache. error_log contains similar information but records error messages instead. For example, if a file does not exist or Apache receives an invalid request (such as those caused by attack scripts), the information will end up in here. It's the first place to look if you suspect something is amiss or you just want to make sure that everything is running smoothly.

Apache separates the SSL side of things from the standard logs. Both ssl_access_log and ssl_error_log contain the same sorts of information; they're just separated out to make them easier to work with.

Setting Up Virtual Hosts

The ability to create virtual hosts is probably one of the most powerful features that Apache offers. It is also no doubt one of the most widely used, and for good reason; it lets you run multiple web sites from a single web server.

There are effectively two types of virtual host. You can create name-based virtual hosts or IP-based virtual hosts. Name-based virtual hosts are by far the most common and most useful because they allow you to have an almost unlimited number of web sites on one IP address. If you are hosting on an ADSL line or similar, chances are that you have only one IP address anyway. Although most hosting providers can supply you with more IP addresses, they often come at a hefty premium.

So, why use IP-based virtual hosts? Well, they do have one very important and critical role. You may remember from the beginning of the chapter when you looked at SSL certificates very briefly that because a secure session is established between the web browser and the web server before the web browser sends its request, Apache has no way to know which SSL certificate it should serve. In effect, it can serve only one SSL certificate on an IP address. Using multiple IP addresses is the only way for the server to hand out separate SSL certificates.

Other than that, IP-based virtual hosts aren't really used that much. Apache already comes with the settings needed to create a default SSL virtual host. You saw this when you accessed the server using HTTPS when you first set up Apache. Although you saw the same page on both the secure and insecure versions, this is because by default Apache looks in the same location for both.

Getting Started with Virtual Hosts

First you need to enable virtual host support in the main Apache config file. Open the config file in nano (`nano /etc/httpd/conf/httpd.conf`), and search for `NameVirtualHost`. You should find it near the end of the file.

This section looks like this:

```
# Use name-based virtual hosting.
#
#NameVirtualHost *:80
#
```

The configuration option `NameVirtualHost` lets you specify the IP addresses and ports that Apache should use for virtual hosts. The `*:80` means that Apache should make virtual hosts available for all possible IP addresses but only on port 80. This default is ideal for most people, so uncomment this line by removing the hash (#) from the beginning of the line, leaving you with the following:

```
#
# Use name-based virtual hosting.
#
NameVirtualHost *:80
#
# NOTE: NameVirtualHost cannot be used without a port specifier
# (e.g., :80) if mod_ssl is being used, due to the nature of the
# SSL protocol.
```

Now that you've told Apache that you want to use virtual hosts, you need to configure one. Directly after the `NameVirtualHost` configuration option is a sample virtual host definition. We will show how to create a new virtual host beneath the example. You could, of course, uncomment the example and use that, but we find it's always a good idea to keep some documentation around in case you ever need to look back and double-check your work.

The example looks like this:

```
# VirtualHost example:
# Almost any Apache directive may go into a VirtualHost container.
# The first VirtualHost section is used for requests without a known
# server name.
#
#<VirtualHost *:80>
#     ServerAdmin webmaster@dummy-host.example.com
#     DocumentRoot /www/docs/dummy-host.example.com
#     ServerName dummy-host.example.com
#     ErrorLog logs/dummy-host.example.com-error_log
#     CustomLog logs/dummy-host.example.com-access_log common
#</VirtualHost>
```

You'll recognize ServerAdmin and ServerName from earlier. They do the same thing within the context of each virtual host, although ServerName has a special function here. In this case, ServerName is how Apache will know which web site it should serve up to the web browser. In the previous example, it will use this virtual host only if the web site requested is dummy-host.example.com.

■Note There is a catch here. Whichever virtual host is defined first will be considered to be the default. This means that if none of the other virtual hosts matches the URL that's been requested, the first virtual host will be used instead. Thus, it's a good idea to make sure that your default virtual host is somewhat safe for public consumption. Otherwise, visitors might get a shock when they expect one web site but get something else altogether!

DocumentRoot tells Apache where to find the files for this web site. Although you can put the files pretty much anywhere, you must make sure that Apache has permission to view them. Apache doesn't have any special access and so can access only those files that have file permissions (and SELinux context if you're using SELinux). If you're not sure about file permissions, flip back to Chapter 3. Most people like to keep their virtual hosts in one location. We tend to keep ours in /var/www/vhosts/. We also name the actual virtual host directory to match the web site name, replacing the dots with underscores. For example, we would keep the web site for test.example.com in /var/www/vhosts/test_example_com/.

ErrorLog and CustomLog allow you to separate log files from each of your different virtual hosts and more important from the main Apache logs in /var/log/httpd/. Some people actually prefer all the logging to go in one place. If you want only one log file to check, all you need to do is leave out these two options from your virtual host configuration. If you want to analyze each site separately or you need to provide information to a third party, it will make your life a lot easier if you do use separate files. You can, of course, still store them in /var/log/httpd/ if you prefer.

Creating Your First Virtual Host

Because the first virtual host is also used as the default, we'll set it up to mirror the original setup. So, at the end of the file, add the following:

```
<VirtualHost *:80>
ServerName localhost
DocumentRoot /var/www/html/
</VirtualHost>
```

Of course, you can set ServerName to whatever you prefer; you don't have to use localhost. This is probably the simplest virtual host definition that you will come across. Any options that you do not specifically set will be inherited from the original defaults. For example, logging will continue to go to the main log files, and ServerAdmin will be set to whatever you used previously.

To test this, save the config file, and restart Apache. Using one of the techniques discussed earlier, take a look to see whether you can still see your web server. All being well, it should look just the same as before. If you receive an error message, look again at the config file, and make sure that everything is as it should be.

Using vhosts.d

Some people prefer to keep all of their virtual hosts in the main Apache config file. For small servers with ten or fewer virtual hosts, that is what we generally do as well. However, if you're thinking of hosting a couple hundred virtual hosts, you might want something a bit easier to manage and use.

Apache has the ability to read in config files from other locations. You saw this at the beginning of the chapter when you looked at how Apache's config files were laid out under CentOS. You can do a similar thing for virtual hosts. We recommend, though, that your first virtual host is always configured in your main config file and is placed before the line that instructs Apache to read in additional configuration files. This way, you can be completely sure which virtual host is the default.

First you need to create our `vhosts.d` directory. This is the most common name for the directory, but as before, there is nothing stopping you from choosing something else. To keep things neat and tidy, create this in `/etc/httpd/` as follows:

```
[root@www ~]# cd /etc/httpd/
[root@www httpd]# mkdir vhosts.d
[root@www httpd]# cd vhosts.d/
[root@www vhosts.d]#
```

Now you can start creating your virtual host files. To see this in action, you'll create a virtual host definition for `www.example.com`. Again, you can call the file anything you want, but to ensure that Apache loads only the files you want, give your virtual host files a `.conf` extension.

So, let's create a new config file for our example web site. You're already situated inside `/etc/httpd/vhosts.d/`, so there's no need to specify the full path to nano. If you aren't in the right directory, you can use the full path instead. We'll use nano to create the new file:

```
nano www_example_com.conf
```

And add this content:

```
<VirtualHost *:80>
ServerName www.example.com
DocumentRoot /var/www/vhosts/www_example_com/
</VirtualHost>
```

Now save the file, and exit nano. All you need to do now is tell Apache that it should look for additional configuration files in your newly created directory. So, edit the main configuration file again (`httpd.conf`), and scroll down to the bottom. Add the following line:

```
Include /etc/httpd/vhosts.d/*.conf
```

Save the file, and exit nano. You should now run a `configtest`, and assuming all is well, you can restart Apache. Congratulations! You're using virtual hosts!

Using SSL

You will no doubt know all about secure web sites. You probably use them every day such as when you order a book from Amazon or log in to an online banking site to check your statements. Depending on the browser, secure connections are shown in different ways. Firefox, Safari, and Internet Explorer, for example, all show padlocks but in different places. For example, Firefox shows the padlock on the status bar at the bottom right of the window, whereas Safari shows it in the top-right corner of the window.

During installation, a self-signed SSL certificate is created for you. This will work perfectly well to encrypt traffic, but it will raise a warning for anyone who tries to use it. If the secure site is going to be used only by a couple of people and you are able to convince them that the certificate is actually valid, then there's no urgent need to change it. If, on the other hand, you want to use the server with the general public (for example, the payment page of your new e-commerce venture), you're going to have to get yourself a certificate that has been signed by a trusted third party called a *certificate authority* (CA).

There are various CAs available ranging from the well known and incredibly expensive (such as VeriSign and Thawte) to the lesser known, better priced, and equally usable (such as DynDNS and GoDaddy).

You will find that there are various services offered to try to tempt you to part with your money. Some will offer high assurance levels or will provide you with a seal to put on your web site to show that your certificate is genuine. None of these features makes your SSL certificate any more or less secure. If you think these features will help convince customers that you're legitimate and upstanding, then by all means give them a go. If you just want a secure site that doesn't flash up a warning, you can safely ignore these extra features and go for a basic certificate.

Installing mod_ssl

Installing mod_ssl is very straightforward on CentOS and requires only one command:

```
yum install mod_ssl
```

As with Apache itself, if you followed the installation instructions in Chapter 2, you will already have mod_ssl on your system. Once it has been installed, simply restart Apache (service httpd restart), and you will be good to go!

Getting Your Shiny New Certificate

Before you can get a certificate from a CA, you need to generate a certificate-signing request (CSR). Before you can do that, you need to generate a key. This key will be password protected and will ensure that even if someone were to steal your certificate, without your password they wouldn't be able to use it. This isn't always as useful as it sounds, and we'll cover removing the password protection a bit later.

First we'll create a directory called /etc/certs/. We prefer to keep our certificates in /etc because it is one place we're always guaranteed to have backed up. From here, any of the various tools that want to use SSL can do so without making the configuration files look strange (that is, the mail server loading SSL certificates from the web server directory).

```
[root@centos conf]# mkdir /etc/certs
[root@centos conf]# cd /etc/certs/
[root@centos certs]#
```

Now you can create the key file. We prefer to name the key the same as the host that the certificate is going to be for. We generally create a separate key for each site so that we can separate them or hand them over to other people if necessary. So, to create your key file, do the following:

```
[root@centos certs]# openssl genrsa -des3 -out www_example_com.key 1024
Generating RSA private key, 1024 bit long modulus
.......................................................................................
.........................................++++++
...................................++++++
e is 65537 (0x10001)
Enter pass phrase for www_example_com.key:
Verifying - Enter pass phrase for www_example_com.key:
[root@centos certs]#
```

You will be prompted for the password twice. When your key has been generated, you'll be returned to the command line.

■**Caution** The key file contains the private part of the key pair and should be kept secret at all costs. You should never give anyone access to your key file, because with this, they could potentially impersonate your server!

Now it's time to create your CSR. You need to create a CSR so that a certificate authority will be able to provide you with a signed certificate. You should answer the questions honestly in this section because the answers form part of the certificate. The big gotcha is that when it asks for the common name, you should put in the full hostname for the web site. If you don't do this or what you enter is not exactly the same as your web server's hostname, people will get a warning message that the certificate is for a different server!

To create your CSR, do the following:

```
[root@centos certs]# openssl req -new -key www_example_com.key -out \
www_example_com.csr
Enter pass phrase for www_example_com.key:
You are about to be asked to enter information that will be incorporated
into your certificate request.
```

```
What you are about to enter is what is called a Distinguished Name or a DN.
There are quite a few fields but you can leave some blank
For some fields there will be a default value,
If you enter '.', the field will be left blank.
-----
Country Name (2 letter code) [GB]:
State or Province Name (full name) [Berkshire]:
Locality Name (eg, city) [Newbury]:
Organization Name (eg, company) [My Company Ltd]:
Organizational Unit Name (eg, section) []:
Common Name (eg, your name or your server's hostname) []:www.example.com
Email Address []:
Please enter the following 'extra' attributes
to be sent with your certificate request
A challenge password []:
An optional company name []:
[root@centos certs]#
```

We've left most of the information blank. If you do this, OpenSSL will use the defaults that it has suggested. As mentioned, you should use your real information here and make sure that the common name is correct. There's no need to set a challenge password or a company name.

You will now have a CSR file. Before you can use this with Apache, you need to create a signed certificate, which is generated from the public part of your key plus the signature from the CA. The exact procedure for doing this will depend on the certificate authority that you decide to use. However, they will at some point ask you to copy and paste your CSR. The easiest way to do this is to use the cat command to display the contents on the screen:

```
[root@centos certs]# cat www_example_com.csr
-----BEGIN CERTIFICATE REQUEST-----
MIIBpjCCAQ8CAQAwZjELMAkGA1UEBhMCR0IxEjAQBgNVBAgTCUJlcmtzaGlyZTEQ
MA4GA1UEBxMHTmV3YnVyeTEXMBUGA1UEChMOTXkgQ29tcGFueSBMdGQxGDAWBgNV
BAMTD3d3dy5leGFtcGxlLmNvbTCBnzANBgkqhkiG9w0BAQEFAAOBjQAwgYkCgYEA
14ccCDnF2/A5ol1JYkv/neAOrV6ou1BtiCo/LrZQNJiVdbHmNINaGSNXUpieSe2H
riJpmzW8xhURkOpPIVgIZa5HmVZVtGpiHIZ4BRyMOHXJKkOEn34Ew9AO92JXrraS
f9bWDQE2pQkDWuSXRNgARUtjCeWohORTk/gtfhnSZbkCAwEAAaAAMAOGCSqGSIb3
DQEBBQUAA4GBAEaM7/92TUDH3Qnq/BqFfJsBpNaq2GjQ5TkyTaKcy8jQrHgUiSAe
/2ZlC9DpYlVf9lLNuHWkuFCVidntffLwJaZhq8KGsM+OwlIbDfpRXPMXMiMYBl9K
JC+9zj+uGdJ3noft1Z/dLrqVzKPcopmr5xJJzW2nUuouI6bRnE2HELFq
-----END CERTIFICATE REQUEST-----
[root@centos certs]#
```

You need to make sure that you also copy the lines with BEGIN and END in them and try not to introduce extra line breaks when pasting the text. At this stage, there is little more you can do until your CA comes back to you with a signed certificate. Alternatively, of course, you can sign your own certificate. We show how to do that next.

Signing Your Own Certificate

Signing your own certificate can be quite useful. Having a third-party CA sign your certificate costs money, and the certificate normally lasts only for a year or two. By signing your own, you maintain complete control over the process. However, if the public visits your secure site, they will get a warning that the person who signed your certificate is not known, and therefore it isn't trusted. Browsers generally come with a selection of CA certificates, which allows them to automatically recognize certificates signed by them. If you self-sign your certificate, your visitors can elect to trust it, and from then on it will work just like one signed by a CA. This isn't a great idea for an e-commerce site, though.

```
[root@centos certs]# openssl x509 -req -days 365 -in www_example_com.csr -signkey \
www_example_com.key -out www_example_com.crt
Signature ok
subject=/C=GB/ST=Berkshire/L=Newbury/O=My Company Ltd/CN=www.example.com
Getting Private key
Enter pass phrase for www_example_com.key:
[root@centos certs]#
```

OpenSSL will show you all of the details that you originally entered in your CSR. Double-check these to make sure everything is as you expect, and then enter your password to approve the request.

If you look at the contents of the directory, you now have this:

```
[root@centos certs]# ls -lh
total 24K
-rw-r--r-- 1 root root 847 Jan 12 14:15 www_example_com.crt
-rw-r--r-- 1 root root 647 Jan 12 13:55 www_example_com.csr
-rw-r--r-- 1 root root 963 Jan 12 13:35 www_example_com.key
[root@centos certs]#
```

This is now enough to configure Apache to use the new certificate. The CSR can now be deleted because it's not needed to actually use the certificate. That said, many people like to keep it around as a record of what they used last time. We must confess that we have a few CSR files hanging around. They don't take up much space and aren't a security risk. You can decide whether you think they're worth keeping.

What to Do with an Intermediary Certificate

Some CAs, notably the cheaper ones, use what's known as an *intermediary certificate*. They may also refer to it as *certificate bundle* or *certificate chain*. Whatever they call it, you need to install it along with your certificate. To establish the chain of trust, the web browser needs to be able to back-track your certificate to an authority that it knows about. Because your certificate was signed by an intermediary, you must also provide that intermediary's certificate so that the browser can see that the intermediary trusts you and that the intermediary in turn is trusted by someone it knows about.

We'll discuss adding this certificate to Apache's configuration as part of the next section. Although you could cut and paste the file, sometimes the intermediaries provide considerably more content than can be comfortably managed. Because the information contained in such a certificate is publicly available, most CAs publish them on their web sites. If yours has done this and you have the URL, you can download it directly to your server by using wget:

```
wget https://www.example.com/intermediary.cert
```

This will create a file of the same name in the current directory. wget is a very useful tool and is ideal for downloading large files directly to your server. This is usually much faster and more convenient than downloading to your home PC and then uploading the file again to the server.

Putting Your New Certificate to Work

Now that you have your certificate ready, you can configure Apache to use it. If you opted to get your certificate signed by a third party, simply use nano to create a new file with the same naming scheme and cut and paste in your signed certificate. OK, let's hook this up!

Open Apache's SSL configuration file in nano (/etc/httpd/conf.d/ssl.conf). You'll need to change at least two things here; you need to tell Apache which certificate and key to use (SSLCertificateFile and SSLCertificateKeyFile). If you also need to use an intermediary certificate, you will need to update SSLCertificateChainFile.

SSLCertificateFile: This will be the .crt file that either was created when you signed your certificate or was returned to you by the CA. You should use the full path. In our example, the path would be /etc/certs/www_example_com.crt.

SSLCertificateKeyFile: This is the key file that we created initially to start the whole process. Apache needs this so it can unlock the contents of the certificate. In our example, the path would be /etc/certs/www_example_com.key.

SSLCertificateChainFile: This file will have been provided by your CA. Not all CAs require this. If you're not sure, leave this out for now. If on restarting Apache your certificate shows up in the browser as invalid but everything looks OK, this would suggest that your CA does need this to be set up. If you still aren't sure, drop an e-mail to the CA explaining what you're trying to do. They're normally very helpful and have in-depth guides on their web sites explaining how to set up a variety of servers with their products.

That should be it. You're ready to give it a go! Remember to run the configtest before restarting Apache just in case. When you do restart Apache, you should see something like this:

```
[root@centos certs]# service httpd restart
Stopping httpd:                                        [  OK  ]
Starting httpd: Apache/2.2.3 mod_ssl/2.2.3 (Pass Phrase Dialog)
Some of your private key files are encrypted for security reasons.
In order to read them you have to provide the pass phrases.
Server www.example.com:443 (RSA)
Enter pass phrase:
OK: Pass Phrase Dialog successful.
                                                       [  OK  ]
[root@centos certs]#
```

You're now running with your own customized certificate!

Removing the Password Protection from the Key

You'll have noticed, of course, that you have to enter your password to restart Apache. This is because the key file is currently password protected and Apache is unable to unlock the key file without the password. This is good for security because it means that if someone stole your certificate, they would not be able to use it without first guessing your password. Unfortunately, it also means that someone has to type the password in every time Apache starts including every time the server boots, even after an unexpected reboot, and that's hardly ideal either.

If you want to remove the password protection, it's easy enough to do. The following command will do just that:

```
[root@centos certs]# openssl rsa -in www_example_com.key -out www_example_com.key
Enter pass phrase for www_example_com.key:
writing RSA key
```

```
[root@centos certs]# service httpd restart
Stopping httpd:                                        [  OK  ]
Starting httpd:                                        [  OK  ]
[root@centos certs]#
```

This time a password wasn't required to restart Apache. This means that Apache will also start up fully functional when the server boots.

Summary

Well, you've reached the end of the chapter. You learned how a web server works and how web browsers interact with them. You now know how to install and configure a basic Apache server and how to configure some of the more basic features. You learned how to configure Apache to serve multiple web sites from a single IP address with virtual hosting and how to use SSL to secure and protect your content. We also touched briefly on how to optimize Apache and why compression provides a quick return on investment.

In the next chapter, we'll be taking a look at mail servers, the second-most popular task for a Linux server.

CHAPTER 6

■ ■ ■

Setting Up Mail

In terms of Internet history, electronic mail is stone old. When the World Wide Web was conceived in the early 1990s, e-mail already had reached its age of maturity. The first electronic mail between two networked computers was sent in 1971, over the Internet's predecessor, ARPANET. Even though e-mail predates most other applications you use on the Internet—with the exception of the File Transfer Protocol (FTP), which is about as old—e-mail is still one of the most popular functions of the Internet today (and this is not only because someone somewhere chose you to help him get his inheritance out of the country). Even with spam mails rising to levels of 70 to 90 percent of all mails sent, most Internet users write and receive mails on a daily basis.

E-mail still is one of the most versatile Internet applications: you can write to your friends without having to wait for the postal carrier to deliver a letter; you can share pictures, sounds, and videos over e-mail; and you can partake in discussion groups set up as mailing lists. And all of this is delivered directly into your inbox without you having to check web pages for newly arrived messages. Well, mostly.

If you want every mail that reaches you to be directly delivered to a computer that you are responsible for, without the need to store mails on a provider's mail server, then you need a mail server. Or if you want to provide mail service for your family and friends, you need a mail server.

A mail server usually consists of two different pieces of software. One is the mail transfer agent (MTA), which basically sends mails from your machine to other mail servers on the Internet and which receives mails that have been sent from other hosts to your domain. The second is a Post Office Protocol 3 (POP3) or Internet Message Access Protocol (IMAP) server, which is used by your mail user agent (MUA) or mail client (such as Evolution, KMail, or Mutt) to retrieve the mails that have been delivered to your mailbox.

In this chapter, we'll go through how to install the mail server software and how to do a basic setup so you can send mails to the outside world. Then we'll show how to set up your machine to receive mails from the Internet, for which you also need to change your firewall settings. After that, we'll discuss some basic antispam settings and how to configure your server to receive mails for multiple domains. Finally, we will show how to install and configure a POP3 and an IMAP server so your family and friends can fetch the mails you receive for them.

Note For sending and receiving mails, you need your own domain, a working Domain Name System (DNS) server set up, and, preferably, a static IP address. Chapter 7 shows you how to set up your own DNS, but if you have a provider that is willing to set up DNS for you, this is fine also.

How Do Mail Servers Work?

Sending mails seems to be easy. You just type an address of the form user@example.com into your mail client, add a Subject line, and write some text. After that, you click Send, and only seconds later the recipient of that message—user@example.com—has that mail sitting in his inbox. But behind the scenes, sending mails is a bit more complex. After clicking the Send button, your mail client does one of two things: either it has a built-in Simple Mail Transfer Protocol (SMTP) client or it hands off the mail to /usr/sbin/sendmail, the so-called Sendmail interface. SMTP is the protocol that defines how mail works on the Internet, and applications with a built-in SMTP client, like Evolution or KMail, have the ability to send mails via this protocol on their own but to only one predefined mail server, normally the one that is responsible for sending out mails for your domain. Others rely on an installed transfer software.

SENDMAIL INTERFACE

The Sendmail program was one of the first largely deployed mail transfer agents on the Internet. To send mails, it used the program /usr/lib/sendmail, which on Linux distributions normally exists as /usr/sbin/sendmail. A complete mail message including all headers and the message body is piped into that program, and a recipient is specified on the command line. So, if you have a completely formatted mail in mail.txt and you want to send this mail to user@example.com, you would use this command line to send mail:

```
cat mail.txt | /usr/sbin/sendmail user@example.com
```

Because many mail clients such as Mutt, Alpine, or even Mail expected this program to be there, Sendmail became a de facto standard. All mail transfer agents that are available on CentOS implement this interface for sending mails.

So, what happens exactly when your mail client sends the mail to the SMTP server you configured in the program's preferences? The client opens up a session on port 25 with the SMTP server and sends SMTP commands to it. Luckily, SMTP is a clear-text protocol, so if you sniffed on the wire, this is what an example session would look like (lines in bold show the output of the server; normal lines are client input):

```
220 mail.example.com ESMTP Postfix
HELO client.example.com
250 mail.example.com
MAIL FROM:<me@example.com>
250 2.1.0 Ok
RCPT TO:<you@example.net>
250 2.1.5 Ok
DATA
354 End data with <CR><LF>.<CR><LF>
From: Me <me@example.com>
To: You <you@example.net>
Subject: This is a mail from me to you

Hi!
.
250 2.0.0 Ok: queued as 48516F8279
```

The server sends an initial greeting to the client, which starts with 220. As you can see here, the server is running Postfix, which is the mail transfer agent you'll install and configure in this chapter. After it sends the greeting, the client says HELO client.example.com, which is not a typo. There's also an EHLO greeting that turns on Extended SMTP, which the server supports, too. The server is content with the client name on the HELO line and says to go ahead with a 250. Mail programs look only at the numbers at the beginning of the lines; the additional text is there for us humans, which makes it easier to debug problems.

Now the client tells the server who sends the mail and who is going to receive it. You do that with MAIL FROM:<user> and RCPT TO:<user>. The angle brackets are required, and there also must be no space between the colon and the opening angle bracket. If the server is satisfied with both—it might tell you that it doesn't want to relay a mail or that it doesn't know the sending user. Depending on configuration, it sends you an OK by saying 250. You could now add a few more recipients to that mail. When you are finished with this, you need to tell the mail server that you want to send the actual mail content now. You can do this with the DATA command. You get back a 354, which means that the server is willing to accept the mail content.

SMTP has a similarity with normal mail: there is an "envelope" around a "letter." As with letters on paper, addresses on the envelope can be different from those on the actual letter inside the envelope. The addresses on the envelope are used for the mail transport, and the addresses inside the mail are displayed by your mail client when you look at the mail. So, for the first two lines after the DATA command, you repeat the sender and recipient. Then a Subject: line follows, which will also be displayed by your mail client.

To separate this header data from the content of the mail you are writing, you insert an empty line.

When you have finished writing the mail, you end it with a . on a single line. This way, the mail server knows that you reached the end of the mail and that it is supposed to send it now. You get another 250 as an answer, with which the mail server tells you that it has received the mail and now will send it to the recipient (which means talking to other mail servers). The SMTP reply codes are explained in section 4.2 of RFC 2821 (http://www.rfc-editor.org/rfc/rfc2821.txt), which describes SMTP.

Why Run Your Own Mail Server?

"Because I want to have control over all my mails" probably is the best reason for setting up your own mail server. How often have you wondered why a mail did not reach the recipient? And who is at fault? Is it your provider's server that delayed the mail? Is it the recipient's provider? Running IMAP on your local machine often is faster than running it over an Internet link to the provider too, so that is another reason. And you can set up your own discussion lists, if you want.

You can also give out mail addresses within your domain to your family or to your friends easily, which means that you will be their provider for their mail. Or you can use as many mail addresses as you want for yourself, which is a great way to control who knows what about you. If you have your own web server running (see Chapter 5 on how to do that), you can run a web front end to your mail server too, which may make it easier to access your mails from wherever you are, because you need only a web browser.

Caveats

Although it is fun to run your own mail server, a lot of responsibility comes with it. If you provide mail addresses for friends and family, there are privacy issues you have to obey—like not looking into their mails or not looking at mail logs to find out who they sent mails to and when or who they receive mails from. Their mails need to be kept secure, too, so that not everyone can read those mails. Normally, the user concept in Linux takes care of that for you.

You also have to keep your mail server software up-to-date as with each public service you are running. That is not a very difficult job, because CentOS will offer you updated packages as soon as a security problem has been fixed—you just have to stay alert and install those updated packages as soon as they are published.

But there is another issue to watch out for. Scammers and spammers are always looking out for misconfigured mail servers to send their mails over—that way it will look like you are the culprit who sent out those pesky mails, not them. It has gotten very difficult to misconfigure modern mail transfer agents, so you should be safe if you use a configuration that is close to the default config. But if you have problems with some aspect of the mail configuration and one of the solutions seems to be opening up access very widely, you should find a better solution, which may be harder to implement. The question is not *if* open mail servers will be found; the question is *when* they will be found. And when an open server has been found, it will be abused.

Also, you will lose the spam filtering offered by your provider: when you run your own mail server, you are the first line of defense, meaning that you are responsible for filtering out spam—and viruses.

But don't fret. It is not that hard to keep your configuration secure. If you follow this chapter, you should have a safe configuration to work with.

When Not to Run Your Own Mail Server

Even if you think you have everything to run your own mail server, there still might be some reasons as to why it might be smarter to let someone else run a mail server for you. If you have your own domain and a hosted server somewhere in a data center, you probably also have a static IP address. You are all set then. If you have your own domain and a static IP address and you want to run your server at your home or at your office, you normally should be set, too.

If you have your own domain name but no static IP address, you can still run a mail server. Dynamic DNS (DDNS) providers will point a hostname at your current IP address so that it is easily reachable. In this case, you have to make sure that the DDNS provider points the name at your new IP address *as soon* as your address has changed. If there is a noticeable delay, someone else might have gotten your old IP address already, and mails will be sent to his computer. If that person has a mail server running and if it takes all mails offered to it, you will lose your mails. So, think twice in this situation. There is a second problem with this setup. Because of spam, many Internet service providers do not accept mails from machines that don't have a static IP address. If this is the situation—or if your Internet provider blocks port 25 outgoing—you can still run your own mail server, but you have to deliver the mails via the provider's mail servers.

If you don't have a domain and aren't planning on getting one, there is no way for you to run a reliable mail service.

Another thing you have to check is that many Internet service providers allow connections to port 25 only to their own mail servers. If this is the case, you cannot run your own server, because there will be no way to reach your server from the Internet.

Finally, you should also check that your Internet service provider's terms of service allow you to run servers on your end of the line.

Which Mail Server to Choose

This is not as easy a question as it looks. The debates between users of different mail servers can become as heated as the vi vs. emacs, Coke vs. Pepsi, or my football team vs. your football team debates. CentOS ships with three mail server applications to choose from: Exim, Postfix, and Sendmail. Sendmail has the longest history of those three and should be the one that is installed if you followed the install guide in Chapter 2. Sendmail is a great mail server, and you can make it do everything you want, but many people deem Sendmail's configuration to be very hard; its main config file isn't readable at all and should be treated as read-only except by real experts. Exim also can be tweaked to do everything regarding mail, but configuring it is not obvious at all times either. The third one, Postfix, is relatively easy to set up and considered to be fast and secure. This doesn't mean that the others aren't secure, even if some people tell you about the bad security history of Sendmail. It has just had more time to be insecure than the other two.

Because Postfix is the easiest of the three mail servers to configure, we're going to use it as the mail server you are going to learn about during the rest of the chapter.

Installing the Mail Server

Installing Postfix would be rather straightforward, if Sendmail hadn't been installed during the installation of the system. Some of the installed packages require a mail server to be on the system, and Sendmail is the one that gets pulled in by default. You can check whether it is installed with `rpm`:

```
rpm -q sendmail
```

The output should be this:

```
sendmail-8.13.8-2.el5
```

You cannot remove Sendmail at this moment, because that in turn would remove packages that rely on a mail transfer agent to be installed. But you can now install Postfix via Yum without any errors. Sendmail still would be left installed and the preferred mail transfer agent. Because several files between those two packages are the same (for example `/usr/sbin/sendmail`), the system uses the alternative system to distinguish between those packages. `/usr/sbin/sendmail` is a symbolic link to `/etc/alternatives/mta`, which in turn is a symbolic link to `/usr/sbin/sendmail.sendmail`. The Postfix package contains this file as `/usr/sbin/sendmail.postfix`. This way, both packages can be installed at the same time without conflicting. To enable Postfix and make it preferred over Sendmail, you only have to switch these links to the correct binaries so that `/etc/alternatives/mta` points to `/usr/sbin/sendmail.postfix`. Luckily, there is a package that does this automatically for you. This package is called `system-switch-mail`.

So, let's install Postfix and make it the preferred mail server. If you haven't updated your system yet, it will ask you for the CentOS `gpg-key` to be installed (see Chapter 4):

```
yum install postfix system-switch-mail
```

To check whether it got installed, use this:

```
rpm -q postfix
```

The output should be similar to this:

```
postfix-2.3.3-2.1.el5_2
```

To switch between mail servers, run the following command. You will be asked for the root password if you run it as a normal user:

```
system-switch-mail
```

This opens the menu that you can see in Figure 6-1. Choose Postfix, and press Tab to select OK. Select OK again on the confirmation screen. If you check /etc/alternatives/ mta now, you will see that it points to /usr/sbin/sendmail.postfix. You can switch back to Sendmail by running system-switch-mail again. Because you are going to use Postfix as the standard mail server now, you can uninstall Sendmail with yum remove sendmail.

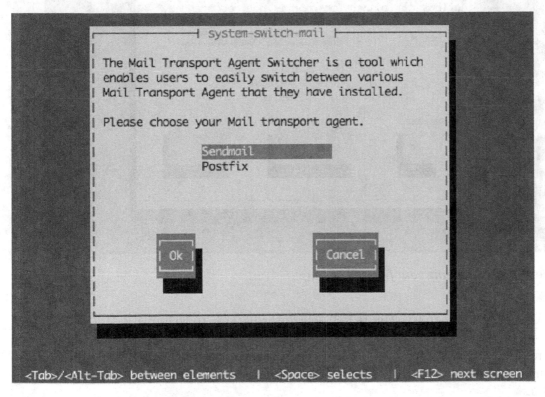

Figure 6-1. *Switching the preferred mail transfer agent*

You now have successfully installed Postfix and configured CentOS to use it as the standard mail transfer agent. But to receive mails, your computer needs to be able to be reached on port 25, which is blocked by the default firewall configuration.

Configuring the Firewall

To configure the firewall, run the command system-config-securitylevel-tui. This will open a text-based menu system in which you will be able to configure your firewall settings (see Figure 6-2). Use the Tab key to select Customize, and press Return.

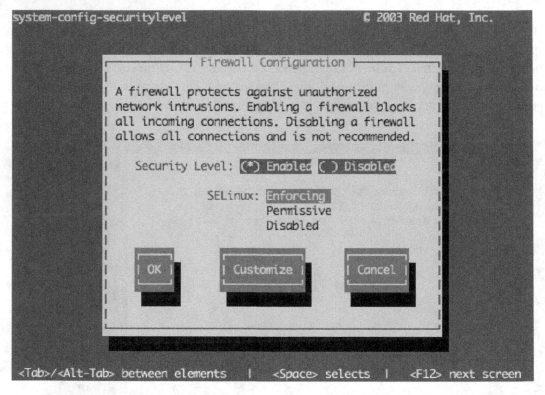

Figure 6-2. *Customizing your firewall settings*

On the next screen (see Figure 6-3), use the arrow keys to go to [ ] Mail (SMTP), and select it with the spacebar. This will put an asterisk (*) in the box. Now use the Tab key to select OK, and press the Enter key. This will bring you back to the first screen (see Figure 6-2). Use the Tab key to select OK on that screen, and press Enter to leave the menu.

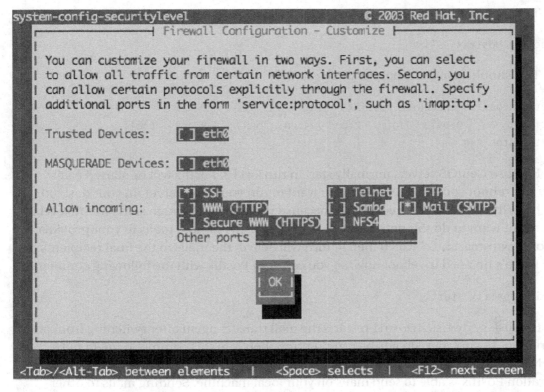

Figure 6-3. *Enable traffic to port 25, Mail (SMTP).*

You are now accepting traffic on port 25 to your machine, which is the port SMTP will use to deliver mails. To check whether it worked, you can use the `iptables` command:

```
iptables -L | grep smtp
```

You should see the following line. If you don't, retry the previous steps.

```
ACCEPT  tcp  --  anywhere   anywhere  state NEW tcp dpt:smtp
```

Making Sure Postfix Starts During Boot

You haven't configured Postfix yet, but you should make sure that it starts when your system boots. Postfix has to be running not only to receive mails on your machine but also to send any mails to other servers. This is often forgotten—and all your users will be left wondering why they didn't get any mails during the last three days—but you can enable it easily. To do so, use the `chkconfig` tool:

```
chkconfig postfix on
```

To check whether this has worked, you can use chkconfig's list option:

```
chkconfig postfix --list
```

This should give some output similar to this:

```
[root@centos ~]# chkconfig postfix --list
postfix         0:off   1:off   2:on    3:on    4:on    5:on    6:off
[root@centos ~]#
```

Because CentOS servers normally start in run level 3, Postfix will be started each time you reboot your system now. If you want to run your mail server on your desktop machine, it will also be started at boot, because your desktop system starts in run level 5. You might want to do this only if you want to use Postfix to send mails to your provider's or your own smart host, which then in turn will deliver the mails to the final recipients.

There's no need to reboot now, so you can start Postfix with the following command:

```
service postfix start
```

Because system-switch-mail restarts the mail transfer agent after switching from one to another, Postfix may already be running, and therefore this command might fail.

Now that you have Postfix started, you are ready to test it. Yes, without further configuration Postfix is able to send mails on your local machine. Sending mails to other destinations should also work, but probably the mail addresses will be off. So, please refrain from trying that until you do at least a minimal configuration.

To test your server, run the following command as your normal user:

```
echo "hello" | mail -s "mailsubject" <username>
```

<username> is your user's name on the system. To see whether the mail got delivered, open /var/log/maillog as the root user. You should see something like this at the end of the file:

```
Mar 22 19:39:24 localhost postfix/qmgr[3395]: 8BD11180D3: ➥
from=<ralph@centos.localdomain>, size=340, nrcpt=1 (queue active)
Mar 22 19:39:24 localhost postfix/local[12127]: 8BD11180D3: ➥
 to=<ralph@centos.localdomain>, orig_to=<ralph>, relay=local,➥
delay=0.16, delays=0.11/0.02/0/0.03, dsn=2.0.0, status=sent ➥
 (delivered to mailbox)
```

To read this mail now, fire up the Mail mail client, which is a very simple, though limited, way to read your mail. To read the mail, just press the Enter key, because there will be only one message in your mailbox. This will give you the following output:

```
[ralph@centos ~]$ mail
Mail version 8.1 6/6/93.  Type ? for help.
"/var/spool/mail/ralph": 1 message 1 new
>N  1 ralph@centos.localdo  Sun Mar 22 19:42  14/488   "mailsubject"
&
Message 1:
From ralph@centos.localdomain  Sun Mar 22 19:42:50 2009
X-Original-To: ralph
Delivered-To: ralph@centos.localdomain
To: ralph@centos.localdomain
Subject: mailsubject
Date: Sun, 22 Mar 2009 19:42:50 +0100 (CET)
From: ralph@centos.localdomain (Ralph Angenendt)

hello

&
```

Just enter q to quit the mail client. This will save the read mail to a file called mbox in your home directory.

Congratulations! You just sent your first mail!

Configuring Postfix

If your computer has a proper hostname, you might not need to do any more configuration to Postfix to just send out mails. In most cases, you need to apply some changes to the default configuration so that hostnames and mail addresses come out correctly. For receiving mails, you have to do a little more configuration. All files you need to touch to configure Postfix are in /etc/postfix. The most important file in there is main.cf, which contains the main configuration, as you might have guessed by the name.

The file master.cf is used to configure the behavior of all the processes Postfix needs to receive and deliver mail. Normally you should not have to touch this file. Some additional software, such as virus- or spam-scanning programs, might require you to configure that file (see the documentation for those programs for the exact entries). You will be introduced to other files in /etc/postfix when they are required for special features.

One config file, the aliases file, does not live in that directory. The reason for that is compatibility with Sendmail, which always used /etc/aliases instead of putting this file into a subdirectory. The aliases file tells your mail transfer agent if a receiving mail address is just an alias for a user on your system. Postfix, for example, does not deliver mails to the user root because of security reasons. You can use the alias file to tell Postfix which user should receive root's mails instead. You can find a more detailed description later in the "Setting Up Users to Receive Mails" section.

Postfix uses `/var/spool/postfix` and the directories below it for handling mail. The structure of this directory is explained in the `qmgr(8)` manual page. Under `/var/spool/mail/`, you will find the user's mailboxes where Postfix delivers mail to.

Configuring Your System to Send Mail

You'll now configure your system for sending mail. You can do it in two ways, covered in the following sections:

- If you are lucky and have a dedicated mail server somewhere or you have a leased line to your home or office, you probably can send out mails directly. In the "Sending Mail Directly" section, you will learn how to do that.

- You can send mail via a so-called smart host. Most, if not all, Internet providers will offer you an SMTP server you can point your mail client to that then will send all mail to the recipient's mail host. Depending on your provider, you might be required to use this host, because many providers block the SMTP port to the outside world. You'll learn how to do this in the "Sending Mail via a Smart Host" section.

Sending Mail Directly

Fire up your favorite editor, and open the file `/etc/postfix/main.cf` as the root user. You will just have to make a few changes to this file to be able to send mails. As you can see, this file is very well documented, and most options are explained. The top of that file states: "A detailed explanation of all options in `/etc/postfix/main.cf` can be found in the `postconf` manual page in section 5." To view this manual page, you can use the command `man 5 postconf`.

If you think your hostname is OK for a mail server, because it is `mail.example.com` or something similar, you can leave it alone. If you want to set a specific hostname for the mail server that is different from the hostname of the machine you are running the server on, then search for the `myhostname` parameter. Set it to the hostname you want to see in outgoing mails, and don't forget to remove the comment sign (#) from the front of the line:

```
myhostname = centos.example.com
```

If you are running a web server on the same machine, your host can have several domain names to it. If this is the case and you want to use a specific domain name for serving mails, you should change the `mydomain` parameter. The default is to strip the first part from `myhostname` and use the rest. In this case, `example.com` would be the domain, because the `centos` would be stripped. The `mydomain` parameter will become important when receiving mails. Let's just leave it alone for now.

The next parameter that you should change is myorigin. This parameter defines from which mail addresses locally posted mails are coming from. For example, many jobs on a CentOS machine send mails. Those mails normally have unqualified sender addresses, meaning that just the part in front of the @ is used. As a default, Postfix fills in your machine's hostname, so the mails seem to come from user@centos.example.com in the previous example. Normally you want to just put your domain name in there, especially if the hostname of your machine is not resolvable from the Internet (think about your workstation here, which sends mails to a smart host). Mail servers normally reject mails if they cannot resolve the host or domain name in a mail address.

```
myorigin = example.com
```

Now mails originating on your machine seem to come from user@example.com. You still have to make sure that example.com is a valid domain name. To make the new configuration active, use the following command:

```
service postfix reload
```

And that's it. You can now send mails from your mail server. If you changed something in your /etc/postfix/main.cf and you have forgotten what you changed, don't be afraid. The postconf program is able to show you which parameters have been changed from Postfix's default settings. Just type the following to see those values:

```
postconf -n
```

This is the output you should see after you make the previous changes:

```
[root@centos ~]# postconf -n
alias_database = hash:/etc/aliases
alias_maps = hash:/etc/aliases
[...]
inet_interfaces = localhost
[...]
myhostname = centos.example.com
myorigin = example.com
newaliases_path = /usr/bin/newaliases.postfix
```

The parameters that are left out here are default parameters for Postfix on CentOS but differ from the parameters the standard Postfix distribution sees by default. Take a look at the inet_interfaces line. This means that Postfix is listening on 127.0.0.1 only, so it cannot receive mails not coming from your local machine. This is a great way to test configuration changes, because those cannot affect mails coming from the outside—because there aren't any.

THE POSTCONF COMMAND

The `postconf` command is able to do more than just show you what is different from the default configuration. Just running `postconf` without any options will show the current Postfix configuration without comments or inline documentation. The following will show you all the default parameters Postfix knows about:

```
postconf -d
```

The following will show the value the parameter has at the moment, so `postconf myhostname` would show you the hostname that is configured within Postfix:

```
postconf <parameter>
```

You can also use `postconf` to set parameters and make them active at once without manually reloading the Postfix server. This is of great use when you deploy computers via core builds (see Chapter 11 on how to do that). Maybe all your computers should use the same relay host to deliver their mails to and let that host do the rest. You could edit the main configuration file on all machines for that—or just put the following line into the %post section of your kickstart file:

```
postconf -e "relayhost = mailhub.example.com"
```

This will set the `relayhost` parameter to `mailhub.example.com` on the machine you are installing.

Using `postconf` for simple changes can save you from firing up your editor and manually changing `main.cf`, and it makes the change active at once.

If you have made those changes, you can now try to send a mail to outside your network. You can use the mail command from earlier to send a mail to your account you have with your Internet service provider, for example.

What happens with your mail now? First Postfix looks at the domain part of your mail. If the domain part is local to your mail server, Postfix will try to deliver the mail locally, just as it did in the previous example. If it is not, Postfix does the following.

Imagine you have found an error in this chapter (which is improbable but not impossible). So, you want to send a mail to support@apress.com to tell them about this error. Please do this *only* if you really have found an error; don't send mails there for fun. This is just an example of how sending mail works. Fire up mail to send that mail:

```
[ralph@centos ~]$ mail -s "Error in chapter 6" ralph
Dear Apress support,

I have found an error in chapter 6.
```

```
Regards,

Your Name
<CTRL>-d
Cc: <ENTER>
```

You press Ctrl+D to end the mail. The mail command then asks you whether you want to add a Cc: to that mail. Because you don't want to do that, just press Enter.

Postfix now looks up which server is responsible for mails going to the domain apress.com. To do that, it asks the domain name system for the MX record of apress.com (see the next chapter if you want to know how DNS works). The MX record defines the mail exchanger for the domain—remember that you will meet this term again when configuring your server to receive mails. You can find out the MX record for yourself by using the host command, which should be installed by default:

```
[ralph@centos ~]$ host -t mx apress.com
apress.com mail is handled by 5 smtp3.intermedia.net.
apress.com mail is handled by 50 mail.uu.net.
[ralph@centos ~]$
```

After having found out that smtp3.intermedia.net is the preferred mail exchanger (lower numbers have priority over higher numbers), Postfix will contact that server and deliver your mail there.

If the mail does not show up, it is time to look at the mail log again. Postfix writes everything it does with a message to /var/log/maillog, and maybe you made a typo in your configuration. Because that happens to everyone sooner or later, it is a good idea to look at the mail log after you change the configuration and reload Postfix with service postfix reload.

Sending Mail via a Smart Host

Because spam from private PCs being part of botnets is a real problem nowadays, many Internet service providers block the outgoing SMTP port. If your provider does that, you cannot send mails directly to other machines as shown earlier. This is not how the Internet is supposed to work, but it is understandable from the ISP's point of view. If many machines in the provider's network send out spam, the amount of complaints about spam is huge, too. But because your provider wants you to be able to send out mail, it normally offers you a *smart host*, where you can drop off your mails. This smart host then in turn will take care of further mail delivery. You will lose one of the main advantages of running your own mail server—control over all your mails.

Again, there are two ways how such smart hosts are implemented. Normally the host knows which IP addresses are allowed to send mail and which aren't, so there is no need for further authentication. The other type requires you to log in with a username and password before it will accept mails from you. There are other configuration possibilities—for example, "POP before SMTP," which requires you to first fetch your mail before you can send mails—but those aren't widely deployed.

You should check with your Internet service provider what kind of smart host it is running if you are required to use one.

If it doesn't require you to log in with a password but takes mails from known IP addresses, there is only one line you have to change in /etc/postfix/main.cf. Instead of editing the file with an editor, you will use the postconf command to make this change.

You should check first whether there already is a smart host definition in your configuration. You can do that with the grep command:

```
[root@centos ~]# grep relayhost /etc/postfix/main.cf
# The relayhost parameter specifies the default host to send mail to
# no relayhost is given, mail is routed directly to the destination.
#relayhost = $mydomain
#relayhost = [gateway.my.domain]
#relayhost = [mailserver.isp.tld]
#relayhost = uucphost
#relayhost = [an.ip.add.ress]
[root@centos ~]#
```

Postfix uses the term relayhost for smart hosts—the term *smart host* comes from Sendmail, and because that is the oldest mail server of them all, it defined many terms. You can see that there are several occurrences of the term relayhost in the configuration file, but all of them are commented out. To add your provider's mail server as a relay host, just type in the following command, and check the configuration again:

```
[root@centos ~]# postconf -e "relayhost = mail.example.com"
[root@centos ~]# tail -1 /etc/postfix/main.cf
relayhost = mail.example.com
[root@centos ~]#
```

Using the command tail -1 /etc/postfix/main.cf, you checked the last line in the Postfix configuration file. Parameters you add with the postconf command always are added to the end of the configuration. If you use postconf to change a parameter, it gets changed where it is defined. You can try this by setting the myhostname parameter to another hostname. But remember what the original setting was, because there is no way to undo those changes.

You should tell Postfix to trust the computers on your local network; otherwise, you will not be able to send out mails except from the local machine. Search for the mynetworks parameter in the configuration and set it:

```
mynetworks = 192.168.1.0/24, 127.0.0.0/8
```

Postfix now trusts every computer in the 192.168.1.0/24 network—and the localhost. Trust in this case means that your mail server will accept mails from all computers that are in this address range, and those mails will be relayed to other mail servers on the Internet. You shouldn't open this up too much to keep your mail server from becoming an open relay for the complete Internet (or even only parts of it).

If your provider's relay host doesn't require a login, you are set now to send your mails. If it does, you are not quite finished with the configuration. You are now going to learn about configuring simple client authentication for Postfix—with the added security of an encrypted connection to your provider's relay host, if supported.

First you should check what your provider expects from you. As you have seen, SMTP is a simple plain-text protocol, which enables you to talk to a mail server "by hand." So, let's see what kind of authentication your provider supports. You can do that with the telnet client program, which should already be installed on your CentOS system. If it isn't, just install the telnet package with Yum:

```
yum install telnet
```

Now open a session to the mail server you want to check. You should see something like this:

```
[root@centos ~]# telnet mail.example.net 25
Trying 208.77.188.166
Connected to example.net (208.77.188.166).
Escape character is '^]'.
220 mail.example.net ESMTP Postfix
EHLO mail.example.com
250-mail.example.net
250-PIPELINING
[...]
250-STARTTLS
250-AUTH PLAIN LOGIN
250-AUTH=PLAIN LOGIN
250 DSN
```

You have been using the EHLO command to greet the mail server, instead of the HELO command shown before. EHLO is the "extended hello," which tells the foreign mail server to run in Enhanced SMTP mode (ESMTP). The output will be a bit longer than this normally, but at the moment only a few lines are of interest. There are two AUTH lines in the previous code, one with a blank between AUTH and the parameters and the other one with = in between. The line with = denotes that your provider also supports older versions of Outlook and Outlook Express, so if you don't see it in the answer to your EHLO request, there is nothing to worry about.

You should see PLAIN LOGIN in the output, which is the simplest way to log in—there are other authentication schemes like GSSAPI and MD5, but those aren't widely deployed. There is more interesting information up there, the STARTTLS line. This means that your provider accepts encrypted connections, and it also means that if you don't see this line, your provider doesn't. If you already worked through Chapter 5 (Apache), you have learned that for accepting encrypted connections, the web server has to listen on port 443 in addition to the standard HTTP port. STARTTLS works differently.

The daemon—in this case the mail server—listens on only one port, port 25. This connection is done unencrypted. The first handshake the servers exchange is unencrypted also. If your mail server detects the STARTTLS line in the answer to the EHLO command, it then can use STARTTLS as the next command. From then on, all configuration is encrypted. You will learn how to enable TLS for receiving mails later in the section "Authenticating Users."

You need the cyrus-sasl, cyrus-sasl-lib, and cyrus-sasl-plain packages if you are required to log in. These should already be installed on your system, but if they aren't, just add them with Yum. Simple Authentication and Security Layer (SASL) is an authentication framework. As with most applications and frameworks that have "Simple" in their name, it really isn't—or you wouldn't have to read this chapter that mostly talks about the Simple Message Transfer Protocol. Now start your favorite editor again, and add the following lines to the Postfix configuration:

```
smtp_sasl_auth_enable = yes
smtp_sasl_security_options = noanonymous
smtp_sasl_password_maps = hash:/etc/postfix/sasl_passwd
smtp_tls_security_level = may
tls_random_source = /dev/urandom
```

The last two lines are needed only when your provider supports STARTTLS. This setting enforces encrypted connections if a remote mail server offers TLS and falls back to plaintext connections if it doesn't. It might be a good idea to add these lines to your Postfix configuration anyway—even if you don't use a smart host.

The first three lines tell Postfix to enable authentication, to disable anonymous authentication, and where Postfix will find the username and password for logging in. This configuration statement needs a bit more explanation:

```
smtp_sasl_password_maps = hash:/etc/postfix/sasl_passwd
```

Postfix stores most external information (aliases, passwords, and the headers it checks against) in map files, which really are small database files. Postfix uses this format to speed up operation, because it can use database operations on those files and does not have to parse them completely when they are read. The password map is of type "hash," where you have a key on the left side of the file and a value to the key on the right

side. Enough theory. Open up your editor, and put the following line into `/etc/postfix/`
`sasl_passwd`:

```
mail.example.net      myname:secretpassword
```

If there is more than one mail server you need to authenticate against, just add more lines to this file. The key Postfix uses is the name of the mail server it connects to, and the value is a username:password pair that it uses to log in. Now you only have to make a map out of this file; Postfix cannot use the plain-text version:

```
postmap /etc/postfix/sasl_passwd
```

This will create a database file from the plain-text file you just created:

```
[root@centos postfix]# ls -l sasl_passwd*
-rw------- 1 root root    30 Mar 23 01:08 sasl_passwd
-rw------- 1 root root 12288 Mar 23 01:08 sasl_passwd.db
[root@centos postfix]#
```

Postfix will use the `.db` file for further operation. It takes about a minute for Postfix to pick up that changed file. If you want it active at once, type this:

```
service postfix reload
```

To see which username and password Postfix uses for a certain mail server, you can query Postfix with the `postmap` command:

```
[root@centos postfix]# postmap -q mail.example.net sasl_passwd
myname:secretpassword
[root@centos postfix]#
```

You should now be able to send mail over your provider's relay host—after logging in. Check with the `mail` command. If it doesn't work, check the log file for errors.

If you just want to send mail over a central server in your network, you are all set now. Local mail will be delivered to your mailbox on your mail server, and all other mails will be sent to the recipient's mail server, either directly or over a relay host. You can now use that server as the SMTP-Server entry in your mail client (hey, this is your own relay host) after one more change.

At the moment, Postfix listens only on the local interface 127.0.0.1, which is fine if Postfix is running on your workstation. If you run it on a server, you have to add the servers IP address to the configuration. Change the following line in `main.cf` accordingly:

```
inet_interfaces = localhost,192.168.10.12
```

Please use the internal interface for the time being. You will open up your server to the rest of the world, after you learn how to configure Postfix for receiving mails in the next section.

Configuring Your System to Receive Mail

Now that you are able to send out mail, you probably also want to receive some directly to your server. You have to check some things before you can begin configuring Postfix for doing so. Most important, do you have your own domain and a static IP address? If you do not have your own domain, maybe a friend of yours has one and would give you a subdomain out of that. In other words, if your friend has the domain example.net and has access to the name servers of that domain, he could give you—for example—good.example.com and create a few hostnames under that: mail.good.example.com, www.good.example.com, and so on.

No matter which way you go, you need to set up your domain name service correctly. You need a hostname for your mail server that has a static IP address, and you should set up a mail exchanger (MX record) for that domain. For DNS configuration, either ask your domain host for help or set up your own official DNS. See Chapter 7 on how to do that.

If everything seems to be configured correctly, you can use the host command to check whether it is indeed correct:

```
host -t MX example.net
```

This should give you something like the following output:

```
[ralph@centos ~]$ host -t MX example.net
example.net mail is handled by 5 mail.example.net
[ralph@centos ~]$
```

mail.example.net has to exist and should have a static IP address (see the earlier discussion about possible problems with hosting mail servers on a host with dynamic IP addresses).

Once you have that configured, you have to make only a few changes to your Postfix configuration. Postfix has to know which domain(s) it should feel responsible for; otherwise, it will not accept the mails. Again, start your favorite editor, and open /etc/postfix/main.cf. The first change you are going to make is a bit of a safety net. Normally if Postfix cannot deliver mails permanently, it will answer the sending machine with a 5xx error (see RFC 2821 for an explanation of SMTP error codes). This means that the remote host will return the mail to the sender; it will not try to send it again. Search for the next two lines and change them:

```
soft_bounce = yes
unknown_local_recipient_reject_code = 450
```

This changes the reply to a 4xx reply, which is a temporary error. Temporary errors can happen when your disk is full or your mailbox is over quota or, in several other circumstances, where Postfix expects the error to be fixed in a short amount of time. When a sending host gets a notice about a temporary error, it will put the mail into the mail queue again and try at a later time. So, setting this is a bit of a safety net against misconfigurations. You should turn this on when you plan to make large configuration changes or when adding a new domain to your server. When everything works as planned, set those two lines to the following:

```
soft_bounce = no
unknown_local_recipient_reject_code = 550
```

Now search for the following line in `main.cf`:

```
mydestination = $myhostname, localhost.$mydomain, localhost
```

This should be changed to the following:

```
mydestination = $mydomain, $myhostname, localhost.$mydomain, localhost
```

What does this do? This tells Postfix that it should regard itself as the last hop for mails that go to `user@example.com`, `user@centos.example.com`, `user@localhost.example.com`, and `user@localhost`. These mails are going to be delivered into local mailboxes under `/var/spool/mail` for each user that exists on your machine. If you plan on hosting several domains on your mail server that even might have different users, so that mails to `user@example.com` and `user@centos.example.com` should not go to the same mailbox, do not enter these domains in `mydestination`. You will learn about virtual domain hosting later in this chapter.

Setting Up Users to Receive Mails

How does Postfix decide which users get mails on your server? It has to make several decisions, depending on the setup of your server. Let's begin with a simple setup. Say you have only one domain. Mail will be delivered only to "real" users on your system, so to be able to receive mails, you have to set up users on your machine. So if Peter, Ralph, Tim, and you are the people who should receive mails, those users must exist on your machine. Make sure their accounts exist with `getent passwd ralph` (and the other users). These users do not need to have a login shell or a home directory on your computer.

Once those users exist, they are ready to receive mails. This also means that you don't have to do anything special when you create a new user. As soon as the user is created, Postfix will accept mails for it. "Hmm," you might say, "what should I do if I want to give my mother a mail address in my domain but want that mail to be delivered to her provider's mail server?" Or, as another example, what if you want to have a mail address that receives mails for Peter, Ralph, Tim, and you? Easy. For this, Postfix (and every other mail server) knows about aliases. An *alias* is a mail address that will deliver the received mails to another mail address. To create your own aliases, you need to edit the alias file. You can easily find out which file Postfix accepts as an alias file with the `postconf` command.

```
[root@centos ~]# postconf alias_maps
alias_maps = hash:/etc/aliases
[root@centos ~]#
```

This file is outside of the /etc/postfix directory. Sendmail and Exim can use the same file for finding aliases, so if you decide to switch your mail server software later, you can reuse that file—both mail servers expect it to be at this location. If you take a look at this file, you will see that several aliases have already been filled out:

```
# General redirections for pseudo accounts.
bin:            root
daemon:         root
adm:            root
lp:             root
sync:           root
shutdown:       root
```

These are all system accounts on your computer used for running software, and you will also find the Apache user in that file. And as soon as a user is there, it will receive mails. But because nobody is going to look through the mailboxes of those users, it has been decided to send all those mails to the root account on your machine. If you look at the last line of that file, you will find the following entry:

```
#root:          marc
```

You should replace `marc` with your username and remove the # at the beginning of the line so you get all mails that are going to the root account because Postfix refuses to deliver mails to the root account because of security reasons. You should not read mails as root.

As you can see, the format of the alias file is dead simple. On the left side, you have the local part of the mail address, and on the right side, you have the user account where those mails should go. And you can override system accounts, too, which happens with the root account, for example. Giving out an address to your Mom is also easy:

```
mom:            mother@example.net
```

So, if you have `example.com` as your domain name but your mother already has a mail account with the large `example.net` Internet service provider, this is all you have to do to send all mails going to mom@example.com to her address mother@example.net. And because Peter, Ralph, Tim, and you are administrating your network together, you want all mails going to support@example.com to be delivered to those three users:

```
support:          peter,ralph,tim,you
```

You can also mix those styles:

```
support:          peter,ralph@example.net,tim@example.com,you
```

What you cannot do is put a fully qualified mail address at the beginning of the line, because the left side is always considered as address@$mydestination. But you are going to learn about virtual domains very soon in the section "Receiving Mails for Several Domains."

The alias file is also a map file like the earlier password file. So, you have to run the following after you make changes to the file:

```
postmap /etc/aliases
```

Or even easier, you can just run newaliases after editing the file. This again is a standard set by the Sendmail mail server. If you just added the support line to your alias file instead of changing the one that already was there, you should see the following error:

```
[root@centos ~]# newaliases
postalias: warning: /etc/aliases.db: duplicate entry: "support"
[root@centos ~]#
```

The first found entry has precedence, so mails to support would go to the postmaster and not Peter, Ralph, Tim, and you.

You can have more than one alias file, which is practical if you need many aliases for several reasons. Just add a second alias file to the alias_maps parameter:

```
alias_maps = hash:/etc/aliases, hash:/etc/postfix/company.aliases
```

The newaliases command will refresh both alias files when run.

Hey, you are all set up now to receive mails! Go ahead and let the Postfix daemon listen to the world! For this, add the static IP address of your server to the inet_interfaces line. Or tell Postfix to listen to all interfaces:

```
inet_interfaces = any
```

Run service postfix reload after that, and in a few minutes you will probably receive your first spam.

Taking a Few Antispam Measures

There is not enough space in this chapter to talk about the integration of antispam or antivirus software into your mail server, so here are a few hints. There is SpamAssassin in CentOS, and there is ClamAV in the RPMforge repository. SpamAssassin is an antispam solution, and ClamAV is an open source virus scanner. You then need Amavisd (available from RPMforge) or MailScanner (available from `http://mailscanner.org`) to integrate those two into your mail server. The documentation for Amavisd and MailScanner should be sufficient to get you running.

But there are a few other things you can do to lower the amount of spam mails you will receive when running your own mail server. Let's begin with a client requesting to send a mail, which is around the `HELO`/`EHLO` phase. Oh, one thing: if you cannot fit everything on one line in the config file, press Return and add a few spaces before you go on typing. Postfix will then recognize it as one line:

```
smtpd_helo_required = yes
smtpd_client_restrictions = permit_sasl_authenticated,
                            permit_mynetworks,
                            reject_unauth_destinations,
                            reject_rbl_client bl.spamcop.net
```

This permits all clients that have authenticated themselves (you will learn about authentication later in the "Authenticating Users" section) to permit all messages from IP addresses that are listed in the `mynetworks` parameter, reject any mails to domains that Postfix does not feel responsible for, and reject any client that is listed in the `bl.spamcop.net` blacklist (see `http://www.spamcop.net/bl.shtml`). The first line tells Postfix to reject all clients that do not issue a `HELO` or `EHLO` before trying to send mail.

The next restrictions are in the `MAIL FROM` phase of sending a mail, and they are defined in the `smtpd_sender_restrictions` parameter:

```
smtpd_sender_restrictions =
        permit_sasl_authenticated,
        check_sender_access hash:/etc/postfix/access
        reject_unknown_sender_domain,
        reject_non_fqdn_sender,
        reject_rhsbl_sender dsn.rfc-ignorant.org
```

Again, authenticated users are allowed to send. The next line checks mail addresses (this again is the address on the envelope, not the one you see in your mail client) against an access file. The third line rejects mails from senders where the domain does not exist. This keeps out pretty much unwanted mail. The next line rejects senders without a fully qualified domain name—like `user@foobar`, for example. And the last line checks the sender's domain against the `dsn.rfc-ignorant.org` blacklist, which rejects all mails from domains that don't accept bounces; see `http://rfc-ignorant.org/policy-dsn.php` for more information.

■**Caution** Although the usage of blacklists is shown here, do not use a blacklist in your configuration except if you understand which rules the list operator uses to blacklist senders. If you use a blacklist, you should regularly check that the blacklist still works as expected. Some blacklist providers shut down their services and answer every request with "sender is listed." This way, every sender is blacklisted. Remember, when you use a blacklist to block mails, you let somebody else decide which mails will not reach your and your users' mailboxes.

The previous configuration shows the usage of an access map, which is a great way to refuse or accept a few mail addresses. Again, it is a map, so you have to run `postmap` after you edit the file. The format is as follows:

```
/^postmaster@.*$/        OK
/^abuse@.*$/     OK
support@example.net          554 FIX YOUR BROKEN GATEWAY. GET LOST.
/^.*@test.example.net/       554 WE DO NOT ACCEPT MAIL FROM YOU.
```

On the left side is a mail address or a regular expression within two slashes. This is the sender's envelope address. On the right side you can put `OK`, which lets the mail go through; `REJECT`, which rejects the mail during the SMTP dialogue; `DISCARD`, which takes the mail but silently throws it away; or an error code with an additional statement there, as shown in the previous example.

With these additions to your configuration, you will stop a fair share of spam. For more information on `smtpd _*_` restrictions, see the `postconf(5)` manual page.

Receiving Mails for Several Domains

Let's say you got your hands on a second domain called `example.org` and want to receive mails for it, too. You have also configured your DNS so that your mail server is the primary mail exchanger (MX) for this domain. If you just want a copy of your other domain, meaning that all addresses in the new domain should be the same as all the addresses in the old domain, you can add the new domain to the `mydestination` parameter:

```
mydestination = $mydomain, $myhostname, localhost.$mydomain,
        ,example.org, $myhostname.example.org,
        localhost.example.org, localhost
```

After reloading Postfix, all your configured addresses and aliases for `example.com` will now also work for `example.org`. You won't be able to differentiate between the two domains when configuring Postfix like that. It's not possible to have `peter@example.org` be another Peter than the one at `example.com` when you do this.

Postfix knows about virtual domains, though, which enable you to do exactly that: have several domains receive mail and have two different Peters in these domains. If you want to set up your second (and third and fourth and fifth…) domain as a virtual domain, you have to remove the entries you just added to `mydestination`.

Directly after this, add the following line:

```
virtual_alias_maps = hash:/etc/postfix/virtual
```

Virtual alias maps are a lot like the normal alias files for Postfix, with a few exceptions. This time you need to have fully qualified mail addresses on the left side, something you cannot do with an alias file. Here's a short example:

```
example.org              #put anything you want here
postmaster@example.org: peter
support@example.org:     peter,ralph,tim
ralph@example.org:       ralph@example.net
```

The first line in this file is important; it tells Postfix that the definitions for a new domain follow after this line. You can really put anything you want on the right side, such as a comment about who is the domain owner, for example. After this, the mail addresses follow. If there is no fully qualified mail address on the right side, Postfix considers these addresses to be in your primary domain, and it checks `/etc/aliases` and your user database for those. This is a map file, `postmap /etc/postfix/virtual`, that must be run after making changes to the file.

If you want to add another domain, just begin a new section at the end of the file:

```
example.net              #This is ralph's domainname
ralph@example.net:       ralph
```

You can also use more than one file for defining virtual aliases. If you want to give Ralph full control over his virtual domain without giving him access to files under `/etc/postfix`, you can do the following:

```
virtual_alias_maps = hash:/etc/postfix/virtual
                     hash:/home/ralph/virtual
```

Make sure that this file is readable by Postfix by giving it to the user Ralph, and give read access to the rest of the world:

```
chown ralph /home/ralph/virtual; chmod 644 /home/ralph/virtual
```

When Ralph uses the `postmap` command to make a database out of this virtual file, it will automatically get the correct access rights.

Authenticating Users

Now you can send mail from your mail server and from the computers that are in the network you configured with the `mynetworks` parameter. But what happens if you are a roaming user and want to send mail when you are with a client or at your mother's house? If those are static IP addresses, you could add them to `mynetworks`, but in the case of your client, that would mean that every user there could send mails over your server—and that is something you don't want, except if you are getting paid for offering them mail access.

Like your provider, you can configure your mail server to let users authenticate themselves before being allowed to send mails—if they aren't in any of the known networks.

Encrypted Connections

Before you learn how to configure authentication, let's configure encrypted connections first, because it never is a good idea to send passwords unencrypted over the Internet. So, like your provider offering `STARTTLS`, you are going to do the same soon. For setting up encrypted connections, you need an SSL certificate for your mail server. If you want to set up business with providing mails, you should get a commercial certificate from a well-known certificate authority. If you are just doing this for family and friends, you can generate a certificate yourself.

You can read everything about creating your own certificate in Chapter 5. A certificate for a mail server looks exactly the same as a certificate for a web server. When you are asked for a "common name" during the certificate creation, please use your mail server's hostname (`mail.example.com`) and not your web server's name.

After you have created your certificate, you should put the files in the correct places now. Since CentOS 5, there is a directory called `/etc/pki` that should be used for storing certificates and keys (PKI stands for Public Key Infrastructure).

If you did everything correctly, you should have two files, apart from the certificate signing request (CSR) file:

```
[root@centos certs]# ls -lh
total 24K
-rw-r--r-- 1 root root 847 Jan 20 14:15 mail_example_com.crt
-rw-r--r-- 1 root root 647 Jan 20 13:55 mail_example_com.csr
-rw-r--r-- 1 root root 963 Jan 20 13:35 mail_example_com.key
[root@centos certs]#
```

Copy `mail_example_com.crt` to `/etc/pki/tls/certs` and `mail_example_com.key` to `/etc/pki/tls/private`. If you put all your certificates you have on your computer under `/etc/pki`, you have just one place to back up, and you know where all your certificates are. Yes, this can become a problem if you need lots of them on a server.

Now that you have your certificate in place, Postfix needs to know about them. Add the following lines to the Postfix configuration:

```
smtpd_tls_security_level = may
tls_random_source = dev:/dev/urandom
smtpd_tls_cert_file = /etc/pki/tls/certs/mail_example_com.crt
smtpd_tls_key_file = /etc/pki/tls/private/mail_example_com.key
```

The last two lines tell Postfix where it can find the certificate and the key. `tls_random_source` defines where Postfix can read random data out of. `/dev/urandom` is the default on CentOS. And the first line tells Postfix to do opportunistic TLS. It doesn't require the client to open an encrypted connection but makes it possible to do so. You have to restart Postfix after you make those changes.

You are now ready to test whether your server can talk TLS. Encrypted protocols are hard to talk "by hand," even with a deep understanding of encryption. `openssl` will help you with that:

```
[ralph@centos ~]$ openssl s_client -starttls smtp -connect  localhost:25
CONNECTED(00000003)
depth=0  /C=DE/ST=Bavaria/L=Munich/O=Unorganized & ➥
Co/OU=dsf/CN=mail.example.com/emailAddress= ➥
ralph@example.com
verify error:num=18:self signed certificate
verify return:1
[...]
Server certificate
-----BEGIN CERTIFICATE-----
MIICpTCCAg4CCQCPkT5jYJ1G8zANBgkqhkiG9w0BAQUFADCBljELMAkGA1UEBhMC
[…]
250 DSN
```

You just made your first TLS connection to your mail server! Don't worry about the verify error; this always happens when you use a self-signed certificate. For personal use this is OK; you just have to tell your other users to expect this kind of certificate. You can continue with a normal SMTP session by using `EHLO` or `HELO` to greet the server.

Usernames, Passwords, and Such

Now that your server supports encrypted connections, it is time to move on to the actual user authentication. The easiest is to use your /etc/passwd for that, because you already have all your users in there and they all have a password. Postfix itself does not do authentication; it uses SASL for this. Cyrus-sasl is the best-known implementation of this. Another SASL implementation is included in the Dovecot POP3 and IMAP server. Setting up POP3 and IMAP access is explained in the section "Retrieving Mails" in this chapter, but we are going to use Dovecot for user authentication right now. The following will install Dovecot and its dependencies:

```
[root@centos ~]# yum install dovecot
```

Open up /etc/dovecot.conf with your favorite editor. This file is heavily commented. Some options are already turned on and some are turned off, so be a bit careful when enabling this in the configuration. Search for auth default, and change the section to look like this:

```
auth default {
    mechanisms = plain login
    passdb pam {
    }
    userdb passwd {
    }
    user = root
    socket listen {
      client {
        path = /var/spool/postfix/private/auth
        mode = 0660
        user = postfix
        group = postfix
      }
    }
}
```

You are going to offer LOGIN and PLAIN authentication mechanisms to your users. Dovecot will use PAM (which stands for Pluggable Authentication Modules; see /usr/share/doc/pam-0.99.6.2/Linux-PAM_SAG.txt for more information) to check the users' passwords, which is standard for CentOS, and your password file will be used as the database for your users. The last few lines define how Postfix and Dovecot will talk to each other. There are tons of other options if you want to keep your users in a MySQL database, for example, or in an LDAP directory. Just follow the comments and documents that are mentioned in dovecot.conf if your users do not "live" in /etc/passwd.

Now turn on Dovecot, and make sure it stays turned on, even after reboots:

```
[root@centos ~]# service dovecot start
Starting Dovecot Imap:                              [  OK  ]
[root@centos ~]# chkconfig dovecot on
[root@centos ~]#
```

You will learn a bit more about Dovecot later; now it's time to get back to configuring Postfix. Add the following lines to the config file:

```
smtpd_sasl_auth_enable = yes
smtpd_sasl_type = dovecot
smtpd_sasl_path = private/auth
broken_sasl_auth_clients = yes
smtpd_sasl_security_options = noanonymous
```

This turns on SASL, tells Postfix to use the Dovecot SASL implementation, and defines the path for authentication against Dovecot. This is the same path that was used in dovecot.conf earlier, but it is relative to Postfix's spool directory. The broken_sasl_auth_clients parameter is there to support broken clients, which do not honor LOGIN AUTH PLAIN but need the = between LOGIN and AUTH. The last line turns off any anonymous login mechanisms. Now add the following lines to your configuration. Recipient restrictions are checked in the RCPT TO: phase of the SMTP dialogue.

```
smtpd_recipient_restrictions =
    permit_mynetworks,
    permit_sasl_authenticated,
    reject_unauth_destination
```

Reload Postfix after you make those changes. Now you should test whether your mail server announces authentication:

```
[ralph@centos ~]$ telnet localhost 25
Trying 127.0.0.1...
Connected to localhost.localdomain (127.0.0.1).
Escape character is '^]'.
220 centos.example.com ESMTP Postfix
EHLO mail.example.net
```

```
250-centos.example.com
250-PIPELINING
250-SIZE 10240000
250-VRFY
250-ETRN
250-STARTTLS
250-AUTH PLAIN LOGIN
250-AUTH=PLAIN LOGIN
```

Et voilà! Now you just need to test whether authentication really works:

```
[ralph@centos ~]$ telnet localhost 25
Trying 127.0.0.1...
Connected to localhost.localdomain (127.0.0.1).
Escape character is '^]'.
220 centos.example.com ESMTP Postfix
EHLO mail.example.com
250-centos.example.com
250-AUTH PLAIN LOGIN
250-AUTH=PLAIN LOGIN
AUTH PLAIN AHRlc3QAMTIzNDU=
235 2.0.0 Authentication successful
quit
221 2.0.0 Bye
Connection closed by foreign host.
```

Oh, it does. But what is this `AHRlc3QAMTIzNDU=` line? The username and password are Base64 encoded—not encrypted; they can be deciphered at this stage—and you can use Perl to encode it. The user has the username test and the password 12345:

```
[ralph@centos ~]$ perl -MMIME::Base64 -e 'print ➥
encode_base64("\000test\00012345");'
AHRlc3QAMTIzNDU=
[ralph@centos ~]$
```

The \000 is a null byte with which the username and password have to be prefixed. Now you are almost ready to offer authentication to your users; you have to make only one more change to the configuration. With the previous configuration, you can authenticate over an unencrypted connection. Sending plain-text usernames and especially passwords over the Internet is very insecure, so you have to make sure that users can log in only when they use an encrypted connection.

Note Most mail clients can be configured to use TLS when sending mails. If you happen to come across one that cannot do this, you can leave out the next configuration step, but you must make sure that users understand that their passwords go over the Internet in plain text. Clients configured to open TLS connections will still do so.

Add the following line to the `sasl` section of your Postfix configuration, and reload Postfix:

```
smtpd_tls_auth_only = yes
```

If you connect to your mail server now, you will see the following:

```
[ralph@centos ~]$ telnet localhost 25
Trying 127.0.0.1...
Connected to localhost.localdomain (127.0.0.1).
Escape character is '^]'.
220 centos.example.com ESMTP Postfix
EHLO mail.example.com
250-centos.example.com
250-PIPELINING
250-SIZE 10240000
250-VRFY
250-ETRN
250-STARTTLS
250-ENHANCEDSTATUSCODES
250-8BITMIME
250 DSN
```

There's no mention of AUTH capabilities anymore. Try again with an encrypted connection:

```
[ralph@centos ~]$ openssl s_client -starttls smtp -connect localhost:25
CONNECTED(00000003)
[...]
250 DSN
EHLO mail.example.com
250-centos.example.com
250-AUTH PLAIN LOGIN
250-AUTH=PLAIN LOGIN
```

```
250-ENHANCEDSTATUSCODES
250-8BITMIME
250 DSN
```

Over an encrypted connection AUTH is advertised. This makes sure that none of your users sends unencrypted passwords over the Internet. Your mail server is now ready for production. Test it well before giving out accounts to other people. If everything works as expected, turn off the safety net:

```
soft_bounce = no
unknown_local_recipient_reject_code = 550
```

Sit back and enjoy the spam.

Retrieving Mails

Your mail server is running now, mails are coming in, your users can send mails to each other and the rest of the world, but something seems to be missing. Nobody can read mails yet! Sure, if you are logged in locally, you can use the mail command to read and send mails, but this is a very limited mail client, even by old standards. CentOS comes with the Mutt mail client, which also is able to read mails from a local mailbox. The same goes for the Alpine mail reader and some other console clients. Although those mail clients are a good choice for many people, other users prefer graphical mail clients such as Evolution and Thunderbird. You probably don't want to give all your users a shell account on your mail server either. How do your users get their mail now?

Two protocols are used to retrieve mails over the Internet. One is POP3, which is described in RFC 1939. The other one is Internet Message Access Protocol, version 4 rev 1 (IMAP4), which is described in RFC 2060. The most obvious difference between those two protocols is that POP3 is like a real post office, where you go and retrieve your mail to take it home with you. If you fetch mails via POP3, your client downloads them to your local computer, stores them there, and then removes them on the server.

IMAP4 is mostly used to manage your mails on the server. Your client does not download the mails but shows you the mails that are stored on the server. You can build up a folder structure on the server to store read mails in another mail folder than new mails or store all your replies in a separate mailbox. This is a good protocol if you regularly read mails from different computers. With POP3, mails get deleted after retrieval and are available only on the computer you retrieved them with; by contrast, with IMAP4, mails stay on the server and can be read from anywhere. This is also great if you want to test different mail clients—your mail stays where it is, as long as you don't remove it from the server.

For you as a mail server administrator, this may look different. When all your users use POP3 and retrieve all their mails before reading, the storage space for mails does not have to be very big. You should take holidays into account, where some users do not retrieve their mails over a longer period. With IMAP4, users will manage their mails on your server. This can use up a considerable amount of storage space on your server, with people sending and receiving holiday pictures, Word documents, and other large attachments on your server.

Note Postfix does not deliver mails to mailboxes that are larger than 50MB per default. This makes it easy to calculate storage space on your mail server but will soon lead to calls from users who cannot receive mails anymore, because of this limit. You can tune this with the `mailbox_size_limit` parameter, which defaults to 51,200,000 bytes. Messages are limited to 10MB, which is reasonable, but if your users complain, you can change it with `message_size_limit`.

It is up to you to decide which type of message retrieval you want to offer your users. IMAP4 is much more powerful than POP3, but it leads to increased storage on your server. Luckily, both servers that are available for CentOS support both protocols.

CentOS 5 ships with Dovecot (`http://www.dovecot.org/`) and the Cyrus IMAP server (`http://cyrusimap.web.cmu.edu/`). Both servers are fast and reliable and offer a reasonable feature set.

Cyrus IMAP is used in large-scale environments with several thousands, or even hundreds of thousands, of users. It is written to be scalable even to the largest setups, and you can spread it across several servers to level the load. It can also be used for smaller setups, because it has at least one feature that the Dovecot implementation available in CentOS 5 does not have: shared IMAP folders. Shared IMAP folders are mailboxes or folders to which several people have access. Think of it as a "reverse alias"—mail gets delivered to one folder, and three users can access this IMAP folder. Cyrus IMAP also natively supports the sieve filtering system with which you can filter out unwanted mails when they are received.

Dovecot is a new IMAP4 and POP3 server that has been written with speed and security in mind. Dovecot's development is very fast at the moment, so the CentOS version lags a bit behind in features. Newer versions of Dovecot also support shared folders. To use the sieve mail-filtering language, you need to download and install a plug-in, which is not available from the CentOS repositories. One of the biggest advantages of Dovecot is that it uses standard Unix `mbox` and `maildir` formats for mail storage, while Cyrus `imapd` uses its own storage format.

Because you already installed Dovecot to provide authentication capabilities to Postfix and because it is very easy to set up, the next sections are about configuring Dovecot for your users.

The nice thing about Dovecot is that it works out of the box after you install and start it. If you already have mails in your mailbox, you can test whether it works:

```
[ralph@centos ~]$ telnet localhost 110
Trying 127.0.0.1...
Connected to localhost.localdomain (127.0.0.1).
Escape character is '^]'.
+OK Dovecot ready.
user ralph
+OK
pass itsasecret
+OK Logged in.
stat
+OK 26 14419
list 5
+OK 5 554
retr 5
+OK 554 octets
Return-Path: <test@example.com>
X-Original-To: ralph@localhost
Delivered-To: ralph@localhost.example.com
Received: by centos.example.com (Postfix, from userid 501)
        id C7AD818242; Tue, 24 Mar 2009 01:30:40 +0100 (CET)
Date: Tue, 24 Mar 2009 01:30:40 +0100
From: test@example.com
To: ralph@localhost.example.com
Subject: mail Nr. 5
Message-ID: <20090324003040.GA24807@centos.example.com>
Mime-Version: 1.0
Content-Type: text/plain; charset=us-ascii
Content-Disposition: inline
User-Agent: Mutt/1.4.2.2i
Lines: 1
Hello
.
quit
+OK Logging out.
```

After logging in, stat tells you that 26 messages are available, using 14,419 bytes. With the command retr 5, you can retrieve the fifth mail, with all headers. Because this mail has been sent from the local box, the header section is quite short. The mail wasn't deleted after retrieval; your mail client will probably do that. Here's the same for IMAP4 where you are going to fetch only the body of the sixth mail:

```
[ralph@centos ~]$ telnet localhost 143
Trying 127.0.0.1...
Connected to localhost.localdomain (127.0.0.1).
Escape character is '^]'.
* OK Dovecot ready.
1 login ralph isasecret
1 OK Logged in.
2 select Inbox
* FLAGS (\Answered \Flagged \Deleted \Seen \Draft)
* OK [PERMANENTFLAGS (\Answered \Flagged \Deleted \Seen \Draft \*)] Flags permitted.
* 26 EXISTS
* 0 RECENT
* OK [UNSEEN 1] First unseen.
* OK [UIDVALIDITY 1237853960] UIDs valid
* OK [UIDNEXT 27] Predicted next UID
2 OK [READ-WRITE] Select completed.
3 FETCH 6 BODY[TEXT]
* 6 FETCH (FLAGS (\Seen) BODY[TEXT] {7}
Hello
)
3 OK Fetch completed.
4 LOGOUT
* BYE Logging out
4 OK Logout completed.
```

The IMAP4 protocol is much more complicated than POP3, but it has to be because it needs to be able to manage your mails on the server itself, while POP3 just lets you download mails.

What is there left to configure if it already works? For one, you will need to open your firewall so other users can access your IMAP server over the Internet. And because your SMTP server already supports encryption, you probably want to turn that on for POP3 and IMAP4 also.

Configuring Your Firewall

Run `system-config-securitylevel-tui` to access the firewall configuration, as shown in Figure 6-4.

Use the Tab key to choose Customize, and press the Return key to access the next menu, as shown in Figure 6-5.

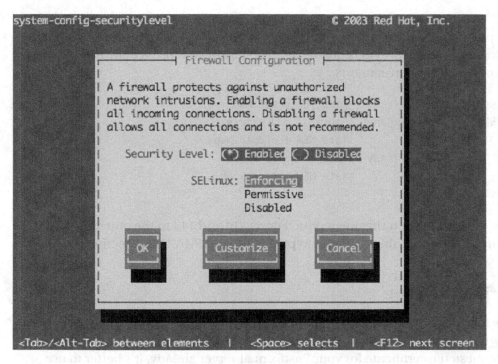

Figure 6-4. *Customizing your firewall settings*

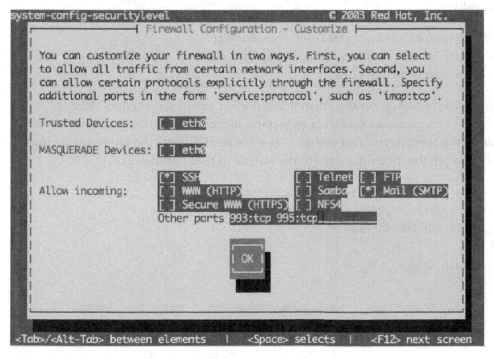

Figure 6-5. *Allowing IMAP4S and POP3S through your firewall*

Use the Tab key to select the line saying `Other ports`. Enter `993:tcp 995:tcp` on this line—these ports are IMAP4 over SSL and POP3 over SSL. Press Tab to select OK, and use the Return key to go to the previous menu. Select OK again, and press Return. Now check whether you opened the correct ports:

```
[root@centos ~]# iptables -L -v | grep -E "pop3|imap"
0     0 ACCEPT    tcp  -- any    any    anywhere  ➡
           anywhere            state NEW tcp dpt:imaps
0     0 ACCEPT    tcp  -- any    any    anywhere  ➡
           anywhere            state NEW tcp dpt:pop3s
[root@centos ~]#
```

There is no need to open the unencrypted ports 110 and 143 to the outside world, because all mail clients are able to use encrypted POP3 and IMAP4 connections.

Configuring Dovecot

All you have left to do is to configure Dovecot correctly so that it uses SSL. Dovecot even brings its own certificates with it, which it stores in `/etc/pki/dovecot/`, but because you created or requested a certificate for your Postfix mail server already, it's better to use that.

Open `/etc/dovecot.conf` with an editor, find the following lines, and change them to the following values:

```
ssl_cert_file = /etc/pki/tls/certs/mail.example.com.cert
ssl_key_file = /etc/pki/tls/private/mail.example.com.key
ssl_cipher_list = ALL:!LOW:!SSLv2
```

Dovecot listens by default on the normal and the SSL ports, so you don't have to change that. Run `service dovecot restart` to restart Dovecot. To see the changes you did to the default configuration, you can run `dovecot -n`, which reflects the changes you just made. You should see the following lines in the output of that command:

```
ssl_cert_file: /etc/pki/tls/certs/mail_example_com.crt
ssl_key_file: /etc/pki/tls/private/mail_example_com.key
ssl_cipher_list: ALL:!LOW:!SSLv2
auth default:
  mechanisms: plain login
  passdb:
    driver: pam
```

```
userdb:
  driver: passwd
socket:
  type: listen
  client:
    path: /var/spool/postfix/private/auth
    mode: 432
    user: postfix
    group: postfix
```

If you have the `nmap` package installed, you can use it to check that Dovecot indeed runs on the needed ports:

```
[root@centos ~]# nmap localhost -p 110,143,993,995
Starting Nmap 4.11 ( http://www.insecure.org/nmap/ ) at 2009-03-24 03:17 CET
Interesting ports on localhost.localdomain (127.0.0.1):
PORT     STATE SERVICE
110/tcp open  pop3
143/tcp open  imap
993/tcp open  imaps
995/tcp open  pop3s
```

You still can reach ports 110 and 143 locally for test reasons. Other users will have to use the encrypted ports, because your firewall configuration denies access to the unencrypted ports. Let's see whether POP3S works:

```
[ralph@centos ~]$ openssl s_client -connect localhost:995
CONNECTED(00000003)
[Lots of output]
Verify return code: 18 (self signed certificate)
---
+OK Dovecot ready.
```

This looks good. You can do the same now for IMAP4 using port 993.

Congratulations. You have just set up a complete mail server with secure connections for SMTP, IMAP4, and POP3. As a cherry on top of that, you are now going to learn how to install a webmail solution on your web server, which will use the mail server you have just set up. With this you can reach your mails from every Internet café without having to start a mail client.

Using Webmail

A webmail interface enables you to read your mails from wherever you are; the only software you need is a web browser. CentOS ships with an easy-to-set-up and fast webmail interface written in PHP, SquirrelMail. If you haven't set up your web server, Chapter 5 explains everything you need to know to get one running. If you want to use your web server for webmail, please configure SSL so you can use encrypted HTTPS connections, because you need to type in usernames and passwords. We'll wait here for you. Back? Everything running? Good. You can install SquirrelMail with Yum, which will also pull in all the needed dependencies:

```
yum install squirrelmail
```

After the installation, you need to restart your web server, because the install drops a configuration snippet in your Apache config directory. To configure SquirrelMail, you need to run the following:

```
/usr/share/squirrelmail/config/conf.pl
```

This opens a text menu in which you can configure all aspects of your webmail interface, like in Figure 6-6.

```
                   Read: config.php (1.4.0)
---------------------------------------------------------

1.  Organization Preferences
2.  Server Settings
3.  Folder Defaults
4.  General Options
5.  Themes
6.  Address Books
7.  Message of the Day (MOTD)
8.  Plugins
9.  Database
10. Languages

D.  Set pre-defined settings for specific IMAP servers

C   Turn color off
S   Save data
Q   Quit

Command >> []
```

Figure 6-6. *Main configuration screen for SquirrelMail*

SquirrelMail has a set of presets for different IMAP servers, which have proven to work best with that server software. Of course, it also knows about Dovecot. Press D on the main screen. This will open the menu shown in Figure 6-7.

```
                       Read: config.php
--------------------------------------------------------------
While we have been building SquirrelMail, we have discovered some
preferences that work better with some servers that don't work so
well with others.  If you select your IMAP server, this option will
set some pre-defined settings for that server.

Please note that you will still need to go through and make sure
everything is correct.  This does not change everything.  There are
only a few settings that this will change.

Please select your IMAP server:
     bincimap    = Binc IMAP server
     courier     = Courier IMAP server
     cyrus       = Cyrus IMAP server
     dovecot     = Dovecot Secure IMAP server
     exchange    = Microsoft Exchange IMAP server
     hmailserver = hMailServer
     macosx      = Mac OS X Mailserver
     mercury32   = Mercury/32
     uw          = University of Washington's IMAP server

     quit        = Do not change anything
Command >> dovecot▯
```

Figure 6-7. *SquirrelMail's presets menu*

Type dovecot at the command prompt, and press Return. This will bring you back to the main menu from Figure 6-6. Press 2 now to get to the server settings (see Figure 6-8). Here you should set the domain (press 1) to the domain you use for mails. If your web server is running on the same host as your web server, you can leave the Sendmail or SMTP value set to Sendmail (which is /usr/sbin/sendmail). If not, you have to set it to SMTP and then configure your SMTP server settings by pressing B. You can now configure your SMTP settings including SMTP-Auth and TLS. The same goes for the IMAP server settings. You can update them by pressing A, which will show the menu in Figure 6-8.

This should be all you have to configure to get SquirrelMail working. You should go through the other menus to see whether there is anything worthwhile to configure for your site such as a different theme or an address book. Save the configuration by pressing S, and quit the setup program by pressing Q. To access your mail, point your browser at https://www.example.com/webmail, which will show a login menu. Enter your username and password, and press the Login button. A window with your mails will open. You can now send and read mail just like you would with a normal mail client.

```
General
-------
1.  Domain               : example.com
2.  Invert Time          : false
3.  Sendmail or SMTP     : Sendmail

IMAP Settings
-------------
4.  IMAP Server          : mail.example.com
5.  IMAP Port            : 993
6.  Authentication type  : login
7.  Secure IMAP (TLS)    : true
8.  Server software      : dovecot
9.  Delimiter            : detect

B.  Change Sendmail Config : /usr/sbin/sendmail
H.  Hide IMAP Server Settings

R   Return to Main Menu
C   Turn color on
S   Save data
Q   Quit

Command >> []
```

Figure 6-8. *Configuring your IMAP settings*

Summary

In this chapter, you learned how to set up the Postfix mail server software to send and receive mails. You can set up a mail server for multiple domains now. You saw how mail works and how to secure SMTP connections with TLS and user authentication. You now know how to set up a POP3 or IMAP4 server and how to configure it so it uses connections over SSL. You also learned how to set up a webmail client for you and your users. You are now all set to run your own mail server on the Internet.

In the next chapter, we will cover the Domain Name System (DNS). This is the glue that makes the Internet work.

CHAPTER 7

■ ■ ■

Understanding DNS

Domain Name System (DNS) is probably one of the most misunderstood technologies in use on the Internet today. Despite that neither the Web nor e-mail would be possible without it, many people do not understand how it works or why it's important. To be fair, that's not all that surprising because DNS is one of those technologies that sits in the background quietly getting the job done. The only time people really think about DNS is when they can't connect to a web site or their e-mail isn't working.

Many professionals use DNS technology passively. Many people who use web hosting with control panels have all the relevant DNS records created for them. They never have to worry about how it all fits together. They simply add a domain, and everything just works. This is all well and good until the day you need to deploy your work onto a machine with a standard install and nothing seems to work.

This chapter starts at the very beginning. It will talk about how DNS came about and why things are done the way they are. We will explain how registries and registrars fit into the mix and why the WHOIS system is vital to how we use DNS today. We will talk about primary and secondary servers and why it's quite possible for a server to be both. We'll also cover master and slave zones, their differences, and why they're important.

We'll continue our foray into the world of DNS by looking at the resolver and the nsswitch file. We'll then move on to working with DNS's predecessor, the hosts file, and show how flexible and useful it is even today. We'll cover how the NSCD service can speed up name resolution and why it's sometimes too efficient for its own good. We'll then show how to set up a proper DNS server to provide a name-caching service and then reconfigure it as a forwarding name server.

After all of that, we'll start to get into the real reason you're here: hosting your own domain names! We'll start by showing how to create a basic master zone for the domain `example.org`. We'll then pad it out by adding the various different types of records that you'd expect to find on a live, working name server. Next we'll cover how to set up a slave server and how you can go about backing up your domains to ensure that they are always available.

DNS, once you've gotten the hang of it, is surprisingly simple. However, so much rests on understanding and configuring DNS that it is crucial that you gain at least a working knowledge of it. Other services work with and rely extensive on DNS. A web site that doesn't work properly or missing or delayed e-mail can often be traced back to an issue with DNS.

So with that in mind, let's get started.

What Is DNS?

DNS is the phone book of the Internet. Quite simply, it provides a mechanism to turn human-readable names into IP addresses. Without this technology, we would have to remember the IP addresses for every single server we wanted to talk to. Humans are notoriously bad with numbers, and although it isn't a problem on small networks, when looking at something as immense as the Internet, it is a problem.

This problem isn't new, and originally the hosts file was a very simple and elegant way to handle it. The hosts file is usually the first port of call when the system needs to convert a hostname into an IP address. This order can be changed, but we'll look at that a bit later in the "nsswitch" section. Most administrators use the hosts file to override any other naming systems that might be in place such as DNS, NIS, or LDAP. More commonly, though, it's used for testing purposes or for setting up an alias for machines the administrator contacts on a regular basis. The key thing to remember, though, is that this file affects only the local machine on which it's running. Two servers managed by the same person could have very different hosts files. There is also no guarantee that a name in one file points to the same IP address that the same name in another hosts file points to.

Confusing? You're not the only person to think so! All you really need to remember, though, is that the hosts file tends to override everything else, so unless you know otherwise, treat them as unique on each machine.

The hosts file is just a simple text file, and originally this file would be maintained and shared among system administrators. This wasn't too bad when there were only a handful of people connected to the Internet. However, it soon became obvious that trying to manage all computer names in a single file was simply not going to work.

One of the big problems was deciding who was going to maintain and manage the hosts file for these people. Who, for instance, gets to decide who gets to use what name? Who decides whether a name is appropriate? Of course, whoever has that thankless job would need to spend time and effort to collate all the new requests, update the hosts file, and then make the file available for people to download.

This was the second issue: distribution. There was no easy way to tell whether you had the most up-to-date hosts file without actually downloading it again and taking a look. As you can imagine, this meant that a lot of resources were required simply to host the file, especially as people kept requesting updates even though no changes had been made.

The hosts file started to get rather large. In effect, it held every single hostname in use on the Internet at the time, and for many people, the vast majority of these names weren't relevant or useful. They had no choice but to download them, however. There was no mechanism to allow partial updates or to selectively take the bits that interested them.

Thus, although the hosts file was fine for an individual system and is still quite effective on a closed network, it was simply too unwieldy to be used on such a large scale. Something needed to be done.

DNS Was Born

DNS was developed by Paul Mockapetris in 1983 to solve this problem. What was needed was a way for the individual organizations to manage their own names in such a way that there was no possibility of naming conflicts. A hierarchical structure would allow responsibility for a given name to be delegated to whoever was best suited to look after it. Today, DNS still follows this hierarchical structure, which allows entire countries to look after their own top-level domains (TLDs) without having to worry about interfering with anyone else. This is called *delegation*.

At the very top of the DNS *tree*, we have what is known as the *root*. This holds all the information on all the top-level domains. A top-level domain is anything that does not have a dot (a period) after it. For example, .com and .org are both top-level domains, whereas centosbook.com is not. centosbook is a *subdomain* of the .com top-level domain. Each subdomain can have one or more subdomains of its own, up to a maximum of 127 levels.

Is it really necessary to learn all this? Generally speaking, you will not need to worry about these finer points when dealing with DNS on a day-to-day basis. You simply add a new subdomain (or hostname), point it at an IP address, and you're done. However, there may be times, especially if you're working in a large organization, where you actually have to delegate control to another party. We'll come back to a specific example later, but for now, take a look at Figure 7-1.

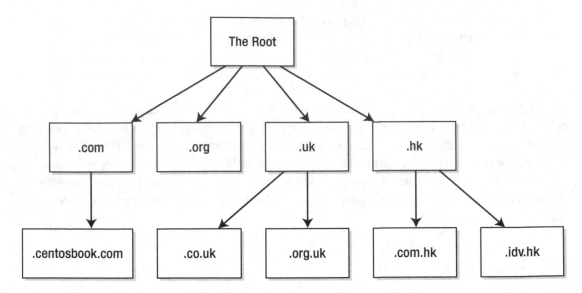

Figure 7-1. *A brief look at how DNS is organized*

Directly below the root you can see all the top-level domains. Two of these are generic top-level domains (.com and .org), and the other two are considered geographical or country code top-level domains (.uk and .hk). In fact, dozens of different top-level domains are available. Check out http://en.wikipedia.org/wiki/List_of_Internet_TLDs for a complete list. The root does not contain any information about any subdomains. Instead, it delegates control over each top-level domain to the relevant authority. When looking up a hostname with DNS, the DNS resolver (the software that actually goes out, finds the name, and runs on every client system on the Internet) starts at the top of the tree and works its way down.

For example, assuming no caching is involved, the resolver will first query the root DNS servers to see who is responsible for the top-level domain of interest. If you're looking up the IP address of www.centosbook.com, it will ask the root servers for information. The root servers, of course, do not have this information, but they do know who controls the .com domain, and they provide a list of DNS servers that are authoritative for it. The DNS resolver then contacts one of these servers and asks again for the information. Again, the DNS servers in charge of the .com do not know about www.centosbook.com, but they do know who is responsible for centosbook.com and, thus, who should be contacted to find the answer. Once more, a set of name servers is sent back to the resolver; this time, though, it is the authoritative servers for the centosbook.com domain. Finally, the DNS resolver requests this information from one of the servers provided. This time, because this server does know the IP address of www.centosbook.com, it returns this value to the DNS resolver, which then passes the IP address back to the software that requested the lookup.

This sounds like a rather long and laborious process, but thanks to caching at all levels of the DNS system, results are usually received pretty much instantly. Now, the delegation you've looked at here happens on an international scale and is not something you usually need to deal with. However, now that you know how DNS finds information in the tree, let's take a look at how those domain names come to be there.

The WHOIS System

WHOIS (pronounced as it sounds, "who is") provides a central record of domain ownership. There are various registries around the world. For example, the Nominet registry manages all .uk domains, and the Hong Kong Internet Registry Corporation (HKIRC) handles all .hk domains. Internet Corporation for Assigned Names and Numbers (ICANN) is responsible for the allocation of all top-level domains as well as IP address delegation. ICANN delegates country code domains to the national registrars (such as Nominet and HKIRC). Depending on the individual registry, the way of purchasing domain names can be very different. They also have their own unique policies and practices.

Both Nominet and HKIRC have restrictions in what domains can be purchased. For example, although .co.uk and .org.uk are open to anyone, you can register a .net.uk address only if you have a RIPE-assigned IP address block. Anyone can buy a domain ending in .hk from HKIRC, but domains ending in .com.hk and .idv.hk are restricted to Hong Kong companies and residents only.

Of course, the majority of domain names purchased today are either .com, .net, or .org. There are hundreds of different registrars offering everything from simple domain name registration to bundled hosting packages for web sites, e-mail, and online advertising. Our registrar of choice is GoDaddy (www.godaddy.com) because it offers good prices and an easy-to-use web site for updating and managing domains.

When looking to choose a registrar, you are in effect getting a simple service, that is, the ownership or the right to use a particular domain name. Because all registrars offer this, you should be looking for registrars that provide good support and allow you to manage your accounts entirely online. Before you choose the cheapest or the most expensive provider, you should do some searches and find out what their customers say about them. Sometimes a really cheap provider will give you amazing support, whereas an expensive provider gives you nothing but grief and hassle. Generally speaking, though, once your domain is set up, you probably won't speak to your registrar until you renew the domain in a year's time.

Why are we discussing the WHOIS system in a chapter on DNS? The WHOIS system is where the authoritative DNS servers for a given domain are listed. These records are not directly queried when looking up a hostname. Instead, the WHOIS record is used by the registry that looks after a given domain name to update their own DNS servers as to which DNS servers are responsible (or authoritative) for a given domain. In other words, it's the first place to look if your domain name doesn't seem to be working the way you expect.

The Root DNS Servers

We're not going to spend too much time on root DNS servers because you will probably never have to use them. That said, you should know what they are because you'll often find documentation that refers to them. There are currently 13 *root servers*, which answer requests from around the world. Their job specifically is to tell people where to find the DNS servers in charge of the top-level domains that we looked at in the previous section.

The Resolver

The *resolver* is a critical part of your computer's network support, but it's not something you are ever likely to deal with directly. The resolver is used whenever a program needs to convert a name to an IP address. Whenever you visit a web site, your browser will make a request to the resolver to find out the IP address to which it should connect. This gives the web browser and the various naming systems great flexibility. The browser wants to exchange a name for an IP address, but it doesn't care (or know) how that process takes place. It doesn't know, for example, whether the name was found in the local hosts file or whether there are two possible IP addresses for a given name.

All of this is hidden in the background, and even as a DNS administrator, this low-level stuff isn't something you'll come across much, if at all. In fact, the only reason I'm even bringing it up is because it shows you how the applications you use on a daily basis interact with the system on which they run. This is important because we'll be looking at various techniques to improve performance, and to appreciate those, you'll need to have a rough idea of how they fit into the grand scheme of things.

Let's start by looking at the hosts file.

The Hosts File

Here is the hosts file from the server we built in Chapter 2:

```
[root@centosbook ~]# cat /etc/hosts
# Do not remove the following line, or various programs
# that require network functionality will fail.
127.0.0.1       centosbook localhost.localdomain localhost
::1     localhost6.localdomain6 localhost6
[root@centosbook ~]#
```

Caution As the comment in the file says, the first two entries should not be altered. In Linux, many programs expect that the local hostname resolves to 127.0.0.1 and will break spectacularly if it doesn't. You can add new entries to this file without needing to worry; just leave these first two lines alone.

The first column contains an IP address, and the second column contains the host that should refer to it. You can add more than one host by separating them with a space. It's very easy to test content in the hosts file by using ping:

```
[root@centosbook ~]# ping localhost
PING centosbook (127.0.0.1) 56(84) bytes of data.
64 bytes from centosbook (127.0.0.1): icmp_seq=1 ttl=64 time=1.75 ms
64 bytes from centosbook (127.0.0.1): icmp_seq=2 ttl=64 time=0.091 ms
64 bytes from centosbook (127.0.0.1): icmp_seq=3 ttl=64 time=0.039 ms

--- centosbook ping statistics ---
3 packets transmitted, 3 received, 0% packet loss, time 2000ms
rtt min/avg/max/mdev = 0.039/0.626/1.750/0.795 ms

[root@centosbook ~]# ping centosbook
PING centosbook (127.0.0.1) 56(84) bytes of data.
64 bytes from centosbook (127.0.0.1): icmp_seq=1 ttl=64 time=0.028 ms
64 bytes from centosbook (127.0.0.1): icmp_seq=2 ttl=64 time=0.053 ms
64 bytes from centosbook (127.0.0.1): icmp_seq=3 ttl=64 time=0.035 ms

--- centosbook ping statistics ---
3 packets transmitted, 3 received, 0% packet loss, time 1998ms
rtt min/avg/max/mdev = 0.028/0.038/0.053/0.012 ms
[root@centosbook ~]#
```

nsswitch

You can find the nsswitch config file at /etc/nsswitch.conf. This is already configured for optimum performance. Specifically, this configuration file determines (at least from a lookup point of view) which service is asked first when a lookup is attempted. The default entry is as follows:

```
hosts:          files dns
```

What this means is that the system will first look in the local files (in this case /etc/hosts), and then, if it can't find what it's looking for, it will try DNS. This setup is very useful because it means you can sneak whatever names you want into /etc/hosts and set them to arbitrary IP addresses. This is very useful for testing and development where you may need to test using specific hostnames but those names are currently in use in production. It's also a very quick and easy way for local administrators to add short names for machines they connect to on a regular basis.

Note There is nothing wrong with putting hosts in /etc/hosts, but you must remember that this data is local to the machine, and not only could it be different on another server, it might also be completely different from what the official DNS system is saying.

NSCD

Name Service Caching Daemon (NSCD) is a useful service that does exactly what its name suggests. Because this is a chapter on DNS, we're going to focus on how NSCD can help us and where it fits into the overall picture. NSCD is very easy to use and should be installed by default. If not, you can install it with the following:

```
yum install nscd
```

So, what exactly does NSCD do? Well, it actually has two caches for each server. The first cache is called the *positive cache*, and this is where name lookups are stored when the hostname is found. For example, the first time you run the command host www.centosbook.com, the resolver will contact your DNS server and look up the name. However, if you're running NSCD, the next time you request that hostname, it will be returned immediately from the cache rather than requiring another lookup. For heavily used machines or those with slow or intermittent Internet connections, NSCD can make a surprising amount of difference.

NSCD also has a negative cache, which as the name suggests is the opposite of the positive cache. If you were to look up the name foo.centosbook.com, you would get a "host not found" error message. That's not overly surprising because there isn't an entry with that name. NSCD will remember this information in its negative cache. The next time you look for this hostname, NSCD will immediately return a failure, saving the trip to the Internet.

As you can see, there quite a few benefits to using NSCD, and you may be wondering why NSCD isn't enabled by default if it's so useful. Well, the answer to that question is that NSCD can be more trouble than it's worth. To be fair, this isn't really NSCD's fault; after all, its job is to remember and cache information. The problem occurs when the cache becomes stale—when the knowledge that NSCD holds and is providing to you is no longer accurate.

Because NSCD "short circuits" host lookups, it's possible for a new host to be created (such as our foo.centosbook.com example) but not be visible to your machine because NSCD has remembered that it doesn't exist and so doesn't check again. The same issue also occurs with the positive cache in that if the IP address of a web site changes, NSCD might not pick up on it and will effectively leave you hanging.

Fortunately, it's really easy to refresh NSCD, and in fact you just need a single command:

```
nscd -i hosts
```

This issue is not unique to CentOS. Windows users may well be familiar with the command `ipconfig /flushdns`, which effectively does the same thing on Microsoft Windows.

So, should you use NSCD? Well, it's a very simple way to improve performance on your machine. If you're connecting via a slow link such as a GPRS modem or even dial-up, running NSCD can actually make a noticeable difference. It's also easy to use (the default config file provided will suit most people very well) and simple to manage. It's also very easy to turn off if you decide it's too much trouble.

■ Tip NSCD caches more than just host lookups; it can also cache user and group information. If you want to cache this information but not host lookups, you can disable the host cache in `/etc/nscd.conf`.

NSCD is a quick way to potentially get a performance boost, but if you have a fast Internet connection, it may not make much difference, and if you deal with domain names that update frequently, you may find that NSCD just gets in the way because it doesn't strictly follow DNS "time to live" instructions.

If you're looking for a performance boost and you don't mind doing an extra bit of work, a caching name server will be right up your street. It doesn't suffer from the issues that NSCD does, and it isn't that much harder to set up and use either.

NSCD supports the usual service commands including `start`, `stop`, and `restart`.

To start NSCD, use this:

```
service nscd start
```

To stop NSCD, use this:

```
service nscd  stop
```

To restart NSCD, use this:

```
service nscd restart
```

If you decide you want to keep on using NSCD, you can enable it so that it starts by default with this command:

```
chkconfig nscd on
```

Now that we've covered these system-level options, it's time to turn your attention to the BIND DNS server.

What Is BIND?

BIND (short for Berkeley Internet Name Domain) is the de facto standard name server on Unix-like systems. It has been in development since the early 1980s, but the current version (BIND 9) is a complete rewrite that fixes a number of issues found in BIND 4 and BIND 8. Because of various security issues with these older versions, you should never run any version of BIND older than version 9. This isn't a problem because this is the version that ships with most modern Unix-like systems, including CentOS.

BIND will allow you to set up and run your own name server. There are four types of name server:

- Caching

- Forwarding

- Master

- Slave

These are actually a bit of a misnomer because there is no reason why a single name server couldn't perform all of these roles simultaneously. In fact, many servers do precisely that, and we'll look at how that can be of benefit in the next section. Really then, each of these is simply a role that a name server can play. It's not as confusing as it sounds because these roles are actually quite distinct, and it will usually be pretty obvious which is meant.

Unfortunately, these aren't the only terms that can be confusing to someone new to DNS.

Primary and Secondary Name Servers

Despite the name, from an outside point of view, DNS servers are treated equally, and requests are distributed among the available servers. It's also possible (depending on the registry's rules) to have only one DNS server or perhaps four or more.

Generally speaking, it's a good idea to ensure that you follow convention. This will make it a lot easier to get help if things go wrong. People who have been working with DNS for many years will most likely assume that these conventions have been followed and that certain terminology is understood. If you choose not to follow these rules without good reason, you may find people are less willing to help you.

Lastly, the terms *primary name server* and *secondary name server* are not very precise in that a DNS server that is the primary for one domain could also be the secondary for another. It is also quite possible for a domain to have a large number of secondary name servers. It is far more precise to refer to *master* and *slave* zones. However, you will find these terms used all over the Internet and in tutorials and books. For the most part, thanks to context, it will be somewhat obvious which term is being referred to. If not, however, you should feel free to ask for more specific information.

Primary Name Server

The *primary name server* should hold the master zone for a given domain. This zone contains "the truth" about the domain. This is known in DNS parlance as being *authoritative*. We'll talk more about authoritative servers in a moment. It is also usually assumed that the first DNS server in the list is the primary. Some registries specifically mention terms such as *primary* and *secondary*. Others just call them name server 1 and 2. So, the primary server should be the first DNS server given, and it should also hold the master zone file.

Secondary Name Server

A *secondary name server* holds the same information as the primary server and is also considered authoritative for any of its domains. However, these servers maintain slave zones rather than master zones. Changes should never be directly made to zones on a slave server. When changes are made on the primary name server, the secondary server is notified and will then download the updates.

Installing BIND

Now that we've covered a large amount of theory, let's put it to use. As usual, we're going to install BIND with Yum. If you are using a system you built with the instructions in Chapter 2, you should already have BIND installed. Most hosted solutions will also come with it pre-installed. Because some installs have explicitly removed BIND, we are going to explicitly install it anyway. Don't worry; if it's already installed, this command won't break anything:

```
yum install bind bind-chroot bind-libs bind-utils
```

This will install (or update) all the relevant packages. The bind-chroot package is actually optional. bind-chroot improves the security of your DNS server by securing it in its own root directory. The idea is that if someone were able to break into your DNS server, they would be locked inside a directory that they can't get out of. This prevents them from being able to access any key system files. Although using this package can cause confusion with some older management tools, generally speaking you will notice no difference in operation, and the extra security you gain is certainly worth having.

That's it really for the basics of running a name server. There is one more optional package that we will be using in the next section. It doesn't do anything that we couldn't do by hand; it just saves us a bit of hassle. Packages like this one are usually referred to as *convenience packages*. We will use the `caching-nameserver` package to quickly and painlessly set up a caching name server.

Setting Up a Caching Name Server

A *caching name server* caches hostname lookups. It's pretty much what you'd expect really. It's different from NSCD in that it honors the time to live (TTL) value. The TTL values tell name servers how long they can remember a record.

Earlier in the chapter, we talked about how DNS works and how a request that starts at your local machine works its way up the DNS hierarchy until it finds a server that can help with the request. Can you imagine how many machines constantly request names such as www.google.com or www.facebook.com? If all those queries had to be answered by Google's or Facebook's own DNS servers, they would be put under tremendous load. It would also mean that there would be constant heavy traffic crossing the Internet, just to resolve names.

To avoid this issue, DNS servers are allowed (and expected) to remember the response for a period of time: the TTL value. Each DNS server in the chain will remember the hostnames that it has looked up. After the TTL value has passed, the DNS server must request the name again. What this means is that because users on your ISP are no doubt constantly visiting Google's web site, when you come to visit it, your DNS request goes to your ISP and can be answered from its local cache. There's no need for your ISP to go hunting on the Internet to try to find it. This not only saves time, but it also helps spread the load from hundreds of thousands of requests across the DNS network rather than focusing on any one server. It also means that network traffic is kept to a minimum.

So, we'll now show how to set up a DNS server on our CentOS machine that is going to perform this task for us. Once you have done the necessary setup (and tested it), you will then tell your machine to start using it. We will also cover how to let other machines use your caching server so that you can benefit from sharing the name cache.

You've already installed the basics of a DNS server. If you try to start it now, you will see the following:

```
[root@centosbook ~]# service named start
Locating /var/named/chroot//etc/named.conf failed:
                                                    [FAILED]

[root@centosbook ~]#
```

This is because in CentOS 5 a default configuration file is no longer provided. You will also note that it looks in /var/named/chroot. You'll recall we touched on this earlier when we showed how to install the bind-chroot package. Fortunately, creating a caching name server is such a common affair that CentOS provides a package that does all of the hard work for you. All you need to do is install it like so:

```
yum install caching-nameserver
```

This will install some key configuration files that we'll cover in a moment. For now, though, simply start up your server with this:

```
service named start
```

and you should find that it now starts without any trouble. That's it as far as the install goes, and for many people, this is as far into setting up a DNS server as they will ever need to go. Let's give it a quick test. Let's look up the details for www.centosbook.com:

```
host www.centosbook.com localhost
```

Notice that instead of just specifying the name, you've instructed the host command to use a particular name server. If you don't specify a name server, the host will use the name servers list in /etc/resolv.conf, which probably points to your ISP. You will update this configuration file in a moment so that it will primarily use your local server before attempting to use the ones provided by your ISP. This is useful because if there is a problem with your local name server (perhaps you forgot to start it, for example), you will still be able to resolve names on the Internet.

The output from the host command should look something like this:

```
[root@centosbook ~]# host www.centosbook.com localhost
Using domain server:
Name: localhost
Address: 127.0.0.1#53
Aliases:

www.centosbook.com is an alias for centosbook.com.
centosbook.com has address 212.13.194.215
centosbook.com mail is handled by 10 mail.doublehelix.hk.
centosbook.com mail is handled by 20 backup.mail.bitfolk.com.
[root@centosbook ~]#
```

The first section just confirms which DNS server was used to look up the request. As you know, localhost points to 127.0.0.1, which is the internal local address (see /etc/hosts), and #53 tells you which port you used, which in this case is the default for DNS.

The next section breaks down some key information such as that www.centosbook.com is actually an alias (or CNAME) for centosbook.com. It then continues to tell you the IP address for centosbook.com and shows you the mail-handling details. You will learn more about these different types of records in just a moment.

If you run the same command again (press the up key and then Enter), you should find that you get a very fast response. The truth is, you might not actually be able to tell any difference. This is partially because DNS is a very lightweight protocol, and there is a good deal of caching going on upstream. Don't be too concerned, though. Browsing the Web can create thousands of individual DNS requests, and all of these will then be cached locally, making them much faster to access next time. Taken individually, the speed benefits are quite difficult to see, but when used on a busy machine, you can often get quite a performance boost. Of course, you also save on bandwidth too, which is very useful if you are being charged per gigabyte!

That said, although DNS caching is a best practice, it's unlikely to make your machine feel like it's had a serious upgrade. Most DNS networks these days are quite fast and have pretty decent response rates. However, if you're stuck on dial-up, GPRS, or ISDN, you might find that DNS caching makes browsing feel more responsive.

Making DNS Available to Other Machines

Right now if you try to access the DNS server from another machine (you can test this using the host command), you'll get an error something like this:

```
[root@doublehelix ~]# host www.google.com www.centosbook.com
;; connection timed out; no servers could be reached
[root@doublehelix ~]#
```

This is because caching name servers are almost always used solely by the machine that's running them. It would be rather unusual to make it publicly available (unless you are an ISP), so by default the config files that we've used specifically listen only on our local IP address. We'll show how to update this configuration so that it listens on all interfaces so that other machines on the network can see it.

Caution This is a bad idea if you're not planning to make the DNS server available to all. If this is on a server on your network behind a firewall, this is perfectly fine. If this server *is* your firewall, you shouldn't open DNS to the outside world unless you are also planning to run your own domain.

To tell BIND to listen on all interfaces, all you have to do is comment out this single line in /etc/named.caching-nameserver.conf (line 15):

```
listen-on-port 53 { 127.0.0.1 };
```

You comment it out by putting a hash (or pound) sign in front of it:

```
#listen-on-port 53 { 127.0.0.1 };
```

If you save the file and restart named (using the command service named restart), attempting to look up the name again should give you this:

```
[root@doublehelix ~]# host www.google.com www.centosbook.com
Using domain server:
Name: www.centosbook.com
Address: 212.13.194.215#53
Aliases:

Host www.google.com not found: 5(REFUSED)
[root@doublehelix ~]#
```

Hmmm, what's this? Well, even though BIND is listening for requests, that doesn't mean it's actually going to answer them. What's happened here is that BIND is refusing to answer you. This is good practice because it means if you accidentally make your cache available to the Internet at large, people wouldn't be able to use it unless you've specifically let them do so. To do this, you need to make some more changes to the configuration file. Specifically, you need to tell BIND to accept queries from everywhere. You should be aware that we're going about this in a bit of an awkward way. You could simply edit the file more extensively to achieve the same effect. However, this way the original options are still available, and you can easily put them back in again by uncommenting them.

First you need to comment out the line that looks like this (line 27):

```
allow-query { localhost; };
```

And then further down, comment out two more lines (lines 25 and 36):

```
match-clients { localhost;};
match-destinations {localhost;};
```

Now if you save and restart the service, you should see this:

```
[root@doublehelix ~]# host www.google.com www.centosbook.com
Using domain server:
Name: www.centosbook.com
Address: 212.13.194.215#53
Aliases:

www.google.com is an alias for www.l.google.com.
www.l.google.com has address 74.125.95.99
www.l.google.com has address 74.125.95.103
www.l.google.com has address 74.125.95.104
www.l.google.com has address 74.125.95.147
[root@doublehelix ~]#
```

Now that's more like it! You can see that lookups have now been enabled for all machines that can connect to the server. Although there are no restrictions in force from a BIND point of view, access can still be restricted by ample use of the firewall. This configuration is quite common in home and small business networks and allows all the machines on the network to benefit from a DNS cache. However, if the server is also the gateway to the Internet (and therefore others can see the DNS server), the easiest way to stop them from using your cache is with the firewall. An additional benefit to this method is that you will still be able to allow certain people to connect remotely by simply updating the firewall rather than having to configure BIND separately.

Configuring BIND to Host Domains

In its current state, BIND is not able to host a real domain name. We've so far been using the handy `caching-nameserver` package to provide you with a working configuration. This is fine as far as it goes, but if you want something a bit more geared to Internet hosting, then you're going to have to create your own configuration file. Don't worry, this is actually pretty painless.

First, we'll show how to create the file `/var/named/chroot/etc/named.conf` using the nano editor. This should be enough to get you started:

```
options {
        directory "/etc";
        pid-file "/var/run/named/named.pid";
        recursion no;
        };
```

If you restart BIND now (with the traditional service named `restart`) and try to run some queries, you'll discover very quickly that your server seems to be broken. This is partly true in that BIND won't resolve any domains currently. This makes sense because you haven't yet told BIND about any of the domains that you have. To start with, we'll show how to create a master zone, and then we'll show how to set up a slave zone so you can see how to configure the master server to allow replication (zone transfers). This should be enough to get you up and running with hosting your own domains, but before we can go much further, we need to talk about what you'll find in your average zone file should you happen to look.

A Records

An *A record* is probably the most common and easiest of all records to understand. Quite simply, whatever is placed on the left will resolve to the IP address provided on the right. Here's an example of an A record:

```
www     IN     A     192.168.1.1
```

Here, www (expanded to include the full domain name) would resolve to 192.168.1.1. If this were the zone file for example.org, www would be expanded to www.example.org. You could choose to be specific in your zone file and use something like this:

```
www.example.org.     IN     A     192.168.1.1
```

The final period (or *dot*) after .org is very important. If you left this out, the record would be expanded to create www.example.org.example.org. That's not quite what you want. This may sound rather obvious, but it can catch people out if they're not careful. There is more information on this in the "Gotchas" section later in this chapter.

CNAME Records

CNAME records aren't used as much as A records, and depending on who you talk to, they either are very useful or should be avoided at all costs. That said, there are some occasions where a CNAME record is definitely the way to go. A CNAME record looks something like this (combined with the A record from the previous example):

```
www     IN     A       192.168.1.1
ftp     IN     CNAME      www
```

This is the shortened form, but you can see what's happening here. It's not unusual, especially with Linux servers, for CNAME records to have more than one job. This is certainly the case with most virtual machines because people tend to give them a huge range of tasks to do. CNAME (short for "canonical name") is a way of creating an alias from one hostname to another. This saves you from the alternative, which is to create two A records like the following:

```
www     IN     A       192.168.1.1
ftp     IN     A       192.168.1.1
```

The benefit with using CNAME is that if you change the IP address of the server (perhaps you're running this particular machine on an Internet connection that has a dynamic IP address), you have to update only one IP address instead of two. This isn't a big deal if you have only two entries, but if you have more, it can save you a lot of time and hassle. Another benefit of CNAME records is that they can point to a completely different host. For example, if you have a mail server that looks after your main domain (example.com) and you want to use the same mail server for example.org, you could do this by creating an A record that points directly to the mail server. Alternatively, you could do this:

```
mail     IN     CNAME     mail.example.com
```

This would in effect tell clients that the mail servers are effectively the same, but it helps keep their identities separate. The biggest downside of using a CNAME record is that a lookup will require two attempts rather than one. In our previous example, the user would need to look up `mail.example.org` and then look up `mail.example.com`. Many people consider this additional overhead to be unacceptable. Others say that the overhead caused is marginal and the benefits gained in making the records clearer and easier to maintain far exceeds any potential performance issues. At the end of the day, use whichever feels right to you.

MX Records

Speaking of mail servers, it's time we took a peek at MX records. These tend to cause a fair bit of confusion among new DNS administrators because their need isn't always obvious. First, you need to understand that MX records are completely separate from either A or CNAME records. MX records are used to tell clients which hosts they should contact in order to deliver e-mail. Some people create an A record for `mail` and expect it to work. Others create an MX record (which ultimately doesn't point to anything) and expect the same. So, without further ado, let's look at an example (we've used the expanded version for clarity):

```
mailserver.example.org.    IN    A    192.168.1.1
example.org.    IN    MX    10 mailserver
```

So, what does this mean? Well, you first create an A record for `mail`. Now this could be anything you wanted. The word *mail* accurately describes the server, but you could call it anything you wanted. Ultimately what you call it makes no difference. The important thing as far as e-mail is concerned is the MX record. The MX record tells mail clients which servers they should use to deliver mail and in which order they should do it. In our example, we have stated that `example.org` e-mail is handled by `mail.example.org` with a priority of 10. Historically, priorities start at 10 and increase by 10 for each new server. In our case, we have only one server, so it makes little difference. Remember, though, that the MX record must point to an existing hostname; in other words, it requires an A record. This doesn't have to be in the same domain, as we'll see in one of the following examples.

First, though, let's add another mail server. This one is going to be imaginatively called `mail2`. Joking aside, although it may seem like a good idea to call your servers things like `gandalf` or `bilbo`, it can get very confusing for people who are not in on your naming scheme, especially because it doesn't provide any useful information. If you want to use such a naming scheme, it is best to do so internally rather than externally. So, our records for two e-mail servers might look as follows:

```
mailserver.example.org.    IN    A    192.168.1.1
mailserver2.example.org.    IN    A    192.168.1.2
example.org.    IN    MX    10 mailserver
example.org.    IN    MX    20 mailserver2
```

What we've done here is create two A records for two different machines (or at least two different IP addresses anyway) and create the relevant MX records to use them. You'll notice that apart from differentiating between the names, `mailserver2` has a much higher priority (20) than `mailserver`. This tells mail clients that `mailserver` is preferred over `mailserver2`. This is the most common arrangement where a business might have its main e-mail server hosted on its premises but has a backup e-mail server somewhere else on the Internet, just in case its Internet connection has problems. If a mail client can't contact `mailserver`, it should try to contact `mailserver2`. It is up to the mail server on `mailserver2` to handle incoming e-mail properly; DNS just provides the ability to find the server.

But what if you want both servers to have the same priority? This is sometimes done for very large companies where a single mail server simply isn't enough to handle all the e-mail needs. In this case, setting both mail server priorities to 10 will create a "round-robin" system. In effect, this means that it is up to the mail client to decide which e-mail server to contact because DNS shows that both can be used interchangeably.

Lastly, you may use a third party to provide your backup e-mail service. This could be a commercial service (for example DynDNS) or provided along with your virtual machine (as is the case for BitFolk). Either way, using these services is very straightforward and follows on from what we've already covered:

```
mailserver.example.org.     IN      A       192.168.1.1
example.org.     IN     MX     10 mailserver
example.org.     IN     MX     20 backup-email.example.com.
```

This works exactly like our previous example, only we've specified a server outside of our domain to handle the task. As with CNAME records, there's no reason why you couldn't create a new A record for `mail2` and then point that IP address at the backup server that's been provided. However, best practice is to point to an already established hostname because this prevents any issues caused by changing IP addresses or DNS load balancing.

NS Records

Last but not least is the *NS record*. NS is short for "name server," and the NS record tells clients which name servers are authoritative (that is, have the official true view) for your domain. Now, in theory, these entries should match the ones listed in the WHOIS record for our domain. Technically this should always be true, and you should ensure your domains follow this best practice. Not doing so won't break anything per se, but it can cause lookup delays and general confusion. An NS record looks like this:

```
example.org.       IN     NS     dns0.example.com.
```

■**Caution** As you can imagine, telling the world that the primary DNS server for `example.org` is `dns0.example.org` has some issues. Mainly, this has you running around in circles because you've created a catch-22 situation. You cannot look up `dns0.example.org` because to do so you need to ask `dns0.example.org`. Now, as long as you have name servers in another domain, this will still work, but it's clearly a bad idea. Stay away from this one, and if you have to, use a so-called glue record that defines `dns0.example.org` in the parent `.org` zone to solve the issue.

Generally speaking, you should have at least two DNS servers. This is good practice because if your DNS server goes down, people won't be able to find your web site or your e-mail servers. Because many people host their web sites in the same place they host their DNS, this won't help much, but it will ensure that e-mail is properly routed to the backup e-mail server. Multiple NS records look like this:

```
example.org.    IN    NS    dns0.example.com.
example.org.    IN    NS    ns1.example.net.
```

■**Note** As per mail servers, the hostname does not specifically matter, and it is how they are assigned using the NS record that's important. Also, like MX records, NS records must point to something that already exists.

Quick Round-Up

So, with that in mind, the following example should now make sense:

```
www.example.org.      IN    A       192.168.1.1
ftp.example.org.      IN    CNAME   www
mail.example.org.     IN    A       192.168.1.2
mail2.example.org.    IN    A       10.0.0.1
example.org.     IN    NS      dns0.example.com.
example.org.     IN    NS      ns1.example.net.
example.org.     IN    MX      10 mail
example.org.     IN    MX      20 mail
```

To summarize then, we have two A records that define our web and mail servers. The FTP service runs on the same server that provides the web site, so we've decided to use a CNAME to alias FTP to www. We have two of our own mail servers (perhaps one in a different building, city, or country) and have created A records for them. We have also created MX records to tell mail clients which e-mail servers should be used and in which order.

Lastly, we have confirmed the authoritative name servers for our domain by creating to NS records.

This is really a whirlwind tour of the types of DNS record you might want to use. There are others, but these are the ones you will most likely work with on a day-to-day basis when hosting your own domains. The BIND documentation provides in-depth information on all of these different types of record, and if you would like to know more, this would be the best place to start. One of us looks after about 100 domain names, and it's rare that we need anything more than what we've talked about so far.

With all this in mind, we are now ready to move on to actually creating a master zone. In reality, we've pretty much done this already, and we will reuse the content that we've already created. There is some additional information that is needed when creating a domain, but this is mostly seen as a template and is rarely altered once a domain has been created.

Creating a Master Server

A *master server* is simply a DNS server that has the master zone for a particular domain. This is the server that provides all the domain information to the slave servers and is where you will make all your changes. There should only ever be one master server for a given domain. This makes sense, and it makes it much easier to keep track of changes if you make them on only one machine. Slave servers will get hold of up-to-date copies very quickly after the changes are applied to the master, so there is no need to worry about delays or try to come up with more efficient alternatives.

First, we're going to update our named.conf file. So far, this has been configured to do nothing except run and ignore queries. That's not overly useful, but note that we'll tell BIND that we want it to be the master server for the example.org. domain. To do this, we need to tell BIND three things. First, BIND needs to know the name of the domain. Second, it needs to know that we wanted it to be a master, and third it needs to know where to find the data for the zone itself. With this in mind, a complete named.conf (/var/named/chroot/etc/named.conf) could look like this:

```
options {
        directory "/etc";
        pid-file "/var/run/named/named.pid";
        recursion no;
        };


zone "example.org" {
        type master;
        file "/var/named/example.org.hosts";
        };
```

If you try to restart BIND now, you'll get an error because this file does not exist. Remember, you installed the chroot package for extra security, so all the paths in this configuration file are relative to /var/named/chroot. This means that although you have /var/named/example.org.hosts in your config file, in actual fact the file name should be /var/named/chroot/var/named/example.org.hosts.

Obviously, you need to put something in there, so add this to that file:

```
$ttl 38400
example.org. IN  SOA     dns0.example.com. pmembrey.example.org. (
                  1187790697   ; serial number
                  10800        ; refresh
                  3600         ; retry
                  604800       ; expiry
                  38400 )      ; minimum


www.example.org.     IN     A     192.168.1.1
ftp.example.org.     IN     CNAME    www
mail.example.org.    IN     A     192.168.1.2
mail2.example.org.   IN     A     10.0.0.1
example.org.     IN     NS     dns0.example.com.
example.org.     IN     NS     ns1.example.net.
example.org.     IN     MX     10 mail
example.org.     IN     MX     20 mail
```

You should now be able to start your name server without errors. You can test your server with host, but remember to specify the name server; otherwise, you won't get the answer you expect. Consider this example:

```
[root@centosbook ~]# host www.example.org localhost
Using domain server:
Name: localhost
Address: 127.0.0.1#53
Aliases:

www.example.org has address 192.168.1.1
[root@centosbook ~]# host -t mx example.org localhost
Using domain server:
Name: localhost
Address: 127.0.0.1#53
Aliases:
```

```
example.org mail is handled by 10 mail.example.org.
example.org mail is handled by 20 mail.example.org.
[root@centosbook ~]#
```

For the most part, the header for our zone file can be used as a template. The only thing you need to change on a regular basis is the serial number. This should be incremented every time you make a change to the zone. If you don't, you'll find that strange things begin to happen such as the new and old addresses both being returned at random intervals. For more information on this, take a look at the "Gotchas" section later in this chapter.

If you're looking to have only one DNS server (perhaps you've created an internal naming system for your own network), then you can stop reading here. A master server can provide everything that a small network needs. Although you really should have at least two DNS servers in a production environment as a backup, you might be able to get away with just one if it's for internal use.

On the other hand, if you want to host Internet domains or you want to ensure that should any one server fail or reboot, name resolution will continue, then you should keep on reading.

Creating a Slave Zone

Creating a slave zone has a lot in common with creating a master zone, only you don't need to create the zone file yourself because BIND will do this for you when it retrieves information from the master server. A slave zone entry that could go into /var/named/chroot/etc/named.conf could look like this:

```
zone "example.org" {
        type slave;
        file "/var/named/example.org.hosts";
           masters {
               192.168.1.1;
           };
        };
```

The big difference here is that we're specifying the server that the information should be requested from. It goes without saying that this example is unlikely to work for you on your network. You will probably need to at least modify the IP address in order to get this to work. Once you're happy with the file, save it, exit nano, and restart named (with the command service named restart).

All going well, your server should have copied the zone information from your master server and is not making it available to everyone who is asking for it. You can repeat this process as many times as you like; there is no limit on how many slave servers you can have. Bear in mind, though, that the key benefits of having slave servers are bandwidth saving (by having servers closer to the people that use them) and redundancy (by having servers that are resilient to localized problems, such as Internet connection failure). Wherever possible, though, you should have at least one slave server, just in case.

Allowing Zone Transfers

When you update a record on your master server, the master server will contact the slave servers and tell them that they need to update their copies of the data. Before the slave servers can do this, though, you need to give them permission on your master server. Giving permission is very straightforward. All you need to do is add the `allow-transfer` statement to `named.conf`. For example, if your slave server had an IP address of 192.168.1.5, you would add this in the options section:

```
allow-transfer {192.168.1.5;};
```

In order for this change to take effect, you need to restart BIND. If you restart your slave name server as well, it will make a new zone transfer request, which will now be allowed.

Tip Another useful statement to remember is `recursion no;`. This statement tells BIND not to make lookup requests for zones for which it is not responsible. This helps secure your server from DNS poisoning attacks (`http://en.wikipedia.org/wiki/DNS_cache_poisoning`) and prevents people from taking advantage of your bandwidth and resources.

Gotchas

Generally speaking, DNS is one of those technologies that you pretty much deploy and forget. Unless you have a very active domain (one that needs lots of changes), chances are you'll set things up and then won't touch it for months. However, you won't be surprised to hear that DNS has a few little tricks up its sleeve. Even when you become familiar with working with BIND on a regular basis, it's still possible to get caught out by these.

Forgetting to Increment the Serial Number

Forgetting to increment the serial number has to be the all-time number-one problem faced by new DNS administrators. It's also likely to cost you a lot of sleep if you're not careful, and you won't be the only one! Because DNS is a distributed system, it is very important that the various servers all have the same data. To ensure the servers stay in sync, each zone has a serial number. The trick is remembering to update the serial number whenever you update the zone file.

This sounds very obvious, and you'd think that nobody would fall for this one, but the simple fact is that they do. All the time. Imagine you're working late and you're just adding a new host to your DNS zone, or perhaps you're updating a variety of different zones. You forget to update one of the serial numbers, but that won't generate any errors. You carry on about your business.

The next day you get a call asking why the DNS change that was requested hasn't been done. Surprised, you look at the file, and sure enough, the new entry is exactly where it should be. You try to look up the name, but it's not there, and your slave servers don't seem to have it either.

This is a dead giveaway that you forgot to update the serial number. Convinced you did update it? No problem, update it again, and you'll be absolutely sure. Remember, having different records for the same serial number is a very bad idea, and although the example we've just presented is somewhat obvious, it often isn't that straightforward when this particular issue bites. The quickest way to ensure you haven't fallen prey to it is to update the serial "just in case" and reload the zone file anyway.

Forgetting the Dot in the Record

When setting up your DNS zone, you don't have to specify the full name if you don't want. This means that if you're editing the zone file for the domain example.org and you add the following record:

```
www             IN          A              192.168.1.1
```

then BIND would assume you were referring to www.example.org. Some people prefer to explicitly state the full name, like so:

```
www.example.org.          IN          A        192.168.1.1
```

This is similar to our first example with one subtle but critically important difference. You'll notice that after .com there is a follow-up dot. This tells BIND that the name is explicit and should not have example.org added to the end. This feature is very important because there will be times when you will need to reference a hostname outside of your domain. Usually, for example, the DNS servers for a given domain have hostnames in a separate domain. This helps ensure that you don't need to look up a server's name in order to find that server's name.

Where people get caught out is that they forget to stick the dot on the end. If we had left off the last dot in our previous example, BIND would have interpreted it as follows:

```
www.example.org.example.org.
```

Again, this would not show up as an error—it is, after all, a completely valid name—it's just not the one you wanted. This one is also hard to debug, because although it looks OK on initial inspection (and often on a much closer inspection), BIND will still insist that www.example.org does not exist.

After updating the serial number and reloading the zone (trust us, it never hurts to start off with this), your next stop should be to carefully scan the zone to make sure that all the dots are in the right places. Again, like the serial number, it is very easy to leave it out. Because it doesn't make much difference to the structure of the file, these issues can be very hard to track down.

Summary

This chapter has been something of a whirlwind tour on how to set up and run your DNS server. We covered how to create a caching and forwarding name server, which is ideal for the home office or small business network. We also talked about how DNS is used throughout the Internet and the different types of record that make up DNS zones. We covered creating both master and slave zones and why it is important to have both. Ultimately, you now know enough to register a new domain name and provide your own DNS.

The next chapter focuses on how to set up Dynamic Host Configuration Protocol (DHCP) so that your CentOS server can automatically configure your workstations. DHCP is one of those services that you really worry about only when it stops working; otherwise, it sits quietly in the background making your life easier. One of areas where DNS and DHCP come together is Dynamic DNS. This is a technology that allows DHCP to directly request an update to a DNS record. This requires DHCP and BIND to work closely together. You will learn more about this in the next chapter. Onward. . . .

CHAPTER 8

■ ■ ■

Setting Up DHCP

DHCP stands for Dynamic Host Configuration Protocol. This name pretty much covers what DHCP is used for: to dynamically configure a host connected to a network so it can use that network. In practice, DHCP is used to give a host an IP address, a subnet mask, a default gateway, a name server, and so on. Basically, it provides a networked device with everything it needs to be able to use the network to which it is connected.

This, of course, makes it clear why you could use DHCP. It allows you to control centrally the configuration of your network and makes it easy to distribute changes of the network configuration to all the hosts in that network. Therefore, it shouldn't come as a surprise that DHCP is used in almost all networks, even in networks where all hosts have a static IP address. You can, of course, configure each host itself with its static configuration, but using DHCP to hand out static IP addresses makes it possible to manage the configuration of these hosts in a central place.

As you can see, DHCP is something that is used almost everywhere, and together with DNS, it is considered to be the basis of a network setup. In this chapter, you'll learn how to use it.

How Does DHCP Work?

Before going into detail on how to configure the DHCP server included in CentOS, we will first cover some basics of the Dynamic Host Configuration Protocol. Knowing how DHCP works may help you understand how to configure it.

If there is a DHCP server, then of course there is a DHCP client. These days, a DHCP client is present in almost all network-attachable devices. When this client connects to a network, it starts by sending a *DHCP discovery packet* to the network. At this moment, the client has no knowledge of the network, so it sends this packet to the broadcast address (255.255.255.255). All devices connected to the network, including the DHCP server, will see this packet.

After encountering this packet, the DHCP server responds by sending a *DHCP offer* to the client. The offer includes, among other things, an IP address and a subnet mask. This offer is called a *lease*, because the IP address is given only temporarily to the client. The lease (and the IP address included) is valid only for a certain time. The lease time is also mentioned in the DHCP offer.

When the client has sent its discovery request, it can receive offers from multiple DHCP servers. The client then selects an offer it wants to accept and replies by sending a *DHCP request* to the DHCP server that sent that offer. What offer the client will accept depends on the configuration of the client.

The DHCP server then responds with a *DHCP acknowledgment packet*, indicating it has approved the request from the client and confirming that the client may use the given IP address. This acknowledgment packet includes, besides the basic IP configuration, the lease time and any other options specified in the DHCP server configuration such as name servers, NTP servers, and proxy servers.

The client has now obtained a DHCP lease, so it can start using the network. However, because the lease expires after a while, the client needs to renew this lease from time to time. To this end, the client sends a new DHCP request packet to the DHCP server when 50 percent of the lease time has passed. The DHCP request packet signals the DHCP server that the client is requesting an extension of its lease. If the DHCP server approves this request, it sends another DHCP acknowledgment packet to the client, and the client then can continue using the lease.

If the client does not receive an acknowledgment from the server by the time 87.5 percent of the lease time has passed, it starts sending DHCP request packages using the broadcast address again. This way, it examines whether other DHCP servers may extend the client's lease. If these other DHCP servers can help the client, they, in turn, reply with a DHCP acknowledgment.

If the client did not get any acknowledgment, the lease expires. Then, the client is required to remove the IP configuration from its network interface. After this, the client is free to restart the whole process by beginning again with a DHCP discovery packet and potentially receiving a different address.

The lease time thus has an important impact on how "available" a DHCP server needs to be. To be able to renew the leases on time, a DHCP server should not be unavailable for a period longer than half the lease time. Setting the lease time is therefore a balancing act between setting a high value to allow the server to be unavailable for a certain period and using a low value to let changes made to the configuration propagate quickly over the network. Notably, it will also take half the lease time before all clients will use the changes made to the system. A small lease time, however, implies a higher load for the server because clients will be making renewal requests more quickly. This is, however, less of a problem with modern hardware, particularly when using DHCP, because it is pretty lightweight compared to some other protocols.

DHCP and CentOS

CentOS provides packages both for being a DHCP client and for being a DHCP server. The DHCP client part has been around for a long time, and it is considered to be a standard aspect of any Linux distribution. To configure the DHCP client, you can either use the `initscript` configuration files located at `/etc/sysconfig/network` and inside `/etc/sysconfig/network-scripts` or use the NetworkManager, which is present inside the GUI of CentOS.

For running a DHCP server in CentOS, you have two choices. The first is the DHCP daemon from ISC (the same people who created the BIND DNS server covered in the previous chapter). This is what is called an enterprise-grade DHCP server that can be used from small to large environments and that allows you to configure a large set of options. This is also the DHCP daemon that we will cover in this chapter.

A second option is the `dnsmasq` daemon. This daemon not only provides DHCP but also, and foremost, a DNS server. It is intended to be used in small and medium-sized networks, such as a home network. Since it is a lightweight application, it is often used inside small (wireless) routers that are frequently used at home. You can find more information about `dnsmasq` inside the package and at `http://www.thekelleys.org.uk/dnsmasq/doc.html`.

Installing DHCP

Like all things that come with CentOS, you can install the DHCP server using the Yum package manager. To install the DHCP server, use this command:

```
yum install dhcp
```

The `dhcp` package as delivered with CentOS comes by default with an empty configuration file for the DHCP server. This configuration file is `/etc/dhcpd.conf`. You can find a sample configuration file at `/usr/share/doc/dhcp-3.0.5/dhcpd.conf.sample`.

A second important file is `/etc/sysconfig/dhcpd`. It allows you to pass certain command-line options to the `dhcpd` daemon. This is, for example, used to restrict on which interfaces the daemon will listen for DHCP requests.

Finally, the DHCP package also includes the file `/var/lib/dhcpd/dhcpd.leases`. As its name indicates, this package is used to store all the leases the server hands out. It is important that you do not change this file yourself. Changes to it are made by the `dhcp` server itself. It may, however, be useful to inspect what leases the server has stored.

Configuring the Firewall

If you have configured a firewall on your system, you will need to allow DHCP requests to go through the firewall. You can find more detailed information on how to do this in Chapter 5. For DHCP, you will need to allow all incoming traffic to UDP port 67. The dhcpd daemon will listen to this port for incoming requests.

The dhcpd daemon will respond to the DHCP client by sending packets to UDP port 68. Since the default firewall configuration on CentOS allows all outgoing traffic, there is, however, no need to configure this explicitly. No other ports are used by the DHCP protocol, so this is all that needs to be set up.

Configuring DHCP

Now that everything is prepared, you can configure the dhcpd daemon. As mentioned, the configuration file for the daemon is /etc/dhcpd.conf. Just like most configurations within CentOS, the configuration file is line based, and the # character can be used to make comments.

The configuration file consists of parameters and declarations. Declarations, also called *sections*, describe the topology of the network, characterize the clients on the network, provide addresses to be assigned to the clients, or apply a group of parameters to a group of declarations. These declarations are followed by curly brackets ({}).

Parameters state whether and how to perform something or what network configuration options need to be sent to the client. Parameters specifying the network configuration start with the option keyword. Parameters that are declared before a section are called *global parameters*, and they apply to all sections after that section. You can specify a parameter in multiple sections, but the most specific one is used.

A Minimal Configuration

So, let's start with a very basic configuration to get a feel for how to configure the dhcpd daemon:

```
ddns-update-style interim;

subnet 192.168.1.0 netmask 255.255.255.0 {
        option subnet-mask 255.255.255.0;
        option routers 192.168.1.1;
        default-lease-time 600;
        max-lease-time 604800;
        range 192.168.1.100 192.168.1.200;
}
```

If you read this example carefully, you probably will have a good understanding of what it means. But let's go over this example line by line:

- The `ddns-update-style interim;` line specifies the type of Dynamic DNS (DDNS) that is used to talk to the DNS server. Even when you don't use DDNS, you have to specify this parameter. The default and preferred DDNS method is `interim`, which is what is shown here.

- The `subnet` line specifies the network to serve IP addresses in. This is a mandatory line; the `dhcpd` daemon will check whether it can find the configured networks on the actual network interfaces of the machine on which it is running. If it does not find them, it will give an error on startup.

- The `option subnet-mask` line tells the DHCP client what subnet mask it must use.

- The `option routers` line tells the DHCP client what default gateway it must use.

- The `default-lease-time` stipulates a time (in seconds) that will function as the lease time if the client does not request a specific lease time.

- The `max-lease-time` is the time (in seconds) that defines the maximum lease time the `dhcpd` daemon will accept from a client.

- The `range` line specifies a range that the `dhcpd` daemon will use to hand out IP addresses to clients.

To summarize, this sample configuration will allow the `dhcpd` daemon in the 192.168.1.0/24 network to hand out dynamic IP addresses between 192.168.1.100 and 192.168.1.200. This configuration has a default lease time of ten minutes and informs the client to use 192.168.1.1 as the default gateway and 255.255.255.0 as the subnet mask.

Starting and Stopping the DHCP Daemon

Once you have a configuration file in place, you will need to start the `dhcpd` daemon. Just like for most other daemons present in CentOS, you can achieve this with the `service` command. Use the `configtest` option whenever you make a configuration change. This will tell you whether the `dhcpd` daemon understands your config file and whether this file is without any syntax errors:

```
# service dhcpd configtest
#
```

If you do not get any output from this command, your configuration is approved, and you can start the daemon. If you do get output, you need to read it carefully and fix all the errors mentioned.

To start the daemon, use the start option:

```
# service dhcpd start
Starting dhcpd:                                    [  OK  ]
#
```

When the command returns "OK," the daemon has started successfully and is running. Once the daemon is running, the dhcpd daemon logs output using syslog; you can find this output in the /var/log/messages file by using the less or tail commands.

The status option allows you to query the current status of the daemon:

```
# service dhcpd status
dhcpd (pid 8715) is running...
#
```

The output of the command will indicate whether the daemon is running.

To stop the daemon, use the stop option:

```
# service dhcpd stop
Shutting down dhcpd:                               [  OK  ]
#
```

When the command returns "OK," the daemon is successfully stopped. There is also a restart option, which stops and restarts the daemon.

If you want the daemon to start when the system is booted, you use the chkconfig command to enable this:

```
# chkconfig dhcpd on
```

Extended Configuration

Now that you have a working minimal configuration, you can take the next step and extend it a bit. One of the nice things of DHCP is that you can send along all sorts of options to the clients. We covered the absolute basics to set up the minimal configuration earlier. But there are a lot more options. So, let's take a look at this configuration:

```
ddns-update-style interim;

subnet 192.168.1.0 netmask 255.255.255.0 {
            option subnet-mask 255.255.255.0;
            option broadcast-address 192.168.1.255;
```

```
        option routers 192.168.1.1;
        default-lease-time 600;
        max-lease-time 604800;
        option domain-name "example.com";
        option domain-name-servers 192.168.1.1, 192.168.1.2;
        option time-offset 7200;
        option ntp-servers 192.168.1.1;
        range 192.168.1.100 192.168.1.200;
}
```

This configuration works the same way as the minimal configuration, but it's sending some additional options to the client. Let's go over these extra options:

- The statement option broadcast-address is an extra specification of the network that includes the client. It is a bit redundant since the broadcast address gets calculated from the subnet mask in case the broadcast address isn't provided.

- The option domain-name line contains the name of the domain of which the client is a part of.

- With the option domain-name-servers option, you can specify the DNS servers that the client can use to resolve hostnames.

- The option time-offset statement specifies the difference between the time zone of the client and UTC in seconds.

- The option ntp-servers statement is used to specify the NTP servers that a client can use.

As you can see, it is possible to send a range of parameters to the client telling where particular services are, what configuration needs to be used to access the network, and so on. You can find the full list of available options in the dhcp-options man page. However, it is important to remember that the client isn't required to follow or use any of the options sent along.

Defining Static IP Addresses

Until now, the configurations used a range, or *pool*, of addresses. You thus cannot predict which IP address a host will receive. For roaming devices such as laptops, and so on, that usually does not matter. For other devices, however, you will always want to receive the same address, for example, to allow the device to pass through a firewall or for systems that run a service that is used by other systems (like a web server).

To this end, it is possible to define hosts with a static IP address in the dhcpd daemon configuration. Consider this example:

```
ddns-update-style interim;

subnet 192.168.1.0 netmask 255.255.255.0 {
            option subnet-mask 255.255.255.0;
            option broadcast-address 192.168.1.255;
            option routers 192.168.1.1;
            default-lease-time 600;
            max-lease-time 604800;
            option domain-name "example.com";
            option domain-name-servers 192.168.1.1, 192.168.1.2;
            option time-offset 7200;
            option ntp-servers 192.168.1.1;
            range 192.168.1.100 192.168.1.200;

            host server1 {
                        hardware ethernet 00:00:00:12:34:AB;
                        fixed-address 192.168.1.10;
            }
}
```

As you can see, this is the same configuration as in the previous section except for the added host entry. This host entry is the way to add static definitions to the dhcpd daemon configuration. These three lines are required for every static host definition.

The host line consists of the word host followed by a name for the host entry. This name is internally only within the dhcpd daemon. To send a hostname to the client, you need to add an option host-name parameter to the host entry.

The hardware ethernet line is used to specify the MAC address of the host. The MAC address is a unique identifier for a network interface. It is fixed inside the hardware. Therefore, it can be used to match a certain host and to give it a static IP address. A MAC address almost always shows as a string of six groups of two hexadecimal numbers (from 0 to F) separated by a colon (:). There are different ways to find the MAC address of a host. Sometimes there is a label on the computer/motherboard with the address. Usually the BIOS also has an option of showing it. When you have already installed CentOS on the host, the command ifconfig can also display the MAC address. In this case, you can find the MAC address next to the word HWaddr.

The final line of the host entry, the fixed-address line, specifies the static IP address that will be given to the host. If you add a host with a fixed IP address in a subnet that also has a range specified, that fixed IP address needs to be outside that range.

It is important to note that all hosts defined in a certain subnet statement will be sent all the different options specified in that section. You can, however, override these options by placing the same option parameter with a host-specific value inside the host definition. You can also add option parameters inside the host statement if needed. Here's an example:

```
ddns-update-style interim;

subnet 192.168.1.0 netmask 255.255.255.0 {
          option subnet-mask 255.255.255.0;
          option broadcast-address 192.168.1.255;
          option routers 192.168.1.1;
          default-lease-time 600;
          max-lease-time 604800;
          option domain-name "example.com";
          option domain-name-servers 192.168.1.1, 192.168.1.2;
          option time-offset 7200;
          option ntp-servers 192.168.1.1;
          range 192.168.1.100 192.168.1.200;

          host server1 {
                    hardware ethernet 00:00:00:12:34:AB;
                    fixed-address 192.168.1.10;
          }

          host server2 {
                    hardware ethernet 00:00:00:23:45:EF;
                    fixed-address 192.168.1.11;
                    option host-name "web1.servers.example.com";
                    option domain-name "servers.example.com";
          }
}
```

Here we added a second host statement with an additional host-name parameter and a different domain-name parameter than the one in the subnet statement.

Using this mechanism, you can add different hosts with static IP addresses and send along different and/or additional options to these hosts.

Grouping Statements

When you have a large number of statements (subnet, host, and so on) sharing a lot of options with the same value, it can be easier to group them in order to avoid having to go over each statement when something needs to be changed. If you have grouped statements, you can implement the changes in the grouped section, and all underlying statements will be changed at once. The grouping feature is used a lot for hosts since these are frequently used. Consider the following example:

```
ddns-update-style interim;

subnet 192.168.1.0 netmask 255.255.255.0 {
            option subnet-mask 255.255.255.0;
            option broadcast-address 192.168.1.255;
            option routers 192.168.1.1;
            default-lease-time 600;
            max-lease-time 604800;
            option domain-name "example.com";
            option domain-name-servers 192.168.1.1, 192.168.1.2;
            option time-offset 7200;
            option ntp-servers 192.168.1.1;
            range 192.168.1.100 192.168.1.200;

            group {
                    option domain-name "servers.example.com";
                    option ntp-servers 192.168.1.5;
                    host server1 {
                            hardware ethernet 00:00:00:12:34:AB;
                            fixed-address 192.168.1.10;
                            option host-name "db1.servers.example.com";
                    }

                    host server2 {
                            hardware ethernet 00:00:00:23:45:EF;
                            fixed-address 192.168.1.11;
                            option host-name "web1.servers.example.com";
                    }
            }
}
```

Here we're grouping the different host statements and adding two options that override values from the subnet statement. It makes sense to start using a group as soon as you have two or more statements that have identical options set. Grouping reduces considerably the length of the configuration, makes it clearer and more readable, and facilitates the administration.

Shared Networks

The final statement that we will touch upon here is the shared-network statement. You can use this statement when multiple subnets are present on a single physical network. Here is an example of such a shared-network statement:

```
shared-network internal {
          option domain-name "test.example.com";
          option domain-name-servers 192.168.0.1;
          option routers 192.168.0.1;

          subnet 192.168.1.0 netmask 255.255.255.0 {
                    range 192.168.1.100 192.168.1.200;
          }
          subnet 192.168.2.0 netmask 255.255.255.0 {
                    range 192.168.2.100 192.168.2.200;
          }
}
```

Here you have defined a shared-network called internal. All the subnets inside the shared network share the options domain-name, domain-name-servers, and routers. You also have two subnets: 192.168.1.0/24 and 192.168.2.0/24.

Because there are no statically defined hosts in this configuration, all hosts will be assigned an IP address in the two available ranges. It is uncertain in what range a host ends up. It depends on the free leases in each of the two ranges.

Relaying DHCP Requests

Larger networks are usually split up into different subnets to restrict the amount of broadcast/multicast traffic going around in a network. The different subnets are then linked to each other by means of routers.

In such a situation, you have two options on where to place your DHCP servers. The first option is to place a DHCP server in each subnet. The advantage of this procedure is that you will have a very simple configuration for each DHCP server. The disadvantage is that you will need a machine inside each network and will need to manage all these machines separately.

The second option is to have a single central DHCP server. The routers in the networks will then have to relay all DHCP requests they encounter on the network to that central DHCP server. This is because DHCP requests are sent to the broadcast address, as you remember. Routers, however, do not forward packets sent to the broadcast address.

The DHCP relay mechanism was invented for such situations. The router serves as a kind of proxy for DHCP traffic between networks. The advantage of using relaying is that you have a central place to configure the DHCP server. The disadvantage is that you will need to configure all the routers to do DHCP relaying and point them to the central DHCP server.

To configure a central DHCP server, you simply add subnet statements for all the different networks. Take this code for example:

```
ddns-update-style interim;

subnet 192.168.1.0 netmask 255.255.255.0 {
            option subnet-mask 255.255.255.0;
            option broadcast-address 192.168.1.255;
            option routers 192.168.1.1;
            default-lease-time 600;
            max-lease-time 604800;
            option domain-name "example.com";
            option domain-name-servers 192.168.1.1, 192.168.1.2;
            option time-offset 7200;
            option ntp-servers 192.168.1.1;
            range 192.168.1.100 192.168.1.200;
}

subnet 192.168.2.0 netmask 255.255.255.0 {
            option subnet-mask 255.255.255.0;
            option broadcast-address 192.168.2.255;
            option routers 192.168.2.1;
            default-lease-time 600;
            max-lease-time 604800;
            option domain-name "example.com";
            option domain-name-servers 192.168.2.1, 192.168.2.2;
            option time-offset 7200;
            option ntp-servers 192.168.2.1;
            range 192.168.2.100 192.168.2.200;
}
```

The router that forwards a DHCP request to the server adds some extra fields to the request indicating from which network the request came. This allows the server to look for the matching subnet statement in its configuration and send back an offer to the router for the correct network. The router then forwards the offer to the client.

PXE Booting

Besides just being used to hand out IP addresses to hosts, DHCP can also be used in a process called *PXE booting* (also sometimes called *network booting* or *netbooting*). In short, PXE booting is a mechanism that allows a computer to boot over the network without using a local disk, floppy, CD, DVD, and so on.

PXE booting is mostly used to do network-based installations. In this process, the computer receives a Linux kernel over the network that starts the installation process. The installer itself then looks for the install files on the network. PXE booting can be used to fully automate installations since all commands then come from centrally managed servers.

This sort of network installation requires a couple of services including DHCP. The others are TFTP, FTP, NFS, or HTTP. The DHCP server is used to bootstrap or start the process. In this case, the DHCP server gives an IP address lease to the server but includes two additional pieces of information. First, the server also includes a server IP address indicating where a particular application can be retrieved. Second, it provides the file name of that particular application. The application's job is then to start a Linux kernel and the rest of the installation process.

For all of this to work, the computer booting the network needs to support this network booting process. Therefore, it needs PXE (from which the name PXE booting comes). PXE stands for Preboot eXecution Environment. It is a standardized environment that can be set up by the network adapter in the computer, in which a small application can run. Most recent network adapters support PXE, but it usually needs to be enabled in the BIOS of the computer. After you have enabled PXE and the computer does a network/PXE boot, three things happen:

1. First, the network adapter will do a standard DHCP request. After receiving a response from a DHCP server, it will configure the network adapter with the information received. Then it can communicate over the network.

2. Second, the adapter will look for two options in the reply from the DHCP server. These are called `next-server` and `filename`. It will then request the file name using TFTP from the address defined as `next-server` and download it into the local memory.

3. Third, it will start this downloaded application and hand control of the computer over to it.

This downloaded application is usually a kind of boot loader (a variant of GRUB or LILO) that can download a Linux kernel over the network and start it. This boot loader is then used to start the normal installation process.

Configuring dhcpd for PXE Boot

How do you then configure the dhcpd daemon to send these two options to the PXE environment so that it can continue the network boot? Well, here is an example:

```
ddns-update-style interim;


subnet 192.168.1.0 netmask 255.255.255.0 {
          option subnet-mask 255.255.255.0;
          option routers 192.168.1.1;
          default-lease-time 600;
          max-lease-time 604800;
          next-server 192.168.1.5;
          filename "/pxelinux.0";
          range 192.168.1.100 192.168.1.200;
}
```

This configuration started from the minimal configuration used earlier and added the two options required for a PXE boot. The first option is the next-server option. As explained, it is the IP address of the TFTP server to get the application to continue with.

The second option is the filename option. This option specifies the complete path to the application on the TFTP server.

With these two additional options, the PXE environment has sufficient information to take the second step of the PXE boot. Setting up the rest of the system requirements to do an installation over the network would take us a bit too far for this chapter. You can find more information about network installations in Chapter 10 and in the installation guide at http://www.centos.org/docs/5/.

DHCP Integration with DNS

DHCP and DNS are closely related. They both contain mappings of hosts to IP addresses. So, it makes sense to try to let DHCP and DNS talk to each other. Dynamic DNS is specifically created for this purpose: it allows external applications, devices, and so on, to update the entries of the DNS server. The dhcp daemon is an ideal candidate to do this. As soon as the dhcp daemon has acknowledged a lease for a client, it sends the hostname of the client and its IP address to the DNS server. Subsequently, the DNS information is updated accordingly to the IP address that the DHCP server has given to the client.

For Dynamic DNS to work, both the DHCP server and the DNS server need to be configured correctly: they both need to allow the use of Dynamic DNS, and the DNS server needs to "trust" the DHCP server. The latter is usually accomplished through the use of a cryptographic key.

For the example in this section, we presume that you have working BIND DNS server available, as explained in the previous chapter.

The first step in linking the DHCP and BIND daemons is to create the key that is used to authorize the DHCP server to make DNS updates. You can do this using the `dnssec-keygen` tool that is part of the BIND package:

```
# dnssec-keygen -a hmac-md5 -b 256 -n USER dyndns
```

This tool will create two files that start with `Kdyndns`. If you check the content of the file that ends in `.private`, the last line should contain a line like this:

```
Key: QvVkTnvBcXy4ssmKHSwmADZ2LQtYxeusl+VqHzDl5jQ=
```

Everything that comes after the `Key:` is the actual key that you will use.

The next step is to configure the BIND daemon to allow dynamic updates from the key you just created. To do this, add the following to the global part of the `named.conf` file (before the zone definitions):

```
key dyndns {
        algorithm HMAC-MD5;
        secret "QvVkTnvBcXy4ssmKHSwmADZ2LQtYxeusl+VqHzDl5jQ=";
};
```

Do not forget to change the secret to the actual key you created. And then for each zone that you want to allow dynamic updates for, add a line like this:

```
allow-update { key dyndns; };
```

When these changes are done, you can reload the BIND daemon so that it reads in the new configuration, and those are all the changes that are needed on the BIND side of things. One thing that you will need to watch out for is that BIND will need to be able to write in the same directory where the zone files are located. So, make sure the permissions for that directory are sufficient.

Next, you can configure the DHCP daemon to perform the actual dynamic updates. First you tell the daemon what key to use and what zones to update. You do this by adding the following to the global section of the `dhcpd.conf` file:

```
update-static-leases on;

key dyndns {
  algorithm hmac-md5;
  secret QvVkTnvBcXy4ssmKHSwmADZ2LQtYxeusl+VqHzDl5jQ=;
}
```

```
zone 244.168.192.in-addr.arpa {
  primary 127.0.0.1;
  key dyndns;
}

zone example.com {
  primary 127.0.0.1;
  key dyndns;
}
```

The first line is needed only if you have static host entries for which you want the DHCP daemon to perform dynamic updates.

The key block defines a key the DHCP daemon can use. In the example, the key is called dyndns.

The two zone blocks define the zones the DHCP daemon should update (example. com and 244.168.192.in-addr.arpa in this case), what server to send the updates to (in this case 127.0.0.1), and what key to use (in this example dyndns).

The next step is then to say for which hosts the DHCP daemon should send dynamic updates and what hostname it should use for it. For this, two options are used, namely, ddns-hostname and ddns-domainname. They specify the hostname and domain name to use for the dynamic update. Here's an example using a static host:

```
host server2 {
    hardware ethernet 00:00:00:23:45:EF;
     fixed-address 192.168.1.11;
    option host-name "web1.example.com";
    option domain-name "example.com";
    ddns-hostname "web1";
    ddns-domainname "example.com";
}
```

If you want to do the same for a range of IP addresses, then you can use this example:

```
subnet 192.168.1.0 netmask 255.255.255.0 {
        option subnet-mask 255.255.255.0;
        option broadcast-address 192.168.1.255;
        option routers 192.168.1.1;
        default-lease-time 600;
        max-lease-time 604800;
        option domain-name "example.com";
        option domain-name-servers 192.168.1.1, 192.168.1.2;
```

```
    option time-offset 7200;
    option ntp-servers 192.168.1.1;
    range 192.168.1.100 192.168.1.200;
    ddns-hostname concat("dhcp", binary-to-ascii(10, 8, "-", leased-address));
    ddns-domainname "example.com";
}
```

Here you're using a couple of internal functions of the DHCP daemon to create the hostname on the fly based on the IP address given in the lease. You can find more information about these internal functions in the dhcpd-eval man page.

Now you can restart the DHCP daemon, and it should send dynamic updates to the DNS server whenever it registers a lease. When testing, keep a close eye on the BIND and DHCP daemon log files; they will tell you whether things have gone wrong.

Summary

In this chapter you learned the basics of DHCP. You learned how to install the DHCP server included in CentOS and how to configure it. We also showed you different configurations, going from simple to more extended ones. You got to know some different options that can be sent to the DHCP client. In the final part of this chapter, we spoke about relaying the DHCP request, PXE booting, and how to do dynamic DNS updates between the DHCP daemon and the BIND daemon.

CHAPTER 9

■■■

Sharing Files with Samba

Samba is one of those open source projects that seems to have been around as long as people can remember (like the Linux kernel or the Apache web server). It also is a showcase of what open source software is capable of doing. Samba started as a file and print server for Windows clients, but it has grown up into a project that provides a bridge between Linux and Windows and makes these platforms integrate as tightly as possible.

In practice, Samba is almost always used as a file and print server. From a Windows machine, a Samba server will look like any other Windows machine that is providing shares on the network. In terms of integration with a Windows network, Samba can do this in three ways. The first method requires no integration, meaning that the Samba server is completely independent. The second method is when Samba becomes part of a Windows domain. The third method is when Samba itself manages a domain and other Windows machines and Samba servers can become part of it. Which mode to use depends on the correct setup of the network and how you want to integrate Samba into it.

Windows Networking Basics

It is a bit strange to talk about another platform in a book about a Linux distribution. But when you want to talk to that other platform, you will need to understand a bit how it works.

The Basic Protocols

The protocol that is spoken by Samba and Windows file servers is Common Internet File System (CIFS). The old name for it was Server Message Block (SMB), which is where Samba got its name from (SaMBa).

The CIFS or SMB protocol is used only for the actual file and print services. Other things we associate with Windows networking are other protocols, but Microsoft has integrated all this tightly inside Windows. One of those other protocols is NetBIOS. This is a network protocol on which SMB/CIFS can run. But these days SMB/CIFS can run directly on TCP/IP. NetBIOS is responsible for naming and addressing hosts in a Windows network. The automatic discovery of other hosts that are part of your network is an example of NetBIOS at work.

In Windows versions since Windows 2000, Microsoft added even more protocols to Windows networking, including Kerberos, LDAP, and DNS. They were added to create Active Directory, but we'll come back to this in a moment.

Workgroups

In the early days of Windows networking, groups of machines could be grouped into *workgroups*. In workgroup mode, there is no central control of who is allowed on the network. The workgroups are created arbitrarily by configuring a Windows machine to be part of a certain workgroup. When browsing the network, all discovered machines will be grouped by the workgroup (or domain for that matter) they are part of.

Windows Domains

To secure Windows networking and to better control what happens inside the network, Microsoft introduced *domains* in Windows NT 3 as a way to centrally control the network. A domain manages a central list of users, and these users can use any computer that is part of the domain if the user's profile is stored centrally. The machine that controls a domain is called a *domain controller*. There is one active domain controller, called the primary domain controller (PDC), and multiple backup domain controllers (BDCs).

Active Directory

In Windows 2000, Microsoft introduced a successor to Windows domains called Active Directory. It allows domains to grow to larger environments. Active Directory uses an LDAP implementation to store all the data related to the domain, and Kerberos is used to provide authentication services.

Samba and CentOS Basics

The version of Samba included with CentOS at the time of writing this book is 3.0.33. There are currently two branches of Samba available, the Samba 3 branch and the Samba 4 branch. The latest stable release of Samba at the moment is 3.3.4. Samba 4 is currently still in development and has not seen a stable release at this time.

Samba 4 is a complete rewrite of Samba 3. It was started to clean up the way that Samba was created. Before Samba 4, the developers did reverse engineering of Windows networking. But doing this for all those years has made it possible to write proper documentation of all the protocols, and even Microsoft has released some documentation about the protocols used. So, the developers thought that it was time to start over again and use the documentation to create a new, cleaner, and simpler-to-maintain version of Samba.

Initially, Samba 4 focused on only one goal, implementing a complete Active Directory–compatible domain controller. They have succeeded in that, and in the meantime, the developers are now focusing on adding the missing pieces so that Samba 4 can be used in production environments. (But only alpha, or test, releases are available at the moment.)

While Samba 4 was being developed, other people were attending to Samba 3, and this has led to some duplication of code. To rectify this, a new branch of Samba 3 (3.2) was created to synchronize all that is possible between Samba 3 and 4, while not impacting the stability and available features of Samba 3. When Samba 3.2 was ready, the 3.0 branch was put into maintenance mode, and it will soon stop being supported. At the time of this writing, the Samba 3 version is up to the 3.3 branch.

So, the Samba version in CentOS isn't the latest version with all the latest features, but like anything else in CentOS, the focus is on stability; therefore, CentOS 5 will probably stick to a Samba 3.0.*x* version for the rest of its lifetime.

What exactly can Samba in CentOS be used for? Samba 3.0 can be used as a stand-alone (or also called workgroup mode) file and print server. It can also be used as a member of an NT-style domain or an Active Directory domain. Finally, it can also be used as an NT-style domain controller.

In this book, we are going cover only the stand-alone and domain member functions of Samba. Setting up a domain controller requires other components besides Samba, which is beyond the scope of this chapter.

Preparing to Set Up Samba

When you set up Samba, you will of course need Windows-based machines, since that is the whole point of Samba. You can also use the clients available in Linux as test tools, but those are not a substitute for the real thing.

For using Samba in stand-alone mode, you need only a client. We suggest you use at least a Windows 2000 machine since you probably won't find any of the older versions still used (or we hope so).

When Samba is used in domain member mode, you will, of course, need a domain and a domain controller. We assume it will be an Active Directory–type domain running on a Windows server since that is the most commonly used type these days. The domain controller itself can be used as a client, but it is preferred to have a separate client for testing.

Installing Samba

Installing Samba is very simple because you can use the Yum tool to install software. To install Samba, you run the following command:

```
yum install samba
```

This will install the Samba server part and all the required dependencies to make Samba function correctly. These Samba packages contain the following things. First there is the directory /etc/samba/. This is the configuration directory for Samba. It includes, besides other things, the main configuration for Samba: smb.conf.

Then there are the three Samba daemons: smbd, nmbd, and winbindd. The smbd daemon is responsible for the actual file sharing and the domain controller functionality. The nmbd daemon is responsible for the NetBIOS protocol, the naming of machines on the network, and the browsing. The winbindd daemon is used when Samba is part of the domain. Then this daemon will make all the users and groups of the domain visible inside the Linux environment.

To start these daemons, you need init.d scripts. But there are only two instead of three, as you might have expected. /etc/rc.d/init.d/winbind will control the winbindd daemon, and /etc/rc.d/init.d/smb will control both the smbd and nmbd daemons since you will need both daemons working to have a working environment for the Windows clients.

You can use many command-line tools to manage the Samba setup. Commonly used tools are net, smbstatus, smbcontrol, and smbpasswd. The net tool is inspired by the command with the same name that is available on Windows. You can use it to configure Samba that is part of a domain and perform a lot of different administrative tasks. You can use the smbstatus and smbcontrol tools to manage the Samba daemons for tasks such as changing the log level, viewing the current connections, and forcing a reload of the configuration.

Finally, the complete Samba documentation, in HTML form, is included and is located in the directory /usr/share/doc/samba-3.0.33/htmldocs. It contains all the man pages, the Samba-HOWTO book, and the *Samba by Example* book.

Configuring Samba

Now that you know what Samba consists of, we'll show you how to configure it. As mentioned, the configuration file for Samba is /etc/samba/smb.conf. The CentOS Samba package includes a sample file that you can use as a basis.

The configuration file works like most text configuration files. It is line based, and the # and ; characters indicate a comment (but only if they are at the beginning of a line). In the example included, a line starting with # is commentary, explaining something. A line starting with ; means that it is a configuration statement that you might enable.

The Samba configuration consists of different sections. The first section is indicated with [global] and, as the name indicates, is the global section of the configuration. All the other sections are configurations for shares. They are indicated in the same manner as the global section but with the name of the share between the brackets.

The actual configuration options are in the format of <parameter> = <value>. There are a lot of these options, but we will go over them in the coming sections. You can use the smb.conf man page as a reference for all the possible parameters. To view this man page, use the following command:

```
man smb.conf
```

Example Configuration

As an introduction, we will go over the included example configuration file. Then, in the next sections, we will show how to set up specific configurations. We suggest that you open /etc/samba/smb.conf and follow along as we go through this example.

The first section of the example is an introduction; it basically repeats what we've already mentioned. It ends with a note that you should use the testparm command when you make changes to smb.conf. We also recommend this.

```
# This is the main Samba configuration file. You should read the
# smb.conf(5) manual page in order to understand the options listed
# here. Samba has a huge number of configurable options (perhaps too
# many!) most of which are not shown in this example
#
# For a step to step guide on installing, configuring and using samba,
# read the Samba-HOWTO-Collection. This may be obtained from:
#  http://www.samba.org/samba/docs/Samba-HOWTO-Collection.pdf
#
# Many working examples of smb.conf files can be found in the
# Samba-Guide which is generated daily and can be downloaded from:
#  http://www.samba.org/samba/docs/Samba-Guide.pdf
#
# Any line which starts with a ; (semi-colon) or a # (hash)
# is a comment and is ignored. In this example we will use a #
# for commentry and a ; for parts of the config file that you
# may wish to enable
#
# NOTE: Whenever you modify this file you should run the command "testparm"
# to check that you have not made any basic syntactic errors.
```

The next section talks about SELinux. When you have enabled SELinux and use Samba, you might need to set certain booleans or labels so that SELinux does not interfere with Samba.

```
# SELINUX NOTES:
#
# If you want to use the useradd/groupadd family of binaries please run:
# setsebool -P samba_domain_controller on
#
# If you want to share home directories via samba please run:
# setsebool -P samba_enable_home_dirs on
#
# If you create a new directory you want to share you should mark it as
# "samba-share_t" so that selinux will let you write into it.
# Make sure not to do that on system directories as they may already have
# been marked with othe SELinux labels.
#
# Use ls -ldZ /path to see which context a directory has
#
# Set labels only on directories you created!
# To set a label use the following: chcon -t samba_share_t /path
#
# If you need to share a system created directory you can use one of the
# following (read-only/read-write):
# setsebool -P samba_export_all_ro on
# or
# setsebool -P samba_export_all_rw on
#
# If you want to run scripts (preexec/root prexec/print command/...) please
# put them into the /var/lib/samba/scripts directory so that smbd will be
# allowed to run them.
# Make sure you COPY them and not MOVE them so that the right SELinux context
# is applied, to check all is ok use restorecon -R -v /var/lib/samba/scripts
```

Then you'll come to the [global] section of the configuration. This is also split up in the example file so that relevant options are together. The first part is about the network. The workgroup option specifies the workgroup or domain that the Samba server will be part of. The netbios name option specifies the name of the Samba server; it is commented out here because Samba will by default use the hostname of the machine. But this option allows you to override this.

```
[global]

# ---------------------- Network Related Options -------------------------
#
# workgroup = NT-Domain-Name or Workgroup-Name, eg: MIDEARTH
#
# server string is the equivalent of the NT Description field
#
# netbios name can be used to specify a server name not tied to the hostname
#
# Interfaces lets you configure Samba to use multiple interfaces
# If you have multiple network interfaces then you can list the ones
# you want to listen on (never omit localhost)
#
# Hosts Allow/Hosts Deny lets you restrict who can connect, and you can
# specifiy it as a per share option as well
#
        workgroup = MYGROUP
        server string = Samba Server Version %v

;       netbios name = MYSERVER

;       interfaces = lo eth0 192.168.12.2/24 192.168.13.2/24
;       hosts allow = 127. 192.168.12. 192.168.13.
```

The following section contains options that control the logging of Samba, such as the name and location of the log file and whether Samba needs to limit the size of the file:

```
# Log File let you specify where to put logs and how to split them up.
#
# Max Log Size let you specify the max size log files should reach

        # logs split per machine
;       log file = /var/log/samba/%m.log
        # max 50KB per log file, then rotate
;       max log size = 50
```

The three sections that follow then put Samba into three different modes of operation. The first is Samba as a stand-alone server, and the second is Samba as a domain member. The third is Samba as a domain controller. Because we will go deeper into these modes later, we will skip these sections for now.

Then you come to the browser control options section. This is one part of the Net-BIOS layer and is what makes servers appear automatically when you "browse the network" in Windows. As shown in this section, the default values are OK in most cases.

```
# set local master to no if you don't want Samba to become a master
# browser on your network. Otherwise the normal election rules apply
#
# OS Level determines the precedence of this server in master browser
# elections. The default value should be reasonable
#
# Preferred Master causes Samba to force a local browser election on startup
# and gives it a slightly higher chance of winning the election
;       local master = no
;       os level = 33
;       preferred master = yes
```

The name resolution section is about another part of NetBIOS, namely, the resolution of names to IP addresses. As explained earlier, Windows networking does use DNS for this but also uses its own protocol. This section allows you to configure how Samba needs to behave in this regard.

```
# Windows Internet Name Serving Support Section:
# Note: Samba can be either a WINS Server, or a WINS Client, but NOT both
#
# - WINS Support: Tells the NMBD component of Samba to enable it's WINS Server
#
# - WINS Server: Tells the NMBD components of Samba to be a WINS Client
#
# - WINS Proxy: Tells Samba to answer name resolution queries on
#   behalf of a non WINS capable client, for this to work there must be
#   at least one        WINS Server on the network. The default is NO.
#
# DNS Proxy - tells Samba whether or not to try to resolve NetBIOS names
# via DNS nslookups.

;       wins support = yes
;       wins server = w.x.y.z
;       wins proxy = yes

;       dns proxy = yes
```

Next is the printing section. If you want to use Samba as a print server, it could be that you need to make changes here. But by default Samba will use CUPS and show all the printers that CUPS knows about to the Windows network.

```
# Load Printers let you load automatically the list of printers rather
# than setting them up individually
#
# Cups Options let you pass the cups libs custom options, setting it to raw
# for example will let you use drivers on your Windows clients
#
# Printcap Name let you specify an alternative printcap file
#
# You can choose a non default printing system using the Printing option

        load printers = yes
        cups options = raw

;       printcap name = /etc/printcap
        #obtain list of printers automatically on SystemV
;       printcap name = lpstat
;       printing = cups
```

The final part of the [global] section is about the interaction of Samba with the file-system and, more specifically, about how certain Windows attributes that don't exist in Linux filesystems are mapped. Either these attributes are mapped using the execute attribute bit (all the different map... options) or Samba uses a new feature present in modern filesystems called extended attributes to store these Windows attributes (the store dos attributes option).

```
# The following options can be uncommented if the filesystem supports
# Extended Attributes and they are enabled (usually by the mount option
# user_xattr). Thess options will let the admin store the DOS attributes
# in an EA and make samba not mess with the permission bits.
#
# Note: these options can also be set just per share, setting them in global
# makes them the default for all shares

;       map archive = no
;       map hidden = no
;       map read only = no
;       map system = no
;       store dos attributes = yes
```

The final part of the example configuration file contains a collection of shares. The first four example shares have special functions in a Windows network. The first share in the example is called [homes] and is used to share the home directory of each user defined on the system. This means that when a user authenticates to the Samba server and that user has a home directory present on the Samba server, the user's home directory will be made available over the network as a share with the name of the user's name.

```
[homes]
        comment = Home Directories
        browseable = no
        writable = yes
;       valid users = %S
;       valid users = MYDOMAIN\%S
```

The second example share is called [printers] and works like the [homes] share but for all defined printers on the Samba server. Samba will ask the CUPS print server for a list of all printers it knows, and Samba will create a printing share for each of these printers.

```
[printers]
        comment = All Printers
        path = /var/spool/samba
        browseable = no
        guest ok = no
        writable = no
        printable = yes
```

The third and fourth example shares are needed only when the Samba server will be used as a domain controller. In that case, these shares are used to provide roaming profiles for users of the Windows network and to allow for scripts that are run when people log in.

```
# Un-comment the following and create the netlogon directory for Domain Logons
;       [netlogon]
;       comment = Network Logon Service
;       path = /var/lib/samba/netlogon
;       guest ok = yes
;       writable = no
;       share modes = no

# Un-comment the following to provide a specific roving profile share
# the default is to use the user's home directory
;       [Profiles]
;       path = /var/lib/samba/profiles
```

```
;          browseable = no
;          guest ok = yes
```

The last share is a standard share called [public], and it points to a certain directory (/home/samba in this case). We will go into more detail on how to define shares in the coming sections.

```
# A publicly accessible directory, but read only, except for people in
# the "staff" group
;          [public]
;          comment = Public Stuff
;          path = /home/samba
;          public = yes
;          writable = yes
;          printable = no
;          write list = +staff
```

Having reviewed the example configuration file for Samba that comes with CentOS, you should have good idea of how configuring Samba works and what the configuration file looks like. It's time to put all this into practice and set up a stand-alone Samba server.

Minimal Stand-Alone Samba Setup

In this section, we will show how to create a minimal configuration file that will let Samba run in stand-alone mode (something also called workgroup mode). It will have no relationship to a domain. It will also contain three simple shares with simple access rules to get the basics covered. This is how the configuration looks:

```
[global]
        workgroup = MYGROUP
        server string = Samba Server Version %v

        security = user
        passdb backend = tdbsam

        load printers = yes
        cups options = raw

[homes]
        comment = Home Directories
        browseable = no
        writable = yes
```

```
[printers]
        comment = All Printers
        path = /var/spool/samba
        browseable = no
        guest ok = no
        writable = no
        printable = yes


[public]
        comment = Public Stuff
        path = /home/samba
        public = yes
        writable = no
        printable = no
```

This configuration is based on the example configuration file included with the Samba packages. So, it should look pretty familiar. But let's go over the different sections again.

The [global] section has only six lines. The workgroup line specifies that the server will be in the workgroup MYGROUP. The server string line shows that this is a Samba server, and the text %v will be replaced by the actual Samba version. The security statement indicates that the authentication of users will be done by the Samba server itself, the passdb backend option tells Samba where to look for/store user information, the load printers = yes line means that Samba will export all defined printers, and cups options = raw means that Samba will pass all printing data directly to CUPS for printing.

The next three sections in this configuration are definitions for shares. The first share, [homes], is used to provide users with access to their home directories using Samba. Only when a user is authenticated will the user see their home directory share, and it will have the same name as the user has.

The [printers] share will, as mentioned earlier, make all defined printers available for the network. The browseable = no statement means that Samba will not tell the network it has this share, or printers in this case, available. The guest ok = no statement means that only users who have authenticated will be able to use the printers that are available.

The [public] share will export the directory /home/samba and all its content. This share will be visible to the users with the name public. Everybody can see the share, but nobody can write in it; they can only read from it. This is because of the writable = no statement.

You have a configuration file now, but you aren't ready to start Samba yet at this point. We have talked a lot about users and the authentication of users. So, you will need to create them. The first step is to create a standard Linux user using the useradd command and give the user a password using the passwd command:

```
# useradd test1
# passwd test1
New UNIX password:
Retype new UNIX password:
passwd: all authentication tokens updated successfully.
```

This will create entries for the user in /etc/passwd, /etc/shadow, and /etc/group. It will also create a home directory for the user with the path /home/test1.

One of the differences between Windows and Linux is the way that passwords are encoded. This means that Samba cannot use the Linux-type encrypted password (present in /etc/shadow) when a Windows client tries to log in since the Windows client will use a different mechanism. The consequence is that Samba needs to maintain its own user database with the passwords encrypted using the Windows methods. The passdb backend option tells Samba what type of database it needs to use for this. In this case, we used the tdbsam type, which is a lightweight file-based database from the Samba project itself. The file used for this is /etc/samba/passdb.tdb.

Another effect of this difference between Linux and Windows is that you need to also give the password of the user to Samba so it can encrypt the password using the Windows method. For this, the command smbpasswd is used. You can add the test1 user to the Samba database like this:

```
# smbpasswd -a test1
New SMB password:
Retype new SMB password:
Added user test1.
```

As you can see, this looks almost the same as the normal Linux passwd command. The -a switch tells the smbpasswd that this is a new user and it should be added to the Samba user database. Now the fact that the password needs to entered again means that the Linux and Samba/Windows password of the user can be different; the choice of whether this should be done or not is for either the administration or the user.

This procedure will need to be done for all users who need to access the Samba server. Without an entry in the Samba user database, they cannot authenticate and log in.

The final thing that needs to be created before you can start Samba is the /home/samba directory that is used for the [public] share. This will be a share that can be used by multiple users, so it cannot be a home directory of a normal user. Also, in this example, the share is read-only, so users who connect to the share cannot write to it. Writing to this share will be covered in the next section. In this example, create this directory as root, and make sure it has the correct Unix permissions so that files can be read from it:

```
# mkdir /home/samba
# chmod 755 /home/samba
```

With the /home/samba directory in place, you can finally start Samba. In this example, you are not part of a Windows domain, and therefore you don't need the winbind service, only the smb service:

```
# service smb start
Starting SMB services:                                    [ OK ]
Starting NMB services:                                    [ OK ]
```

Now Samba is started. You can check the smbd log file /var/log/samba/smbd.log to see whether it started correctly. If it has, it is time to start up a Windows client and see whether you can find the Samba server and use its shares. To find the Samba shares, first make sure the Windows machine is in the same workgroup as Samba (MYGROUP in this case). You can change this using the System entry in the Windows Control Panel (remember that changing the workgroup requires a reboot).

Then you should be able to find the Samba server by going to My Network Places and clicking View Workgroup Computers (in Windows XP Professional). When you access the Samba server, you will be prompted for a username and password; you can use the test1 user and its password you created earlier. Then you can see the public share and a share called test1, which is the user's home directory.

Shares and Security

When adding shares to Samba, you will probably want to have control over who has access to the share and what they can do (read or write). For this, Samba has a large set of options that allow you to fine-tune the behavior of Samba.

Before we go over some of these options, you will need to take care of the permissions on the filesystem level. Because Samba runs as a normal Linux process and uses normal Linux filesystems, any restrictions set on the filesystem level can interfere with the permissions you set inside the Samba configuration. When an authenticated user uses a share, Samba will access the filesystem as that user (like the user test1 in the example earlier). For an unauthenticated user, Samba will use the user nobody. So, you will need to make sure that the permissions on the filesystem are sufficient for these users. You can always set all the directories completely open (mode 777 or drwxrwxrwx), but this isn't a good idea security-wise. If there is an error in the smb.conf file, users could potentially access files they are not allowed to touch.

The first level of control available is if a share is read-only or read-write. For this, two corresponding options are available: read only and writeable. If neither of these is specified, the default will be that the share will be read-only. Setting read only = no or writeable = yes will make the share read-write.

You can also control this on a per-user level using the read list or write list option. These options allow you to specify a list of users or groups that will have read-only access (when using read list) or read-write access (when using write list) independent of the earlier read only or writeable settings. This allows you to force certain users to always have read-only or read-write access.

A second level of control that is available is setting whether users have access to a share. This is done using the valid users and invalid users options. If neither of these options is specified, the default for Samba is that both are empty, and in that case, all users will be allowed access to the share. If users or groups are specified for the valid users option, then only these users are allowed access to the share and everybody else is denied. If the invalid users option is used, then only these users or groups are denied access while everybody else is allowed. If both options are used and a user or group that is present in both lists is specified, then that user is denied access.

Then there is the browseable option. This can be set to yes or no, and it determines whether the share will be visible when browsing the Windows network like in the previous section. If it is not made visible for browsing, it can still be used if you know the name of the share. In Windows, you can do this using the Add a Network Place task, for example, which allows you to type in the name of the server and share. This option is not really a security measure but just a way to prevent people from finding out the existence of a share by simply browsing.

Another useful option is admin users. You can use this option to specify a list of users or groups that will have administrative privileges on the share. This means that all operations done by this user will be executed as the superuser (root).

A final option we will cover is username map, which specifies a file that contains a mapping between Linux users and Windows users. You can use this to allow certain Windows users to access the Samba server without that user needing to have an account on the Samba server. An example of such a mapping is root = Admin Administrator. Here the Windows users Admin and Administrator will actually use the root user when accessing the Samba server.

Some of these options allow you to specify users or groups. All these type of options use the same mechanism to do this. For users, just use a space-separated list of each user, such as valid users = root test1. Here only the users root and test1 will be allowed to use the share.

If you have a lot of users, this method can quickly result in very long lists that are not easy to use. To solve this, Samba also allows you to use groups, and this is done by using the @ character followed by the name of the group such as write list = root @admins. Here only user root and all members of the group admins will be allowed to write to the share. This greatly reduces the amount of changes you need to do to the Samba configuration; you can assign a user certain rights just by putting the user in the right group, instead of each time needing to change the Samba configuration file.

Extended Stand-Alone Example

Now that you have seen how to manage permissions on shares, it is time for an extended example that uses these new options. It is based on the previous minimal example. Here is how it looks:

```
[global]
        workgroup = MYGROUP
        server string = Samba Server Version %v

        security = user
        passdb backend = tdbsam

        load printers = yes
        cups options = raw
        username map = /etc/samba/smbusers

[homes]
        comment = Home Directories
        browseable = no
        writable = yes

[printers]
        comment = All Printers
        path = /var/spool/samba
        browseable = no
        guest ok = no
        writable = no
        printable = yes

[public]
        comment = Public Stuff
        path = /home/samba
        public = yes
        writable = no
        printable = no
        write list = root @admins

[accounting]
        comment = Accounting files
        path = /home/accounting
        writable = yes
```

```
        printable = no
        browseable = no
        valid users = root @accounting @management
        read list = @management

[apps]
        comment = Applications
        path = /home/apps
        writable = no
        printable = no
        browseable = yes
        write list = root @admins
        admin users = @admins
```

In the [global] section, we only added the username map option and pointed it to the file /etc/samba/smbusers. This file contains the following:

```
# Unix_name = SMB_name1 SMB_name2 ...
root = administrator admin
nobody = guest pcguest smbguest
```

Here we map the administrator and admin Windows users to the root Linux user. The same principle is used for the nobody Linux user.

In the definition of the [public] share, we added the line write list = root @admins. This means that the share that is normally read-only can be written to by the user root and members of the group admins.

Then we added two new shares, [accounting] and [apps]. They follow the same pattern as the [public] share. The [accounting] share is not browsable, meaning that it is hidden from view and can be accessed only if you know its name. The share is accessible only by the user root and members of the groups accounting and management. All users except those of the management group have write access to the share.

The [apps] share is browsable and read-only for all users except for root and members of the group admins. Also, the operations of members of the group admins will be done as the superuser.

As you can see, using the options explained and using groups wisely allow you to easily manage access to shares, control who can write to a share, and so on.

Samba As a Domain Member

Now that you have seen how Samba is used on itself and how to configure shares, we will show how to put your Samba server inside an Active Directory domain. The biggest difference between stand-alone mode and member mode is that in member mode all authentication is done by the domain controllers of the domain and not by the Samba server itself. The main consequence of this is that Samba will no longer have a database of all user accounts. This also means that the Samba server will not have Linux user accounts for all the users who can use the server. This can be a problem since Samba needs a user to perform operations on the filesystem.

There are two solutions for this. The first one is that you can force Samba to use a certain Linux user or group. You can do this using the force user and force group options. The user and group given will be used for all operations on the filesystem instead of the user who is authenticated to use the share.

The second solution is to use the winbindd daemon. This daemon makes all users and groups that are present inside a domain available inside a Linux system. It accomplishes this by using Name Service Switch (NSS). This is an interface in the core Linux libraries that allows for different ways to store and retrieve a list of users and groups (besides others). You can find the configuration for NSS in the file /etc/nsswitch.conf. By default, it will use only the standard Unix files for users and groups (/etc/passwd, /etc/shadow, /etc/group, and so on).

The winbindd daemon will use NSS to inject all domain users and groups into the Linux environment. This way, there is no need to create separate user accounts for all domain users. Using winbind gets around the problem of having to create an account for every user who logs in to the Samba server. In this example, we will be using the winbind service.

To set this up, you will of course need an Active Directory domain controller. You will also need to know the name of the domain and the name of the realm. For example, if the realm is testdomain.com, then the domain name is testdomain. You will also need the password of the domain administrator account to add the Samba server to the domain. Finally, you need to install the krb5-workstation package using Yum.

The first thing we will show how to set up is Samba. We will show only the [global] section of the configuration file. The way that shares work remains the same; only the names of the users change. This is the Samba configuration:

```
[global]
workgroup = TESTDOMAIN
realm = TESTDOMAIN.COM
server string = Samba Server Version %v
security = ADS
load printers = yes
cups options = raw
template shell = /bin/bash
idmap uid = 5000-100000
idmap gid = 5000-100000
winbind use default domain = Yes
```

The biggest difference from the stand-alone example is that the security option is set to ADS instead of user. We also added the realm option to indicate what Kerberos realm to use. The final four options configure how the winbindd daemon behaves. Specifically, the two idmap parameters tell winbind what UID and GID numbers it can use for the domain users and groups. The template shell option says that winbind should give the domain users /bin/bash as shell. The winbind use default domain option tells winbind to not add the domain name in front of the name of a domain user (this makes the names a bit shorter).

Next you edit the /etc/nsswitch.conf file so that the Linux environment gets to know the domain users and groups. Add the word winbind to the following lines:

```
passwd: files winbind
shadow: files winbind
group:  files winbind
```

Next you need to initialize Kerberos to allow the Samba server to become member. To do this, run this command:

```
# kinit administrator@TESTDOMAIN.COM
```

Then you can join the Samba server to the domain using this command:

```
#  net ads join -Uadministrator%password
```

Replace the password string with the real password of the domain administrator. If the command returns a line Joined domain TESTDOMAIN, then it succeeded, and the Samba server is now part of the domain. Now you can start the Samba daemons. First start the winbindd daemon and then the others:

```
# service winbind start
Starting Winbind services:                              [  OK  ]
# service smb start
Starting SMB services:                                  [  OK  ]
Starting NMB services:                                  [  OK  ]
```

To check whether the winbindd daemon is doing its job, you can run the wbinfo command, which directly talks to the daemon and can tell you, besides other things, the users and groups it sees from the domain. You can also use the getent command. This can ask the NSS directly for all information it knows. The getent passwd command should show all users, including those present in /etc/passwd and those present in the domain. The getent group command does the same but for groups.

Now the Samba server is ready for normal use, and you can add shares like in the previous examples.

Summary

In this chapter, you were introduced to Windows networking and to the Samba server and its components. Then we explained how to configure Samba and reviewed the example configuration file included in the Samba package as delivered by CentOS. We also showed how to set up a minimal configuration of Samba in stand-alone mode. Then we covered how to secure shares that the Samba server offers and what options are available for this. We then showed an extended configuration example that used some of the options. Finally, we showed how to configure Samba as a domain member.

For more in-depth knowledge about Samba and more information on how to configure Samba, we refer you to the documentation that is included in the Samba package and available on the CentOS and Samba web sites.

CHAPTER 10

Setting Up Virtual Private Networks

If you need an explanation of what the Internet is, here's a simple one: the Internet is the aggregation of all connected networks that use the Internet protocol. This also means that you can run your personal internet (lowercase *i*) by connecting a group of networks together that all use the Internet protocol. And many companies do exactly that. They have their own private internet, often called an intranet, of which only a small part is really connected to the Internet (capital *I*). Clients in the private internet normally connect to the "real thing" over proxies or routers that translate the private addresses to routed addresses. To the Internet, this looks like there is only one machine connected to it that does a huge amount of traffic. For the client, this looks like they can connect to the Internet, but the Internet cannot connect back; those clients just don't exist there.

You, like most people, probably do the same at your home or in your office. There is a machine storing your music and pictures and documents, another machine that acts as a mail server, another machine that is a web server, and then your desktop machine or laptop. And in most installations there is a machine that connects this network to the Internet, known as a *router*. These machines mostly do network address translation (NAT) from a private IP address range as described in RFC 1918 to the official address that is reachable from the Internet (see Figure 10-1).

Note As the Internet grew larger, more and more companies created their local internets that weren't connected—at least not directly—to the Internet. Still, most computers on these networks used IP addresses that were supposed to be reachable from the Internet directly. RFC 1918 defines three networks that are not supposed to be routed over the Internet but can be used in private networks. First, 192.168/16 is probably the best known one; many home WiFi routers use 192.168.0.0/24, for example. Second, 172.16/12 includes all addresses from 172.16.0.0 to 172.31.255.255. Finally, the 10/8 network contains 16,777,214 IP addresses and is meant for large internal company networks. See `http://www.faqs.org/rfcs/rfc1918.html` for the RFC and `http://en.wikipedia.org/wiki/Private_network` for a more extensive discussion about private networks.

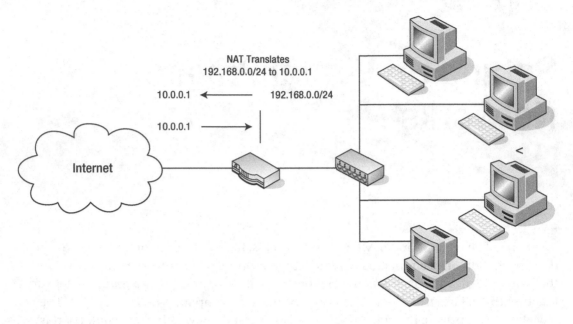

Figure 10-1. *Network address translation*

Normally there also is a firewall in place that disallows traffic from the Internet to the private network, except for a few applications. Because your mail server would be useless if it couldn't receive mail, your web server would be useless if nobody could see your web site. This often is done via port forwarding, so all connects to the router on port 80 are forwarded to the web server and connects to port 25 are forwarded to the mail server.

And there are good reasons to do that. You do not want the internals of your network exposed to the Internet. Imagine if someone was able to access the machine on which you store your private documents. And imagine the outcry of certain companies if the whole world was able to access your music collection. The same is true for companies: nobody should have access to the internal network from the outside, because the information that is stored on this network is too important to share with the whole world.

On the other hand, if this information is so important to you or to the company, you don't want this information to leave your network. You don't want people to store that information on their laptops when they are visiting customers or taking the machines home. If any laptops were stolen, this could be a catastrophe for the company and the company's customers. Who doesn't remember some privacy scandals big companies have gotten into because they lost customer data? And much of the information you store on your private network should be as important to you, too. Nobody has to know how much you pay in taxes, who you do business with, and where your money is stored (okay, there are a few exceptions to that rule).

One possible solution to that would be to store everything you need on your laptop, encrypt the laptop's hard disk, and work with only this set of data. If you choose a good and strong password, your documents are secure—but what if your laptop gets stolen? I guess you want to keep a copy of the document on your network at home, where it gets backed up.

But when you work on a document on your laptop, you have to synchronize the differences between that document and the one you left at home. Wouldn't it be better if you could work like you were at home or in your office at your desktop computer?

And for administrators, sometimes it is enough to use SSH to log into one of the machines at work. But what if you need to mount an internal share to the machine you are working on?

There is a better solution to those problems: virtual private networks (VPNs).

In this chapter, you'll learn what a VPN is and how to set up a VPN. You'll take a look at three different ways to set up VPNs, although there are many more. Also, you'll learn how to give out VPN access to other people and how to generally configure your client and your VPN server.

What Is a Virtual Private Network?

A *virtual private network* is a network that connects two private networks over another network like the Internet or that connects your local machine to a network over the Internet. You can use a virtual private network when sitting in a hotel room and you absolutely need to access your music collection because you forgot to take that one album with you that you want to listen to. Or you want to connect site A of your company with the main office's intranet so people working at site A can edit documents that are available only on the file server located at the headquarters. Connecting machines of employees to the internal network is the most likely reason that you want to use a VPN, because this gives them the ability to work on internal data from (nearly) wherever they are.

Because those connections go over the Internet, you want to protect them as well as possible: encrypted and without a real chance for other people to see what you are doing. With a virtual private network, anyone who is trying to snoop your traffic cannot see whether you are sending a mail, editing a file on your file server, or browsing the intranet pages in your company. All traffic is tunneled through the one connection, which makes your VPN happen, and this connection is the only thing the intruder can see.

To make a VPN work, you need to have an endpoint in your network that you can connect to. From this endpoint on, you should be able to see the rest of your (RFC 1918) network. If you have a Linux machine acting as a router on your network, this would be the perfect machine for setting up such an endpoint.

Next, you'll learn how to use SSH for creating VPNs.

Using SSH for Virtual Private Networks

You are probably already using the Secure Shell client to connect to other machines on your network. Most administrators do their daily work via SSH when connecting to mail or web servers for changing configurations there or watching log files on the remote computers. If all you need is text-based access to another computer anywhere in the world, SSH is really a great way to work. There are mail clients for the console, and editors like vim, nano, and emacs also work without a graphical user interface. If this is all you need, you probably do not need a real VPN at all.

But what if you need to use a web browser on the remote machine to get to some data from your web server? Or what if you have to run an Office program to edit a document you don't want to copy over to the laptop you have with you in your hotel?

SSH has a solution for that: it enables you to do X forwarding through an existing SSH connection. The X Window system is a network transparent system, where the server—the part displaying the graphics—runs on your local machine, while the client application can run anywhere on the network. This works great if you have a reasonably fast link available and not so great if you are sitting behind a slow line.

Make sure that you have the xorg-x11-xauth package installed on the remote machine:

```
[ralph@centos ~]$ rpm -q xorg-x11-xauth
xorg-x11-xauth-1.0.1-2.1
[ralph@centos ~]$
```

If it isn't, just install it via Yum:

```
yum install xorg-x11-xauth
```

Now you have to enable X11 forwarding in SSH on the remote side. Become root and check your sshd config:

```
[root@centos ~]# grep X11Forwarding /etc/ssh/sshd_config
#X11Forwarding no
X11Forwarding yes
[root@centos ~]#
```

X11 forwarding is turned off by default in SSH, but CentOS turns it on during the installation of the OpenSSH server package. This is because the system-config-* applications need a working X11.

If you need to change the X11 forwarding setting, you have to restart the SSH daemon with this:

```
service sshd restart
```

This will restart the SSH daemon but leave your running session intact. Let's start `xclock` on the remote machine:

```
ssh -l user -CX machine.example.com xclock
```

This will display the output of the `xclock` program—a graphical clock—on your local machine. The `-X` option tells SSH to turn on X11 forwarding, and the `-C` option turns on compression, which really helps on slower connections.

Note `ssh -X` opens an untrusted X11 connection to the remote host. This prevents someone who is also logged in on the remote machine from capturing or even sending keyboard or other events. Most X11 clients work great with untrusted connections. There are some applications that have problems running over untrusted connections. If you start a program and it doesn't display correctly on your screen, you have found one of them. If you can really trust the remote machine and all users who are logged onto this machine, you can open a trusted connection with SSH. Just use `ssh -Y` instead of `ssh -X` in this case.

Using SSH this way is not really a VPN solution, but it works in many situations. The greatest problem with this approach is that you transfer the X display commands—these are the commands your X Server uses for drawing windows and their content—over the network. This can be really slow on DSL connections and isn't usable at all on dial-up networks. Wouldn't it be much easier to transfer data instead of graphics over those links? Of course. And you can do it with SSH, too. Since OpenSSH version 4.3, which is included in CentOS 5, you can create network tunnels with SSH. Up to then you could tunnel ports through a connection, meaning that you could connect port 80 on the remote machine—your web server—with port 8080 on the local machine. Using a web browser, you can go to `http://localhost:8080/`, which will be redirected to port 80 on your web server.

This is fine for one application, but if you need more than one service, you will have to enable those tunnels for every service you want to access. OpenSSH version 4.3 solves that by providing you with a complete network tunnel.

Caution There are still many how-tos on the Internet that tell you how to create a VPN with SSH and the `pppd` daemon by creating a tunnel between two ports and then running a PPP "dial-up" session through the tunnel. Although this is really easy to set up, it never is a good idea to run TCP/IP through another TCP/IP session, because it can cause long delays and connection abortions. See `http://sites.inka.de/~W1011/devel/tcp-tcp.html` for a discussion of this phenomenon. And the tunnel solution included since OpenSSH 4.3 is even easier to set up anyway.

There is one big drawback to this solution: you need root access on the remote machine, so you have to permit root logins within SSH. Many people forbid root to log in from a remote machine, which normally is a good idea. In this case, the user logging in as root will be allowed to start the tunnel on login only. And because you forbid root access via a password, you need to have a valid private SSH key to connect.

If you haven't done so already, create an SSH key pair for your root user on the local machine:

```
[root@client ~]# ssh-keygen -f /root/.ssh/id_rsa -N my-passphrase
Generating public/private rsa key pair.
Your identification has been saved in /root/.ssh/id_rsa.
Your public key has been saved in /root/.ssh/id_rsa.pub.
The key fingerprint is:
a6:d7:98:28:b1:fd:d4:b9:bb:3b:ac:92:03:b6:08:38 ➥
 root@client.example.com
[root@client ~]#
```

Choose a strong passphrase for your keys! Copy the public part of your key to the server you want to connect to. You will need it later.

You are now going to create a tunneling TUN device to which the SSH tunnel will be attached. A *TUN device* is a virtual point-to-point network device that behaves like a normal interface and can also be configured like one. But let's set up SSH correctly first. You need to edit the sshd configuration on the server, because you have to allow tunneling, permit root logins, and turn off password authentication. Open /etc/ssh/sshd_config in your editor to change or add the following configuration directives:

```
PermitRootLogin yes
PasswordAuthentication no
PermitTunnel yes
```

Don't restart the SSH daemon yet. Now copy the public key from your client to /root/.ssh/authorized_keys:

```
cat id_rsa.pub >> /root/.ssh/authorized_keys
```

Make sure that .ssh belongs to root:root and allows only the root user to access it. The same goes for the key file:

```
[root@centos ~]# chmod 0700 .ssh ; chmod 0600 .ssh/authorized_keys
[root@centos ~]#
```

To see whether you did everything right, try to SSH into the server as root:

```
[ralph@client ~]$ssh admin@centos.example.com
Enter passphrase for key '/home/ralph/.ssh/id_rsa':
CentOS release 5.3 (Final)
[root@centos ~]
```

You should be asked to enter the passphrase for your key and not for the root password on the remote machine. If this works, then restart the SSH daemon. If it doesn't work, you should look at /var/log/secure or /var/log/messages on the remote machine to see what has gone wrong. Check .ssh/ and .ssh/authorized_keys for correct access permissions. sshd is very picky regarding them, and they have to be as strict as possible.

Open authorized_keys in an editor, and add the following to the beginning of the line, which contains the key you just added. Be careful that your editor does not break lines when doing so. The part you are adding and the key *must* be on one line.

```
tunnel="0",command="/sbin/ifup tun0" ssh-rsa … example.com
```

This limits the key to only start the tunnel with the ID 0, and it will automatically pull up the tun0 device if you connect. The root user cannot run any other commands via SSH now, making this solution rather secure even though you allow root access to your machine via SSH.

It's time to configure the network devices. Say your network at home is 192.168.70.0 with a netmask of 255.255.255.0. It also has a public interface with an official IP address (see Figure 10-2). Because this is your router, I'm assuming that you have already configured IP forwarding on that computer. If not, open /etc/sysctl.conf with your editor, and change net.ipv4.ip_forward = 0 to net.ipv4.ip_forward = 1. Run sysctl -p to apply this change. Open /etc/sysconfig/network-scripts/ifcfg-tun0 with an editor:

```
DEVICE=tun0
BOOTPROTO=static
ONBOOT=no
TYPE=IPIP
MY_INNER_IPADDR=10.0.0.3
PEER_INNER_IPADDR=10.0.0.2
```

Now edit the same file on the client side:

```
DEVICE=tun0
BOOTPROTO=static
ONBOOT=no
TYPE=IPIP
MY_INNER_IPADDR=10.0.0.2
PEER_INNER_IPADDR=10.0.0.3
```

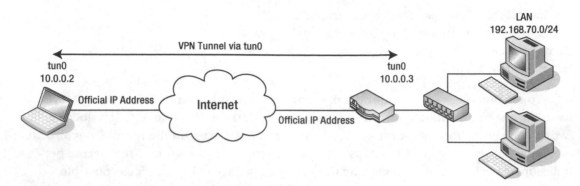

Figure 10-2. *A VPN via SSH tunneling*

These are normal sysconfig network description files. The device is called tun0, it is not started on boot, you use static IP addresses, and the type of the interface is IPIP (IP over IP, which basically encapsulates IP packets into IP to create a tunnel). The two IP addresses are the addresses of the tunnel endpoints: 10.0.0.2 on the client side and 10.0.0.3 on the server. The directives MY_OUTER_IPADDR and PEER_OUTER_IPADDR are the addresses of the public interfaces. You don't need to set these directives, especially because you often won't know the public address of the client. You can set it on the client side, because the public IP address of your router probably does not change.

Note If you are curious about the various settings you can use in files under /etc/sysconfig and especially under /etc/sysconfig/network-scripts/, there is help. In /usr/share/doc/initscripts-8.45.25/ sysconfig.txt, all usable options are listed, sometimes with a terse explanation of what these options do. It's definitely worth a read.

Theoretically everything should work now, but practice might say otherwise. To set up a tunnel with SSH, you use the following command:

```
ssh -w 0:0 server
```

with server being the computer to which you want to connect. The first 0 is the local tunnel interface, and the second 0 is the one on the remote side. If you want to use tun1 instead of tun0 on the remote side, because tun0 already exists, the command is as follows:

```
ssh -w 0:1 server
```

This command does not detach from the command line, though. You can do so with ssh -f server command, which detaches the SSH process but still asks for a passphrase if you set one. You can specify any command you want here. By specifying command="/sbin/ ifup tun0" in authorized_keys, the SSH daemon will start the tunnel device only on connect, ignoring each other command you send to it.

```
[root@client ~]# ssh -fw 0:0 server /bin/true
Enter passphrase for key '/root/.ssh/id_rsa':
[root@client ~]#
```

On the server side, the tunnel interface should already exist, because SSH starts it:

```
[root@centos ~]# ifconfig tun0
tun0      Link encap:UNSPEC  HWaddr 00-00-00-00-00-00-00-00-00-00-00-00-00-00-00-00
          inet addr:10.0.0.3  P-t-P:10.0.0.2  Mask:255.255.255.255
          UP POINTOPOINT RUNNING NOARP MULTICAST  MTU:1500  Metric:1
```

On the client side, the interface is missing; you have to start it with ifup tun0 first. Check with ifconfig to see whether the interface is there. If it is, the tunnel is there, and you should be able to ping 10.0.0.2 from the client. To be able to reach machines in your network, you need only a network route.

```
[root@client ~]# ping 192.168.70.3
PING 192.168.70.3 (192.168.70.3) 56(84) bytes of data.
--- 192.168.70.3 ping statistics ---
3 packets transmitted, 0 received, 100% packet loss, time 2000ms
[root@client ~]# route add -net 192.168.70.0 netmask ➥
255.255.255.0 dev tun0
[root@client ~]# ping 192.168.70.3
PING 192.168.70.3 (192.168.70.3) 56(84) bytes of data.
64 bytes from 192.168.70.3: icmp_seq=1 ttl=64 time=1.95 ms
--- 192.168.70.3 ping statistics ---
1 packets transmitted, 1 received, 0% packet loss, time 0ms
rtt min/avg/max/mdev = 1.956/1.956/1.956/0.000 ms
```

You can now reach your web server at 192.168.70.7, your file server at 192.168.70.9, and so on. You can mount Samba or NFS shares and browse your music collection, just like you would be able to when you are at home. If you want to use name resolution and you have a DNS resolver on your home network, you can change the name server entries in /etc/resolv.conf to use it. If you are the only one using the tunnel, you might even think about adding tun0 as a trusted interface to your firewall policy so that you can get everywhere in your LAN without being subject to your firewall configuration. You can do this with the following command:

```
lokkit -q -t tun0
```

lokkit is a command-line interface to the firewall and SELinux configuration tool. The previous command sets the tun0 interface as a trusted interface from where all traffic is accepted.

Using SSH to create a VPN is a good idea when you are in need of a VPN fast and when it doesn't have to be extremely reliable. There are better solutions for regular use. Especially if you want to connect two company sites, VPN over SSH is not the solution you should be using. IPSec was created for this—and that is what you are going to implement in the next section: a VPN via IPSec.

Using IPSec

Internet Protocol Security (IPSec) is a standard that was developed by the Internet Engineering Task Force (IETF) to secure Internet connections. IPSec is a required part of the IPv6 protocol. Most of this has been back-ported to the IPv4 protocol. IPSec works right at the IP level of the network. IPSec not only offers encryption of traffic over the Internet, but it also provides a means of controlling data integrity, access, and authentication. Keys for authentication and encryption are exchanged via Internet Key Exchange (IKE). IKE sets up a session secret from which keys for encryption are derived. For authentication between hosts, certificates or preshared keys can be used. Certificates can be stored in files or in the DNS infrastructure. IPSec can be used between two hosts, two networks, or a host and a network.

In this section of the chapter, you will learn how to connect two networks with IPSec in place. You will learn how to configure the network interfaces and how to set up racoon, which is needed for IKE.

Note   racoon is a daemon that is responsible for the key exchange between IPSec endpoints. You need to configure racoon, but there is no need for you to start it separately. It gets started automatically by the kernel when you try to establish an IPSec connection. racoon is also responsible for establishing the security associations (SAs) between two IPSec hosts. So after you have configured racoon, all the work it does happens transparently.

There are several implementations of IPSec for Linux, such as openswan, freeswan, and an implementation in kernel 2.6. CentOS ships with openswan and the kernel implementation, plus the ipsec-tools package. The kernel implementation and the ipsec-tools package will be used in the following sections.

IPSec Explained

IPSec is a suite of protocols, with two protocols being the primary protocols. One is Authentication Header (AH), and the other one is Encapsulating Security Payload (ESP). AH is protocol 51, and ESP is protocol 50 (see /etc/protocols). The preconfigured firewall in CentOS is configured to let these two protocols pass; otherwise, IPSec wouldn't be usable:

```
[root@client ~]# iptables -L RH-Firewall-1-INPUT
Chain RH-Firewall-1-INPUT (2 references)
target     prot opt source              destination
[…]
ACCEPT     esp  --  anywhere            anywhere
ACCEPT     ah   --  anywhere            anywhere
```

AH provides authentication of an Internet packet by adding a checksum header around the original packet, which can then be checked on the other side of the IPSec tunnel. By running IPSec in AH mode, you can make sure that nobody on the route between your networks tampered with the packages, but the packages themselves are not encrypted. You might use this mode because you have very fast links between two sites and want to make sure that the data that went in on one side comes out the same on the other side, but you don't want encryption because of performance issues.

If you need encryption, ESP is the protocol to use. ESP encrypts the content of the original packet and adds its own header around it. Depending on if you use IPSec in transport mode or in tunneling mode, ESP does things differently.

In transport mode, ESP puts its headers around the payload and encrypts that. Headers for routing the package are left intact. An intruder would be able to see the control information of these packets—routing information, for example—but would not be able to see the actual data.

In tunneling mode, ESP encrypts the complete packet, not only the payload. Thus, nobody except the endpoint of the tunnel is able to see the control or data information of the packages.

What happens when you initiate an IPSec connection? The initiation takes place in two phases. When you activate the IPSec interfaces, IKE does the following: it authenticates that both peers really are who they pretend to be via the shared secret—either a preshared key or a certificate. If phase 1 has finished successfully, it negotiates security associations between the two peers. After that, it generates a symmetric key for encryption of payload or packages using a Diffie-Hellman key exchange. This is phase 2.

The security associations are then stored in a security association database (SAD). This keeps information about the two tunnel endpoints including IP addresses, information about the mode IPSec is run in (AH or ESP), and information about secret keys and the encryption algorithm that is used. Among those algorithms are AES, 3DES, and Blowfish.

Note IPSec on CentOS 5 supports the following three symmetric encryption cyphers in phase2: Triple Data Encryption Standard (3DES), Rijndael, and Blowfish 448. IPSec uses symmetric encryption after the initial key exchange, because this is much faster than public key algorithms. Rijndael is the cipher that is used in the Advanced Encryption Standard (AES), which is the successor to DES. You can find more information about Rijndael at http://csrc.nist.gov/archive/aes/rijndael/wsdindex.html. Blowfish is a cipher developed by Bruce Schneier, and is a fast but secure algorithm. You can find more information about Blowfish at http://www.schneier.com/blowfish.html. Triple DES is explained in http://en.wikipedia.org/wiki/Triple_DES. Watch out, because most of these documents are pretty heavy on mathematics.

Virtual Private Networks with IPSec

Make sure that the ipsec-tools package is installed:

```
[ralph@centos ~]$ rpm -q ipsec-tools
ipsec-tools-0.6.5-13.el5
[ralph@centos ~]$
```

If it isn't installed, use yum install ipsec-tools to get it on your machine. Everything else you need is already in the kernel. IPSec devices are set up in a similar fashion as normal network devices by editing /etc/sysconfig/network-scripts/ifcfg-ipsec*. The exchange of keys and security associations is done by the racoon daemon, which is called by the security policy database (SPD) in the kernel when an IPSec interface comes up. On CentOS, authentication is done via preshared keys. To set up an IPSec connection, you need to define and configure the IPSec interface, you have to configure racoon, and you have to generate the preshared key that is needed for the authentication between the hosts.

Let's assume the following network configuration: you have two sites, site A and site B. At both sites you have a Linux router that has a public network interface facing the Internet and a second interface that acts as a gateway to the LAN at the site. Site A has 10.0.3.0/24 for the LAN, and site B has 10.0.7.0/24. The IP address of the router's internal interface is 10.0.3.254 for site A and 10.0.7.254 for site B. The public address of site A is 192.168.1.104, and site B has 192.168.1.105 (these aren't "official" IP addresses, but they will have to do for documentation purposes). See Figure 10-3 for a schema drawing of this network.

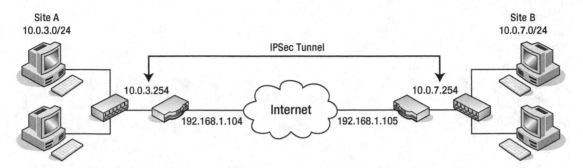

Figure 10-3. *An IPSec network*

Both routers need to be able to route packages, meaning that IP forwarding has to be enabled. To enable it, open /etc/sysctl.conf with your editor, and change net.ipv4. ip_forward = 0 to net.ipv4.ip_forward = 1. Run sysctl -p to apply this change. Log in to the router on site A.

■**Caution** If you do everything correctly, you can configure IPSec "online." But everybody makes mistakes, even experienced system administrators. If you set up an IPSec connection, make sure that there is someone at the remote site who you can talk to and who has the right access level to the machine so that person can correct the mistake you made. Another way to do that is out-of-band administration, over an ISDN or a modem backup line, for example.

Create the file /etc/sysconfig/network-scripts/ifcfg-ipsec0 on the router at site A:

```
TYPE=IPSEC
ONBOOT=yes
IKE_METHOD=PSK
SRCGW=10.0.3.254
DSTGW=10.0.7.254
SRCNET=10.0.3.0/24
DSTNET=10.0.7.0/24
DST=192.168.1.105
```

The type of this network interface is IPSEC, and you want to start the IPSec interface when the router boots. The method for the key exchange is PSK, which defines a pre-shared key. 10.0.3.254 is the gateway to the LAN at site A, and it's 10.0.7.254 at site B—the DSTGW. The next two lines define the networks for both sites. The last line holds the IP address of site B's public interface. The ifcfg-ipsec0 file on site B's router looks like this:

```
TYPE=IPSEC
ONBOOT=yes
IKE_METHOD=PSK
SRCGW=10.0.7.254
DSTGW=10.0.3.254
SRCNET=10.0.7.0/24
DSTNET=10.0.3.0/24
DST=192.168.1.104
```

Now you need a preshared key as a secret password so IKE is able to do phase 1 of the key exchange. This key should be readable and writable only by root, and it is stored in /etc/sysconfig/network-scripts/keys-ipsec0. If you used a different number for defining the interface, you have to set this for the key file, too. If you chose ifcfg-ipsec1, the appropriate key goes into keys-ipsec1. Choose a secure key that cannot be guessed.

```
[root@client ~]# dd if=/dev/random bs=1 count=20 status=noxfer ➥
  | base64
20+0 records in
20+0 records out
FkxUD30peU2JCQBZ8fhYHRODsb8=
[root@client ~]#
```

This reads 20 bytes from /dev/random and pipes the random data into Base64, which encodes it. Use the resulting string as a password at both sites. And do not use FkxUD-30peU2JCQBZ8fhYHR0Dsb8=, because other people might read this book, too.

```
[root@centos ~]# cd /etc/sysconfig/network-scripts/
[root@centos network-scripts]# echo ➥
 'IKE_PSK=FkxUD30peU2JCQBZ8fhYHRODsb8=' > keys-ipsec0
[root@centos network-scripts]# chown root:root keys-ipsec0
[root@centos network-scripts]# chmod 0600 keys-ipsec0
[root@centos network-scripts]#
```

Do the same on site B's router. You now need to configure racoon. Open your editor, and edit /etc/racoon/racoon.conf:

```
path include "/etc/racoon";
path pre_shared_key "/etc/racoon/psk.txt";
path certificate "/etc/racoon/certs";
```

```
sainfo anonymous
{
        pfs_group 2;
        lifetime time 1 hour ;
        encryption_algorithm 3des, blowfish 448, rijndael ;
        authentication_algorithm hmac_sha1, hmac_md5 ;
        compression_algorithm deflate ;
}
```

There is not much to change in that file. The short explanation is that `sainfo anonymous` defines that two hosts can securely associate anonymously if they know the same secret—a preshared key in our case. With `lifetime` you can specify how long a security association is valid, before it has to be renewed. You can put either a time value here or the number of bytes that have to be transferred.

`pfs_group 2` defines that group 2 of the Diffie-Hellman key exchange protocol is used, which uses 1,024 bits of keying material. The `encryption_algorithm` parameter lists the available encryption algorithms and their preferred order of usage. If you prefer Rijndael (which is the algorithm AES is based on) over 3DES, put `rijndael` at the beginning of the list. You should do that on both routers. `authentication_algorithm` chooses the hash algorithm used for creating checksums. You should prefer SHA1, because the MD5 algorithm is known to be weak. The last line tells `racoon` to negotiate payload compression, which can result in a speed gain. There will be a line like this at the bottom of the file when the tunnel is up:

```
include "/etc/racoon/X.X.X.X.conf"
```

The `racoon` daemon changes this file when IPSec is running, so be sure to not leave the config file open after changing it. This is a very basic `racoon` configuration but still a good starting point for network-to-network connections. If you want to use IPSec to connect your laptop to an IPSEC gateway—a so-called road warrior configuration—you can set policies within this file, such as giving out the DNS server the client should use.

Now that everything is configured, you can bring up the tunnel by running this on both routers:

```
ifup ipsec0
```

If you take a look at the /etc/racoon directory on site B's router, there will be a file called 192.168.1.104.conf. This is the configuration that will be used for the tunnel.

```
remote 192.168.1.104
{
        exchange_mode aggressive, main;
        my_identifier address;
        proposal {
                encryption_algorithm 3des;
                hash_algorithm sha1;
                authentication_method pre_shared_key;
                dh_group 2;
        }
}
```

You can use `tcpdump` to check whether the tunnel works. Site A has SSH enabled on the gateway address to the LAN, which means that you should be able to SSH to site A's LAN interface from site B. Start `tcpdump` on site A, and run `ssh 10.0.3.254` on site B's router after that:

```
[root@centos ~]# tcpdump -i eth1 host 192.168.1.105
tcpdump: verbose output suppressed, use -v or -vv for full protocol decode
listening on eth1, link-type EN10MB (Ethernet), capture size 96 bytes
06:06:22.368328 IP 192.168.1.105 > 192.168.1.104: ➥
AH(spi=0x045529f8,seq=0xbe): IP 192.168.1.105 > 192.168.1.104: ➥
ESP(spi=0x0cdb1d46,seq=0xbe), length 92 (ipip-proto-4)
06:06:22.368328 IP 192.168.1.105 > 192.168.1.104: ➥
ESP(spi=0x0cdb1d46,seq=0xbe), length 92
06:06:22.368550 IP 192.168.1.104 > 192.168.1.105:➥
AH(spi=0x06247830,seq=0xae): IP 192.168.1.104 > 192.168.1.105: ➥
ESP(spi=0x0ca0bae7,seq=0xae), length 92 (ipip-proto-4)
```

Someone listening on the wire will see the packages listed here. All packages have an AH header and are ESP packets, meaning that they are encrypted. You cannot see that this is SSH traffic or to which host the traffic inside the tunnel is routed.

You can also use `setkey -D` to see what has been negotiated between the two hosts; `setkey` shows the SAD:

```
[root@centos ~]# setkey -D
192.168.1.105 192.168.1.104
        esp mode=tunnel spi=215686470(0x0cdb1d46) reqid=0(0x00000000)
        E: 3des-cbc   d83142ca 00706bdb 16da1fd1 39f92b74 f816d048 b63fb881
        A: hmac-sha1   83c06fba ffdd6a7c 6a231e78 b142696f 21555916
        seq=0x00000000 replay=4 flags=0x00000000 state=mature
```

```
created: Apr  4 05:35:16 2009    current: Apr  4 06:21:48 2009
diff: 2792(s)   hard: 3600(s)    soft: 2880(s)
last: Apr  4 05:35:17 2009       hard: 0(s)        soft: 0(s)
current: 27833(bytes)    hard: 0(bytes)  soft: 0(bytes)
allocated: 290   hard: 0 soft: 0
sadb_seq=7 pid=7280 refcnt=0
```

In this case, there is an esp connection in tunneling mode. 3DES is used for encryption, and hmac-sha1 is the hash algorithm. It was created on April 4, at 5:35:16 a.m. Below that are a few statistics. There is another entry for the AH protocol that looks similar.

You might wonder why there are no new interfaces created after you brought up the tunnel. When you initiated the SSH tunnel earlier, you had to create a tun0 interface, which had a point-to-point connection to the other side of the tunnel. IPSec does all of this transparently. If there is traffic between the two networks you defined in the ifcfg-ipsec0 files, it will be encrypted. All other traffic going through the public interfaces of the two routers is not encrypted. This means you cannot set the public interface as a trusted interface in your firewall configuration as you could do with the tunnel interface you configured for the SSH tunnel.

Configuring IPSec has some pitfalls: not all implementations of IPSec are happy to work together, which makes it a good idea to run the same operating system on both sides of the tunnel—maybe even the same version. When running between two hosts or a host and a network, this could be problematic if you want to use your Mac or your Windows PC as a client. And road warrior configurations with IPSec aren't as obvious as this example.

If you want a VPN to connect two sites or two hosts with a static IP address configuration and you have the same operating system on both endpoints, IPSec is a stable and proven solution. For road warrior setups, where you have one static host or network and one machine that is traveling, there is a better solution: OpenVPN. OpenVPN is available for several operating systems, including Linux, FreeBSD, OS X, and Windows. In the next section of this chapter, you will learn how to configure and implement OpenVPN for such a scenario.

Configuring OpenVPN

In the previous section, you saw how you can transparently encrypt traffic and ensure data validity between two networks by using IPSec without any additional software packages besides those available in CentOS. IPSec is a great protocol suite for creating VPNs, but it has some drawbacks. It is not easy to implement on the protocol side, which sometimes makes two IPSec solutions from two different vendors incompatible with each other. IPSec isn't easy to debug either, and the setup for more complicated solutions than the one shown earlier isn't easy.

Enter OpenVPN (`http://www.openvpn.org/`). OpenVPN is an SSL/TLS-based VPN solution, which works similarly to the tunneling solution with OpenSSH shown earlier in this chapter. But while the OpenSSH tunnel is for when you suddenly need a small VPN solution, OpenVPN is a proven, scalable solution for creating VPNs. It scales from normal home usage over small businesses up to large VPN concentrators for big enterprises. One OpenVPN daemon can take care of up to 128 simultaneous clients.

It has several advantages over IPSec. For cryptographic operations, it uses the standard TLS/SSL libraries, which are available on many, if not most, operating systems. Because of this, OpenVPN on a Windows computer has no problems talking to OpenVPN on a CentOS computer. It completely operates in the user space, which makes it easier to debug than kernel-based IPSec. If OpenVPN crashes, it won't take the rest of the system with it. And its biggest asset on the plus side is that it is easy to configure.

However, it is not available in the base CentOS repositories. OpenVPN is available in the RPMforge (`http://rpmforge.net/`) and in the Extra Packages for Enterprise Linux (EPEL, `http://fedoraproject.org/wiki/EPEL`) repositories, so if you have one of those two configured, just use it. In this section, the EPEL repository is preferred, because it has some accessories that aren't available in RPMforge. If you haven't configured the EPEL repository, install the `epel-release` package: `http://fedoraproject.org/wiki/EPEL`.

```
rpm -Uvh http://download.fedora.redhat.com/pub/epel ➥
/5/i386/epel-release-5-3.noarch.rpm
```

This will set up everything needed to install packages from the EPEL repository:

```
yum install openvpn
```

For installing this package, Yum requires a GPG key to check that the package is signed correctly. You will be asked if it is OK to install the key with the key ID 0x217521F6. Respond with y to that.

It's time to configure OpenVPN! OK, let's poke a hole in the firewall first. OpenVPN operates over one UDP port on the server side. The IANA assigned port 1194 is for OpenVPN traffic, so check `/etc/services`.

Note Why UDP? Encapsulating TCP sessions into other TCP sessions is a bad idea, because both layers—the inner and the outer one—check for correct network transmissions, try to reget packets they have lost, and so on. If the outer layer has problems with connectivity, the inner layer also will. Then both layers will try to work their magic, which normally leads to connection loss or at least slows down the connection. UDP doesn't check for that; it is a stateless "fire-and-forget" protocol. So, it makes sense to encapsulate TCP packets in a UDP tunnel—only the inner protocol will check for correct transmissions. The outer layer does not care. You can use OpenVPN with TCP for the tunnel, but this configuration is not advisable.

To open port 1194, you can use `lokkit`:

```
[root@centos ~]# lokkit -q -p 1194:udp
[root@centos ~]# iptables -L | grep open
ACCEPT  udp  --  anywhere    anywhere    state NEW udp dpt:openvpn
[root@centos ~]#
```

There will be only one OpenVPN daemon listening on that port, even with many clients connecting to it.

Looking at an Example

In this section, we will use the following scenario: say you have a LAN at home, with a router in front of it. This router will become the endpoint for all OpenVPN sessions into your LAN. Your LAN has the network 10.0.3.0/24, and your router has the IP address 10.0.3.254 in this LAN. The public IP address of your router is 192.168.1.104. The other machine with which you will connect to the VPN is your trusty old laptop, which runs CentOS 5 as the operating system. For OpenVPN's TUN interface, we will use the network 10.10.10.0/24, which needs to be a network that is not in use on either side of the tunnel. Figure 10-4 shows this scenario.

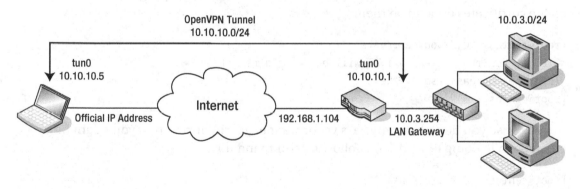

Figure 10-4. *A VPN done with OpenVPN*

Although OpenVPN can work with preshared keys, just like IPSec earlier, this time you will use X.509 certificates to manage authentication

Using X.509 certificates means that you need a public key infrastructure (PKI) for managing, signing, and checking these certificates. The easiest PKI would be using OpenSSL for creating a certificate authority (CA), for certificate requests, and for certificate creation. This can be a tedious task, and because of that, most administrators write scripts for that.

OpenVPN brings a set of scripts with it, which can be used to manage certificates very easily. The openvpn package installs those in /usr/share/openvpn/easy-rsa. You should copy those scripts to /etc/openvpn in case a package update accidentally overwrites those files:

```
[root@centos ~]# cd /etc/openvpn/
[root@centos openvpn]# cp -a /usr/share/openvpn/easy-rsa .
```

Now edit the vars file, because that defines a set of basic variables and shouldn't change. You can find the vars file in /etc/openvpn/easy-rsa/2.0. At least change the settings on the last five lines:

```
export KEY_COUNTRY="DE"
export KEY_PROVINCE="Bayern"
export KEY_CITY="Muenchen"
export KEY_ORG="Unorganized Inc."
export KEY_EMAIL="ralph@example.com"
```

Depending on whether you set this up for your private use or for corporate use, you might also want to look at KEY_EXPIRE, which is set to ten years, and at the KEY_SIZE, which is set to 1024 bits. You can set this to 2048 bits if you are as paranoid as me. These variables have to be exported to your current shell, and the other programs you need to create certificates depend on them:

```
[root@centos 2.0]# source ./vars
NOTE: If you run ./clean-all, I will be doing a rm -rf on ➥
 /etc/openvpn/easy-rsa/2.0/keys
[root@centos 2.0]#
```

Because you don't have any keys yet or want to get rid of keys that you might have created while doing tests, run the following command now:

```
[root@centos 2.0]# ./clean-all
[root@centos 2.0]#
```

This removes all keys and sets up an index and a file with serial numbers in the keys/ subdirectory. Next build the certificate authority.

■**Note** Chapter 5 also talks about creating SSL certificates, using OpenSSL to do so. The approach here uses the same techniques, and the resulting certificates behave the same. We are using the scripts provided by the OpenVPN package for ease of use here; you can create those certificates any way you like.

```
[root@centos 2.0]# ./build-ca
Generating a 2048 bit RSA private key
............................+++
...................................................+++
writing new private key to 'ca.key'
[…]
Organization Name (eg, company) [Unorganized Inc.]:
Organizational Unit Name (eg, section) []:
Common Name (eg, your name or your server's hostname) [Unorganized Inc. CA]:
Name []:
Email Address [ralph@example.com]:
[root@centos 2.0]#
```

This creates the files ca.crt and ca.key in the keys/ subdirectory, which are the certificate for your CA and the appropriate key, respectively. As you can see, it uses the settings
you entered into the vars file. Now that you have a certificate authority, you can create a
certificate for the server. This certificate is needed so that the client can check whether the
OpenVPN server really is the machine it purports to be. There are three questions you have
to answer. When the script asks for the common name, enter server. When it asks whether
you want to sign the certificate, answer y. Enter y after the 1 out of 1 certificate requests
certified, commit? [y/n] prompt as well.

```
[root@centos 2.0]# ./build-key-server server
Generating a 2048 bit RSA private key
[…]
Common Name (eg, your name or your server's hostname) [server]:server
[…]
Sign the certificate? [y/n]:y
[…]
1 out of 1 certificate requests certified, commit? [y/n]y
[...]
```

The rest of the values are taken from the vars file again. This leaves a server.crt and a
server.key in the keys/ subdirectory. The number in the serial file has been incremented,
and in the index file you will find an entry for the certificate you have just created.

Now it is time to generate a certificate for the client. There's a script for that, too. You
have to call this script for every client that should be accessing the VPN. Remember to
give each client a unique name. You can go with "client1," "client2," and so on, or just use
their (ideally) unique hostnames. Any way you do it, you should keep a file somewhere in
which you record each host or person you created a certificate for. Again, answer y when
you are asked whether you want to sign the certificate and when the script asks for com-
mitting the request. As you can see, the name you gave to the script on the command line
ends up in the Common Name entry:

```
[root@centos 2.0]# ./build-key client1
Generating a 2048 bit RSA private key
.......+++
[…]
Common Name (eg, your name or your server's hostname) [client1]:
[…]
Sign the certificate? [y/n]:y
[…]
1 out of 1 certificate requests certified, commit? [y/n]y
```

The last thing to do is to generate some Diffie-Hellman parameters, which are needed for the key exchange between the client and server. This is the same as with IPSec; the client and the server do authentication with a public key encryption method, and the actual encryption of the packets in the tunnel is then done with a symmetric key that both sides negotiate from time to time. Public key encryption could be done for encryption, too, but symmetric encryption is much faster than its public key counterpart.

```
[root@centos 2.0]# ./build-dh
Generating DH parameters, 2048 bit long safe prime, generator 2
This is going to take a long time
........+...............................................
[it will]
[root@centos 2.0]#
```

Let's take a look at the keys/ directory now. The ca.crt file is needed on all machines, clients and server, so they can check the identity of each other. The client files are needed only on the clients, while the server files are needed on the server, as is dh2048.pem. The rest of the files in there are administrative files that the CA scripts need to work. Now would be a good time to put the contents of keys/ into your backup plan.

If you need to revoke a key for a client, there are scripts, too. You should read the README file in /etc/openvpn/easy-rsa/2.0 for more information on the rest of the scripts.

Configuring the Server Side

It is time now to configure the server side of your VPN. There is an example config file in /usr/share/doc/openvpn-2.1/sample-config-files/, called server.conf. You can copy that to /etc/openvpn, or you can just start a new config file and use that as a reference. Let's begin with a fresh one. Copy ca.crt, server.crt, dh2048.pem, and server.key to /etc/openvpn or use the respective places in /etc/pki; then you need to rename those files. Open your editor, and create /etc/openvpn/server.conf. You can call the file any way you want; it just needs to end in .conf.

■Caution If you leave a second `.conf` file in `/etc/openvpn/`, the init script will try to start another instance of OpenVPN with that file.

```
# listen on the public interface
local 192.168.1.104
port 1194
proto udp
# use a TUNnel interface
dev tun
# X.509 certificates
ca ca.crt
cert server.crt
key server.key # chmod 0600 server.key
dh dh2048.pem
# This is the network for the tunnels
server 10.10.10.0 255.255.255.0
# keep a list of client->IP address records
ifconfig-pool-persist ipp.txt
# Push routes to the client
push "route 10.0.3.0 255.255.255.0"
# Enable compression on the VPN link.
comp-lzo
# drop privileges
user openvpn
group openvpn
persist-key
persist-tun
# Status file
status openvpn-status.log
verb 3
```

A few directives might need explanation. `push "route 10.0.3.0 255.255.255.0"` sets a route on the client that points into the network of your LAN. You need to make sure that there is a route back to the network that the tunnels are in from your LAN. This should happen automatically on the router once the TUN interface comes up. `comp-lzo` enables compression on the link, which can make the connection faster. You need to set this on the client, too. `user openvpn`, `group openvpn`, and the two `persist` lines tell the `openvpn` daemon to drop privileges after starting. The persist lines are there because the daemon cannot change network interfaces or read keys anymore after it has dropped privileges.

Try to start the server with the following:

```
service openvpn start
```

This should create a new TUN interface on your computer with an IP address from the network you defined in the server configuration:

```
tun0      Link encap:UNSPEC  HWaddr 00-00-00-00-*
          inet addr:10.10.10.1  P-t-P:10.10.10.2  Mask:255.255.255.255
          UP POINTOPOINT RUNNING NOARP MULTICAST  MTU:1500  Metric:1
```

Once you have everything configured correctly, make sure that openvpn starts when the machine boots:

```
chkconfig openvpn on
```

Configuring the Client

Install the openvpn package first if you haven't already done so. Again, there is a sample configuration file for client configuration in the documentation for OpenVPN. But first you need to copy over ca.crt, client1.crt, and client1.key to your laptop's /etc/openvpn/ directory.

Note When you are giving out certificates to many people, you need to find a way to do this securely. There are several ways to do that. If every user has a home directory on your server and can reach this via SSH, put the certificates there. You can also use encrypted mail to send out the certificates or think about putting them behind password-protected HTTPS links.

Start with a fresh client configuration file, called client.conf:

```
client
dev tun
proto udp
# The server
remote 192.168.1.104 1194
# Try to resolve the remote infinitely
resolv-retry infinite
nobind
user openvpn
```

```
group openvpn
persist-key
persist-tun
# SSL parameters
ca ca.crt
cert client1.crt
key client1.key
#verify the server
ns-cert-type server
comp-lzo
```

Most parameters are the same as the ones on the server side. Note that there is no mention of the LAN's network parameters—these will get pushed by the server to the client side. The ns-cert-type server entry protects against a potential man-in-the-middle attack; see http://openvpn.net/howto.html#mitm for an in-depth discussion.

To start the client, just run the following:

```
openvpn /etc/openvpn/client.conf &
```

and you should see this output:

```
[root@client openvpn]# openvpn /etc/openvpn/client.conf
[…]
Sat Apr  4 11:37:39 2009 UDPv4 link remote: 192.168.1.104:1194
Sat Apr  4 11:37:39 2009 [server] Peer Connection Initiated with 192.168.1.104:1194
Sat Apr  4 11:37:41 2009 TUN/TAP device tun0 opened
Sat Apr  4 11:37:41 2009 /sbin/ip link set dev tun0 up mtu 1500
Sat Apr  4 11:37:41 2009 /sbin/ip addr add dev tun0 local 10.10.10.6 peer 10.10.10.5
Sat Apr  4 11:37:41 2009 GID set to openvpn
Sat Apr  4 11:37:41 2009 UID set to openvpn
Sat Apr  4 11:37:41 2009 Initialization Sequence Completed
```

There is a TUN interface now, and there's a route set to the network of your LAN at home:

```
[root@client ~]# ip addr show tun0
6: tun0: <POINTOPOINT,MULTICAST,NOARP,UP,LOWER_UP> mtu 1500 ➥
qdisc pfifo_fast qlen 100
    link/[65534]
    inet 10.10.10.6 peer 10.10.10.5/32 scope global tun0
[root@client ~]# ip route show 10.0.3.0/24
10.0.3.0/24 via 10.10.10.5 dev tun0
```

You should now be able to ping the gateway or any of the other machines in your LAN from your laptop. Hey, your VPN works!

Some Security Considerations

If you look closely at the routing table of your computer, you will see that only traffic between your laptop and your LAN will go through the VPN tunnel. All other traffic is still routed through your default gateway to the Internet. This might be no problem if you just want to use the tunnel for connecting to your private LAN at home, because you need some files from there or need to use the web server in your LAN. When setting up a VPN for an enterprise, this might be a violation of its security policy, because it might require outgoing traffic to go through a corporate proxy, for example.

In a case like this, you want the default route to also point to the VPN tunnel you just built. You have seen that the route to your LAN gets pushed to the client by the OpenVPN server. OpenVPN can do the same for the default route. The following line in the configuration on the server side will take care of that:

```
push "redirect-gateway def1"
```

This opens up a problem, though. When you connect your laptop to the Internet, it normally receives the name server setup from the Internet service provider you connect to. When you redirect the default gateway so that all traffic goes through the VPN, you probably will not be able to reach those DNS servers. OpenVPN can take care of that, but you need to add the following to the server-side configuration:

```
push "dhcp-option DNS 10.0.3.2"
```

Replace 10.0.3.2 with the IP address of the DNS server in your LAN. If you use Windows on your laptop to connect via OpenVPN, this will set the DNS information automatically. On a CentOS client some scripting is required to do that. Add the following two lines to your client.conf:

```
up setdns.sh
script-security 2
```

script-security 2 allows openvpn to execute scripts, and up sets the script that is run after the tunnel is created, which is setdns.sh in this case. Then create this script in /etc/openvpn on the client:

```
#!/bin/bash
dns=empty
#save old configuration
```

```
cp /etc/resolv.conf /etc/resolv.conf.orig
# pushed options are in $foreign_options_1 to
# $foreign_options_x, so cycle through them.
for option in ${!foreign_option_*}
do
    # Match $option for "dhcp-option DNS" and return
    # the remaining of the line which is the nameserver's
    # IP address. If no match returns, $dns equals "empty".
    eval "dns=\${$option#dhcp-option DNS }"
    if [ "$dns" != "empty" ]
        then
            cat >/etc/resolv.conf <<EOF
nameserver $dns
EOF
            exit 0
        fi
done
```

Make the script executable. You could also set a down script, which copies back the saved DNS configuration, but that doesn't work the way you configured openvpn. Because the process is dropping privileges as soon as possible, this script would be run as the user openvpn, which is not allowed to write in the /etc/ directory.

Now it is time to restart the openvpn client. Your resolver configuration should look like this:

```
[root@client ~]# cat /etc/resolv.conf
nameserver 10.0.3.2
[root@client ~]#
```

You also should be seeing a new default route through your TUN device. The old default gateway is preserved, but no packets will ever reach that route:

```
[root@client ~]# route -n
Kernel IP routing table
Destination Gateway     Genmask      Flags Metric Ref    Use Iface
[...]
0.0.0.0     10.10.10.5  128.0.0.0    UG    0      0        0 tun0
128.0.0.0   10.10.10.5  128.0.0.0    UG    0      0        0 tun0
0.0.0.0     172.16.170.2 0.0.0.0     UG    0      0        0 eth0
```

When the openvpn daemon stops, these two routes will be deleted, so the old default route works again. You have to manually copy over the old resolver config, though.

Doing It the Even Easier Way

If you are running CentOS 5 on your laptop, chances are good that you are running Net-workManager for connection management. NetworkManager lets you connect to wireless networks, remembers networks you have already visited, keeps passwords in a password store, and so on. Several extensions are available for NetworkManager; one of them is an extension to create and manage OpenVPN connections. Make sure that the EPEL reposi-tory is enabled, and use Yum to install the extension:

```
yum install NetworkManager-openvpn
```

Tip If you are using your laptop to go places and have to connect to different networks during the day or week, you should be running NetworkManager, because it makes connection management much easier. To launch it, run `service NetworkManager start`. If you are running GNOME, a new icon should pop up in the notification area. If you like NetworkManager, make sure that you use `chkconfig NetworkManager on` to start it when the computer boots.

You might need to restart NetworkManager after you install the OpenVPN extension. To use OpenVPN, click the NetworkManager icon, and select VPN Connections ➤ Con-figure VPN. Copy `ca.crt`, `client1.crt`, and `client1.key` to your user's home directory, and make them readable for the user. Click the Add button to create a new VPN connection. When asked to choose a VPN connection type, select OpenVPN, and click Create.

Type your gateway—either name or IP address—into the first field (see Figure 10-5). Use the buttons to select your client certificate, your client key, and your CA certificate. If your client key has a password, which it doesn't by default, you can enter it here. Now click the Advanced button.

As you configured LZO data compression on the server side, you should also config-ure it here (Figure 10-6). Click OK after you select this box. Now select the IPv4 tab (see Figure 10-7). Leave Method at Automatic (VPN), or select it if it is different from that. This setting provides for automatically changing everything the server side pushes to the cli-ent. If you didn't change your server-side configuration, NetworkManager takes care of changing `/etc/resolv.conf` and sets your default route through the VPN tunnel. There's no fiddling with scripts on the client side.

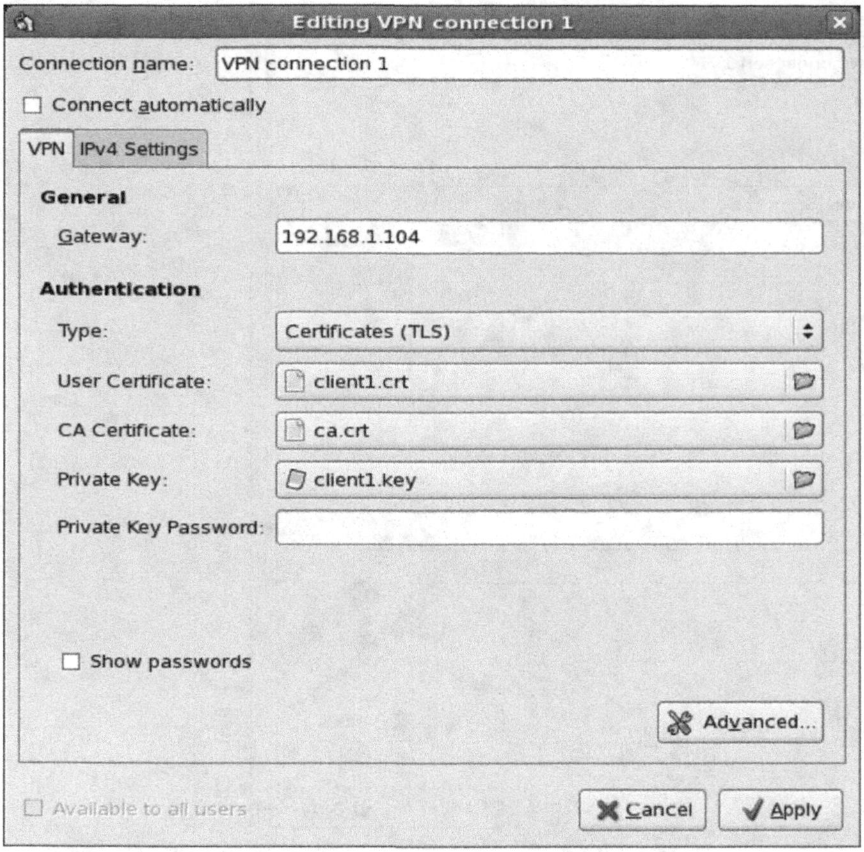

Figure 10-5. *Configuring authentication*

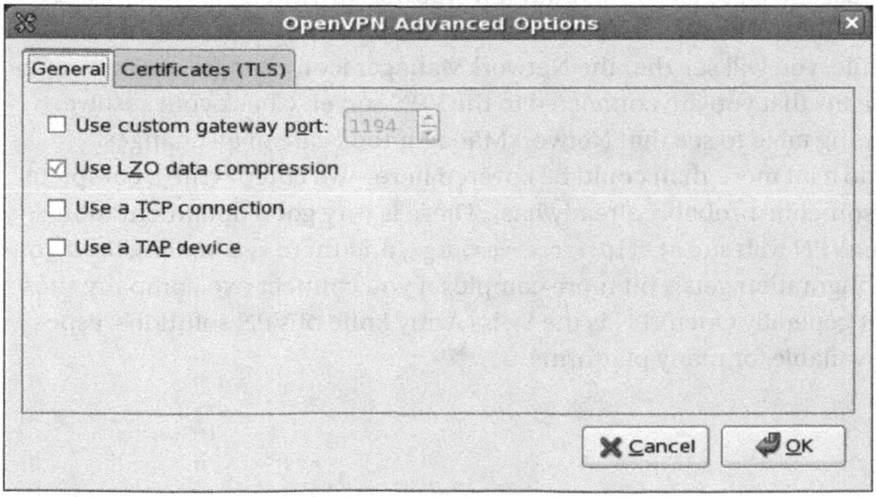

Figure 10-6. *Select LZO data compression*

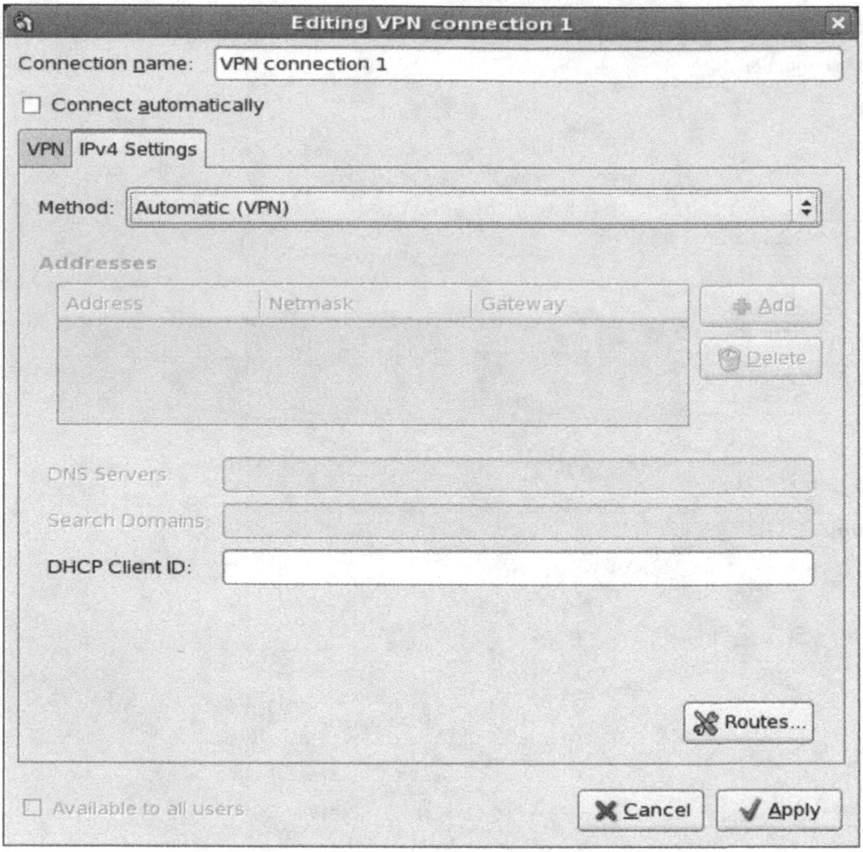

Figure 10-7. *IPv4 settings*

Click OK after this, and close all configuration windows. Now click the NetworkManager button, and choose VPN Connections ➤ VPN Connection 1.

After a short while, you will see that the NetworkManager icon changes and now contains a lock. This means that you are connected to the VPN server. Check your resolver config and your routing table to see that NetworkManager took care of all changes.

OpenVPN can do a lot more than could be covered here—we could write a complete book about it (and someone probably already has). There is very good documentation available at the OpenVPN web site at `http://openvpn.org/`, and there is a mailing list if you have questions. Configuration gets a bit more complex if you connect two company sites with each other. But generally OpenVPN is the Swiss Army knife of VPN solutions, especially because it is available for many platforms.

There are a lot more VPN solutions than the three we covered in this chapter. There is VTun (`http://vtun.sourceforge.net/`), for example, and we already talked about Open-Swan being another IPSec solution that is included in CentOS. There are commercial VPN solutions, such as the VPNC software by Cisco—for which a NetworkManager extension is available. People use the Point-To-Point-Tunneling Protocol (PPTP), and there is also Layer 2 Tunneling Protocol (L2TP).

Summary

In this chapter, you learned what a VPN is. You learned how to set up VPNs with SSH, with IPSec, and with OpenVPN. You now know when to deploy an SSH VPN and when a VPN with IPSec or OpenVPN is preferable over the SSH solution. We covered using shared secrets for VPNs and how to use SSL certificates for OpenVPN solutions. We also looked into integrating OpenVPN into your desktop by using NetworkManager.

The next chapter is about core builds, which is a way of installing and setting up CentOS servers without user intervention.

PART 3

■■■

Enterprise Features

Although CentOS does have many features that Linux users have come to expect, it also has some features that set it apart as an enterprise operating system. These features include a core builds system for customizing and automating installs, high availability, and tools for system and network monitoring.

## CHAPTER 11

Using Core Builds

This chapter will be of most use to you if you have had the pleasure of building multiple servers. We cannot recall the number of times we've looked at a customer install checklist that was a good ten pages long. Every time a server is built, this checklist is followed step-by-step, and each piece of software is copied over and then installed by hand. Apart from being extremely time-consuming and error prone, it's a thankless task. If you get it right, then what's the big deal? You had step-by-step instructions, and it's not that hard. If you get it wrong or miss a single item on that list from hell, you're not going to hear the end of it. The best-case scenario is going back through the same list trying to figure out which bit you missed. Surely, there has to be a better way.

What Are Core Builds?

Core builds are a great way to install your CentOS systems. In short, they are usually a customized install media (usually a DVD) that contains additional scripts and software packages that build a machine to a particular specification. This is considerably better than using imaging products (such as Partimage or Symantec Ghost) because they take a byte-for-byte copy of a server's hard disk. This makes it much more difficult (sometimes impossible) to restore onto a machine that has different hardware. It also requires one server image to be maintained for each type of server that you build. For example, you may have a standard build for your web servers and a different build for a database or an application server. These different builds may have only subtle changes between them, such as including a package here or taking away a package there. But they can also be completely different, having nothing in common with each other.

A *core build* at its most basic is a standard CentOS DVD image with an Anaconda kickstart file. A kickstart file is a text file containing instructions to Anaconda, the CentOS installer. Instructions vary, including how to lay out the hard disk, which keyboard to install, and what to set the root password to. It also has provisions for selecting packages and package groups that you want to install. This is effectively a way to preprogram the answers that you would normally give during the install process. If you're coming from a Windows background, the equivalent would be the *answer* file. If this were all that you could do, core builds would still be very useful. They'd boot from DVD, install, and reboot, and you'd have a machine ready to customize. But wait! There's more!

What makes the kickstart file so powerful is that you can embed scripts at key stages of the install process. This means that you can automate a lot of the work that you'd normally do by hand and have the installer run all of those steps for you. You'll want to do most of the work after the install has completed, and here Anaconda does not disappoint. At this stage you have access to everything on your freshly installed machine. You can download files from another server, restore files from a backup, or do anything else that has the potential to be scripted.

What Can't Core Builds Do?

Part of the beauty of a core build is that it's a fully automated process. That means that software that requires manual intervention (such as installing the Sun JDK, which requires you to accept a license agreement) is not really a good fit. There are also times when you simply have to provide network information. For example, if you are starting a network install but the network does not provide DHCP, you will need a way to specify your IP address and so forth. These can all be circumvented, though. For example, when installing Java, it is possible to find all the related files on a freshly installed system, put them in a TAR archive, and then use the archive to automatically install it in your core build. For the network details, you can provide a script for Anaconda to run right at the beginning of the install process. This means you can enter information, save it to a text file, and pull it back in again at a later time for use in your scripts.

So, the only thing core builds cannot do are things that really do require human interaction. If you do have a tool that simply has to be done by hand, perhaps you can still benefit from a core build by automating as much of the process as possible. For instance, the core build could set the machine up and copy the install software for the program over. That way, all you have to do is actually run the installer rather than going through the whole setup process.

Why Create a Core Build?

Core builds save time. Once you have a core build, you can kickstart ten or more servers, and they will all install themselves to perfection. You won't need to do anything or at the most very little. You will also be able to ensure that your server configuration is reproducible. They will all have been built from the same scripts, so you can rest assured that nothing has been forgotten. It's also a great way to document your systems. What better documentation can you have than the script that actually builds the machine?

What Are Kickstart Files?

As mentioned, a *kickstart file* is a simple text file that Anaconda uses to determine how it should install a system. We will show the inside of a kickstart file in a moment, but first we'll discuss something very important. Few people who create their own kickstart files do so by hand. When you complete a new system install, as part of the final cleanup Anaconda creates a kickstart file based on your selections during the install and places it in the root home directory (/root). This means that if you need to build a new system, by far the easiest way is to start by installing the system normally first and then hacking the kickstart file that Anaconda comes up with.

■**Note** There are lots of funky things you can do with Anaconda and kickstart files. Fortunately, you can find a complete online manual available at http://www.centos.org/docs/5/html/Installation_Guide-en-US/ch-kickstart2.html.

Anatomy of a Kickstart File

A kickstart file has a natural order that most people tend to follow. Most are created from the automatically generated file provided by Anaconda, so this isn't particularly surprising, but you might come across some kickstart files "in the wild" that don't follow this format for some reason. They will usually still work without any trouble, but if you're creating your own, it makes sense to follow the Anaconda standard.

The first part of the kickstart file is called the *command section*. This is where the options for the install itself are set. Some are just keywords such as install or upgrade. Others take options and parameters such as selinux --enforcing. Anything that starts with a # character is a comment and will be ignored by Anaconda. If the kickstart file doesn't contain the information that Anaconda needs during the install, it will prompt the user for it.

■**Note** When doing a network install (an install that pulls the CentOS packages from a network resource rather than from a CD or DVD), if IP address details weren't specified, Anaconda will attempt to request an IP address via DHCP. In previous versions of CentOS, if the DHCP request failed, the end user would be prompted for the network details. In the current version, however, Anaconda's behavior has been modified so that instead of prompting for details, the install simply fails. There is a workaround for this, which we'll cover in the "network" section of this chapter.

The second section is the *packages section*. This is where all the packages you want to install (and in many cases omit) should go. Although you can (and probably will) end up tweaking this by hand, it's much easier to do the hard work in the graphical installer because you'll be able to simply select check boxes and let Anaconda worry about writing out all the details. One thing to be wary of is that if you remove a package that another package depends on, Anaconda will install the package regardless. This is because, unlike in previous versions of CentOS where you had to explicitly tell Anaconda to resolve dependencies with the `--resolvedeps` option, in CentOS 5 Anaconda will resolve dependencies automatically.

The third section is where you place `%pre` and `%post` scripts. The `%pre` script is executed as soon as the kickstart file has been read by Anaconda. You can access the network at this stage, but you won't be able to use DNS to look up names because the name resolver hasn't been configured yet. This section is especially useful for checking hardware or configuring things in advance of the main install. For example, you could provide network configuration information or supply details for partitioning a hard disk. The `%post` script does the opposite of the `%pre` script. Once the system is fully installed (and before a reboot), the `%post` script will be executed. More important, though, is that this script will be executed from the perspective of the installed machine as if you were working on a live system. The `%post` section has a neat little option called `--nochroot`. This allows you to execute scripts from the perspective of the installer. This is really handy because it allows you to copy files from the source media onto the new server. When using this option, most people will copy or set things up and then run the `%post` section. This allows you to do some setup before you finalize your install.

The Command Section

In Chapter 2 we showed how to install a server with a few basic options. As you now know, Anaconda will have stored those settings for us in a kickstart file for future use. You can find this file here:

```
/root/anaconda-ks.cfg
```

Our kickstart file will probably look at least a little different from yours. For a start, our time zone is set to Hong Kong, and we're using a British keyboard layout. Here is the command section of the kickstart file that Anaconda created:

```
# Kickstart file automatically generated by anaconda.

install
cdrom
lang en_US.UTF-8
keyboard uk
xconfig --startxonboot
```

```
network --device eth0 --bootproto dhcp --hostname centos
rootpw --iscrypted $1$wAUSiwsP$k..saSPrjzcW77FwDgUpe/
firewall --enabled --port=22:tcp
authconfig --enableshadow --enablemd5
selinux --enforcing
timezone --utc Asia/Hong_Kong
bootloader --location=mbr --driveorder=hda --append="rhgb quiet"
# The following is the partition information you requested
# Note that any partitions you deleted are not expressed
# here so unless you clear all partitions first, this is
# not guaranteed to work
#clearpart --linux --drives=hda
#part /boot --fstype ext3 --size=100 --ondisk=hda
#part pv.2 --size=0 --grow --ondisk=hda
#volgroup VolGroup00 --pesize=32768 pv.2
#logvol swap --fstype swap --name=LogVol01 --vgname=VolGroup00 --size=256 \
--grow --maxsize=512
#logvol / --fstype ext3 --name=LogVol00 --vgname=VolGroup00 --size=1024 --grow
```

The first line starts with a #, so it is a comment that's ignored by Anaconda. The last part of the command section is also commented out, but we will return to that in a moment. We will give an overview of each of the options used in the command section. The majority of them are straightforward and don't require much in the way of explanation.

install

This tells Anaconda that the kickstart should be used to install a machine. Alternatively, you could have requested an upgrade, but the requirements for an upgrade kickstart file are slightly different from ones used for installation. Fortunately, the upgrade kickstart is a lot simpler; for example, it doesn't have a %packages section to worry about.

cdrom

This tells Anaconda that you want to source the packages from a CD or DVD. You actually have quite a few options here because you can also install CentOS (well, at least fetch the packages) from NFS, FTP, or HTTP. By far the most common are CD/DVD-based and HTTP-based network installs. This is probably because they are the simplest to use, very easy to set up, and work well in most computing environments. We will focus on these two install methods when we look at how we can source our kickstart files and source files from the network.

lang

This option sets the language that you want your system to use. There are plenty of languages to choose from, but you must make sure that you get the language precisely as it is used in CentOS. By far the easiest way to do this is to make sure that your language of choice is picked when you do your initial install. That way, Anaconda will have recorded your choice in the correct format, and you won't need to make any changes.

keyboard

This one is nice and easy. Simply tell CentOS which keyboard layout should be used by the system. Again, you must make sure that you use the same name as used internally by CentOS, and again the easiest way to set this is during the install. If you configured your server the way you wanted it during the initial install, you'll probably find that both the keyboard and language are already correctly set up.

xconfig

This option allows you to specify whether you want the graphical interface (X) to start on boot. This is really down to personal taste. On one hand, having the full graphical interface available is quite nice, and you can log in and work on the server as you would any other machine. However, some people are adamant that this takes up too much in the way of resources that could instead be used to service requests. If your server is going to be sitting in a data center somewhere or if at least the monitor, keyboard, and mouse are going to be plugged into your desktop rather than the server, there's probably little point starting X when the server initially boots. You can always start it on demand if need be.

network

The network option allows you to specify how CentOS should configure your network card(s). You can choose automatic configuration through either DHCP or BOOTP, or you can specify the IP address manually. One thing to watch out for here, unless you have created a kickstart file for each server or you have a dedicated build environment, is that chances are you don't want to assign each server the same address. Otherwise, especially for servers in situ, when they are rebooted for the first time, they will conflict with the other server, and this could lead to all sorts of strange network-related errors that may not obviously point to an IP address conflict.

You have a couple of options here. As already mentioned, you can create customized kickstart files for each server and then hard-code the IP address into them. This isn't too bad if you have only a handful of services, but it will become unmanageable quite quickly if you have more than that. You could also use DHCP to assign the IP address initially and then on reboot configure the IP address by hand. This one requires manual intervention after the install but is probably the most common method of setting the IP address. If neither of those takes your fancy, you can of course do anything you like in a script in the %post section. This could involve looking up the IP address on a remote server or anything else that you come up with. The network configuration tool that comes with CentOS does accept command-line arguments, so it is possible to script this quite happily. Of course, for this to work, the server would need some form of network connectivity to start with, either a fixed IP that all machines being built use (although that really restricts you to building one machine at a time) or ideally DHCP.

rootpw

This is another straightforward option. This allows you to specify the password that should be used for the root account. It can be stored either in plain text or encrypted. Obviously, plain text isn't recommended, because it means that anyone who can see the kickstart file can see the password.

firewall

This is a very flexible option, and it allows you to configure a basic firewall very easily. Some of the key services such as SSH and HTTP are available as shorthand options. Others will need to be specified manually, but that's easy enough to do. As before, if you have set this up during the install, this section will already be configured the way you want it.

authconfig

This command sets the various options for authentication. The standard (and hence the default) is to enable shadow passwords and use MD5 encryption. You can also set any network authentication services such as Kerberos or enable LDAP support for user information.

selinux

Deciding whether to use SELinux still comes down to personal taste. For the most part, it works very well and provides an additional layer of security for your server. Generally speaking, all the software that comes as part of the CentOS distribution will work as expected. Third-party software, though, sometimes has trouble with SELinux. Because of the security benefits, you're encouraged to use SELinux in enforcing mode, but permissive mode is still beneficial because it highlights any potential problems even though it doesn't act on them. This option can either enable SELinux (enforcing), disable it (disabled), or run it in permissive mode (permissive).

If at all possible, you should choose `selinux --enforcing`.

■**Caution** Disabling SELinux at this stage will make it extremely difficult to get it to work properly after the system is installed because of missing file contexts. If you really don't want to use SELinux, you should install the system with it enabled, and then switch it to permissive later. This will make switching later between permissive and enforcing possible.

---

timezone

This option does exactly what it says on the tin. This sets the default time zone for your server. In our case, the time zone is set to Hong Kong, and the internal clock is set to UTC. The recommended practice is that all servers be set to UTC for their base clocks and then use `timezone` to determine what time they should actually use for logs and so forth. This is especially useful on Internet-facing servers where you will need to easily convert between different time zones such as with web applications and localized "last login time." For day-to-day use, this doesn't make an awful lot of difference, so most people follow the recommended practice. You need to pick from a list of available time zones, which you can find under `/usr/share/zoneinfo`. For example, the time zone for Hong Kong is `Asia/Hong_Kong`.

bootloader

This tells Anaconda where you want the boot loader to be installed. Normally it is installed in the master boot record (MBR) of the first bootable device. In our example, the server has IDE hard disks, which is why the disk is referred to as `hd`. On newer systems that use SCSI, SAS, or SATA drives, the disks will show up as `sd`. This is just the way CentOS differentiates between the disks and doesn't affect how the disks themselves are used.

■**Note** Make sure that you get this setting right, because without it, the server will not be able to boot after the installer reboots the machine. If you aren't sure what to set this to, try completing a manual install on the machine and take a look at what Anaconda set this to.

---

part

This section, the disk partitioning section, is commented out by default in automatically generated kickstart files. This is because, depending on what's on the machine before you do the install, this configuration may or may not work. Generally speaking, going through the hassle of defining individual disks is not worth it unless you have a specific need to create partitions of a particular size or you have a corporate standard to which you need to adhere. A far easier way to do this is to use the autopart option, which like the initial installer sets up the system with a large root partition (at least 1GB), swap space, and the relevant boot partition. This is generally fine for most servers, but if you need anything specific or more complicated (such as software RAID), you will find it far easier to create the partitions through the graphical installer and then use what Anaconda provides.

Caution One thing worth mentioning is the clearpart option. Be very, very careful with this! People have been known to accidentally wipe all of the partitions on their SAN or external USB disk by telling Anaconda to clear all the partitions. We know of one company that did this and lost its entire Oracle RAC system. Be warned, it can and has happened before. If you want to be on the safe side, you can do what we do, and that is physically remove any devices that you aren't willing to see wiped clean. This may require a bit more work when you hook them back up after the install, but at least you won't accidentally install on the wrong disk.

%packages Section

Here is an excerpt from our kickstart file:

```
%packages
@office
@editors
@text-internet
@virtualization
@legacy-network-server
@dns-server
@gnome-desktop
@dialup
@core
@base
@ftp-server
```

```
@network-server
@games
@base-x
@graphics
@web-server
@smb-server
@printing
@mail-server
@server-cfg
@sound-and-video
@news-server
@graphical-internet
bridge-utils
device-mapper-multipath
vnc-server
xorg-x11-server-Xnest
libsane-hpaio
-sysreport
```

This section is vital for the install (although ignored completely if present during an upgrade) because it defines what exactly Anaconda should install on your server. This is the entire package list that was generated based on the installation we did in Chapter 2. Don't worry if yours is slightly different, because there may be packages required for our system (such as hardware support) that your machine doesn't need.

Every entry in this list must resolve to either a known package group or a package name. If you include packages or groups that don't exist, Anaconda will halt the install and complain about unknown packages. The easiest way to install third-party packages is to do so during the %post section, although it is possible to customize comps.xml where the packaging information is stored. This is generally avoided because it tends to be a lot of effort getting it to work and will need updating again for the next CentOS release.

Package groups all start with an @. These groups are broadly defined based on the functionality that they provide. For example, @virtualization provides all the packages needed for virtualization support. This saves you having to figure out what packages you need and then installing them all individually. As you can imagine, this is a real time-saver, and it prevents the %packages section from taking up huge amounts of space.

Individual packages that you want to install are just the name of the package without any prefix. This is most often used when you need a particular feature (such as a VNC server) but you don't want the rest of the stuff that the group will install. You can also specifically tell Anaconda not to install a package. You can see that at the end of our package list, sysreport is listed with a minus in front of it. This will prevent Anaconda from installing it.

Note As mentioned previously, Anaconda will attempt to resolve dependencies automatically. This means that if one of the groups installs a package that depends on `sysreport` being installed, Anaconda will install `sysreport` despite that you told it not to. The theory is that you've told Anaconda what you want your system to run and then it looks at how to provide that functionality. In CentOS 4, if you removed a package that the system would depend upon, the install would halt, and you would receive an error message that the package could not be installed because not all of the dependencies were available. The option `resolvedeps` told Anaconda to remove everything we told it to, but if something we wanted relied upon a package we'd removed, then Anaconda put it back in. This made sense and is now the default in CentOS 5.

Picking groups and packages by hand is not a fun task and can take a lot of trial and error. The easiest way is to customize the package list during the install process. This does mean going through every item and selecting what you do and don't want, but it is a lot easier selecting check boxes and reading helpful descriptions than trying to remember everything and write it out by hand. Of course, once you've done that, it is a lot easier to tweak and work with what Anaconda has provided.

There's not really much more to say about the `%packages` section. It does exactly what you'd expect it to do, and now that it automatically resolves dependencies, one of the biggest gotchas has been taken care of. You can be as specific as you like, but we've found that most people prefer to include the groups first and then specifically remove what they don't want rather than specifically defining which packages to install. This is mostly because you can install, say, Apache and then find that SSL or PHP hasn't been included, so you need to go back and add them. You might then discover that you didn't install MySQL support for PHP. Installing in groups tends to avoid this particular problem and also helps keep the `%packages` section easy to read. Because hard disk space usually isn't at a premium, it's better to install a bit more than you need rather than spending hours trying to make sure you have everything you want. Of course, it's also best practice to install only what you need, so if you want to follow that or you just want a minimal install, your best bet is to go through the package list and manually tell Anaconda what you want your server to be able to do.

The Scripts Section

You'll find two types of scripts in the scripts section. As already discussed, `%pre` scripts run before Anaconda uses the file (and before it processes any included files), and the `%post` script runs after the install is complete but before the reboot. The `%post` script can be run either from the installer's perspective (that is, you can still see all the packages and contents of the install media) or from the new server's perspective. These two are usually used in combination with the `%post --nochroot` script, copying data onto the new server, and the `%post` script, installing and configuring it.

■**Caution**   Currently Anaconda seems to execute these scripts in the order in which they appear in the kickstart file. However, this is *not* guaranteed. This behavior could change in the future, although realistically, it's not likely to change.

These scripts are usually written in bash, but they can be written in any language where an interpreter is available. During the %pre and %post --nochroot sections, you are pretty much restricted to bash and Python. In the %post section, though, you can make use of any language that you have installed as part of your system such as Perl or Ruby. As you can imagine, this gives you a tremendous amount of flexibility. Both the %pre and %post sections potentially have network connectivity, so there is nothing preventing you from writing scripts that contact remote servers or download and install packages from another machine.

The network connectivity available during the %pre section depends entirely on what type of install is being conducted. Under normal circumstances, a DVD-based install will not activate networking unless something requires it (such as specifying that you want to use a kickstart file hosted on your web server). This can catch people unaware, because it is quite common to develop a working kickstart by hosting it on a server and then in the final version put the kickstart on the DVD, which, if the scripts require networking, will fail to run correctly. Of course, immediately rerunning it with the known working version, that is, the one hosted on the web server, shows that nothing is wrong, and the install completes happily. This little gotcha is definitely one to look out for!

By and large, though, in the %pre section, assuming that you're using a network-hosted kickstart file or network-hosted media, you should have access to basic networking. However, you won't have access to DNS at this stage, so everything you do must use IP addresses. In the %post section, you will be able to use DNS but only if you configured static networking during the install (that is, a fixed IP address). Otherwise, like the %pre section, DNS won't be available because the name resolver hasn't been configured yet.

So, let's create a couple scripts. We're going to be using bash to demonstrate the sorts of things that you might like to do. Of course, you are really limited only by your imagination and can do far more complex things than we're attempting here.

■**Note**   In future versions of Anaconda, it will become necessary to place %end markers at the end of your scripts. This isn't required yet, but to prevent your scripts spontaneously combusting when you try them on a future version, it makes sense to start using them now.

%pre Scripts

The %pre section is optional but is extremely useful in very specific (and usually advanced) situations such as removing kernel modules or adding some of your own. This isn't ideal as an example because it relies on topics that we haven't covered and doesn't show how to use the %include statement, which is very useful. So, this example is a bit contrived, but it does show how a %pre script can dynamically alter a kickstart file.

This example will configure the server to use a fixed IP address. In a real-world scenario, your %pre script might have a list of valid IP addresses or perhaps request an IP address by contacting a remote server. In our example, we're just going to set the IP directly. There are two stages to doing this. First, you have to create a %pre script that will write the necessary configuration to a file, and then you have to modify the kickstart script to load in that file at the appropriate juncture.

Here is our %pre script:

```
%pre
#!/bin/sh

# Write out the network configuration to a text file using cat

cat > /tmp/network-config << EOF

network --bootproto=static --ip=192.168.0.2 --netmask=255.255.255.0 \
--gateway=192.168.0.1 --nameserver=192.168.0.1

EOF
```

This will create a text file called /tmp/network-config with everything up until EOF. This is a very handy way to create inline configuration files and is quite common in kick-start scripts. Of course, just because we have a file with that in it doesn't actually mean that Anaconda is going to know about it. The %pre script runs completely independently from Anaconda, but because it runs before Anaconda processes the %include statements, we can get Anaconda to pull in the changes. Here's a kickstart file that pulls in our new network configuration (based on the previous example):

```
xconfig --startxonboot
%include /tmp/network-config
rootpw --iscrypted $1$wAUSiwsP$k..saSPrjzcW77FwDgUpe/
firewall --enabled --port=22:tcp
```

When processed by Anaconda during the install process, the ultimate result is that our kickstart file will look like this:

```
xconfig --startxonboot

network --bootproto=static --ip=192.168.0.2 --netmask=255.255.255.0 \
--gateway=192.168.0.1 --nameserver=192.168.0.1

rootpw --iscrypted $1$wAUSiwsP$k..saSPrjzcW77FwDgUpe/
firewall --enabled --port=22:tcp
```

As you can see, this a handy way of dynamically updating a kickstart file from within the system. Although you'll see how to dynamically create the kickstart later in the chapter, some things aren't available using this method. For example, the server doesn't necessarily know the machine's disk configuration or what hardware is attached to it. Using a %pre script, you can modify the kickstarts based on local information during the install.

%post Scripts

%post scripts (also optional) are by far the most common form of script in a kickstart file. They are generally used for fine-tuning and software installation. As discussed, there are two types of %post script: one that runs chroot and one that doesn't. We'll give an example that uses both to show how they can be used together to great effect. Generally speaking, %post --nochroot is used to copy files and content from the install media. This isn't really much use if you're using a standard CentOS DVD or you're installing via HTTP. If, on the other hand, you've created a custom DVD (perhaps for installs where the network is not available) or you're using an NFS-based install where additional packages are available, it is often easier to copy the files over first rather than try to remount or set things up on the freshly installed machine.

You'll now copy across the Hello World application from the install DVD that we have put in a directory called /custom. You will place this in the /tmp/ directory on the server. You need to do this because once you chroot into the new system, you will no longer be able to see the contents of the DVD. To copy this directory over, you need to do the following:

```
%post --nochroot

cp /custom/hello-word.rpm /mnt/sysimage/tmp/
```

The newly installed system is fully mounted under /mnt/sysimage. This is the exact filesystem as it will be when the server reboots. The script copies the file from the installation disc and then places it in the /tmp/ directory. This is important because once Anaconda chroots into the new server, you won't be able to see the DVD anymore because everything will be running under /mnt/sysimage, and hence, you won't be able to access the file. Now that you have the file in situ, you can write the %post script to install it:

```
%post
rpm -Uvh /tmp/hello-world.rpm
```

That's it—that's all you have to do. You have now copied the file to the new server and then installed it. This is exactly the same as installing it by hand, with the only difference being that this is much easier and of course completely automated. Because the package places its files in specific locations on the filesystem, it makes sense that you have to create the illusion that the server is running from its own disk. If you didn't do this, at best RPM would not be able to work out where to place the files, and at worst, it would place them in the wrong place without you knowing.

Using a Kickstart File on a Web Server

Installing CentOS using a kickstart file that's located on a web server is very straightforward, especially if you're using DHCP. If you're not using DHCP, you'll need to specify your network details on the command line. Although this is slightly more work, it doesn't make it any more difficult, as you'll see in a moment. When you start a CentOS install, you will see the initial CentOS menu that looks like Figure 11-1.

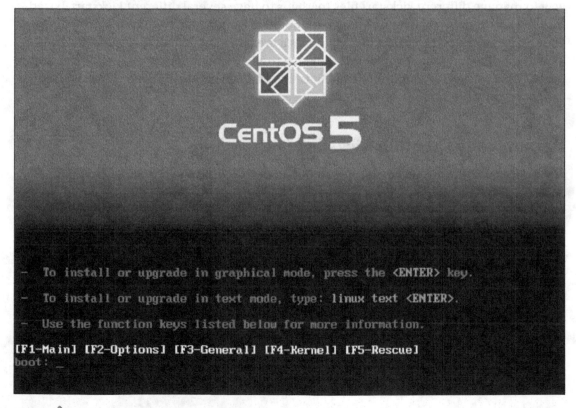

Figure 11-1. *CentOS 5 install boot screen*

If you're using DHCP, all you need to type is the following:

```
linux ks=http://192.168.0.1/ks.cfg
```

Anaconda will then obtain an IP address and try to pull the kickstart file called `ks.cfg` from the web server running on 192.168.0.1. All you need to do is change the URL to point at your kickstart file, and you're off. If you want to use static IP addressing, that's also quite straightforward. Here's an example:

```
linux ks=http://192.168.0.1/ks.cfg ip=192.168.0.2 netmask=255.255.255.0 \
gateway=192.168.0.1
```

This will instruct Anaconda to use those network details to configure the network and then try to download the kickstart file.

One thing to watch out for, though, is that if Anaconda cannot find that kickstart file for any reason, it will simply prompt throughout the install process as if a kickstart were never provided. If this happens, look at virtual terminal 3 (Ctrl+Alt+F3), because this is where you will find debugging information. This will tell you, for example, whether Anaconda was able to find the file or whether something else went wrong.

Apart from that, there is little more to say about kickstart files over HTTP. It is a great way to manage different kickstart files (perhaps to have several different kickstart-based installs) and allows you to boot from an unmodified CentOS DVD while still providing your own customized kickstart file. This gives a great deal of flexibility because you will be able to modify or update your kickstart files centrally without needing to update anything in another location. An additional benefit is that you can create dynamic kickstart files, which as you'll see can be very powerful indeed.

Dynamically Creating Kickstart Files

Dynamic kickstarts are exactly as they sound. Remember, a kickstart file is just plain text, and hence any language that can output plain text can be used to generate a working kickstart file. This allows your web server to generate content on the fly based on where the machine is connecting from (its IP address) or even the time of day. You can also add more information by using a custom URL. For example, the following kickstart URL could be used to tell the remote server which machine is being built:

```
linux ks=http://192.168.0.1/ks.php?server=web
```

In this case, you'd have a PHP script that would look at the content of server and decide which kickstart file should be returned. You can add as many arguments as you want, so you could also have this (the \ character shows where a line break has been added, but normally this would be a single line):

```
linux ks=http://192.168.0.1/ks.php?server_name=goliath&server_type=database&\
server_location=hk
```

Your script could analyze this information and determine what to do about it. Perhaps it will have a profile stored for the server called goliath. Maybe it has different profiles based on the work the machine has to do (such as database or web server). It can also discover where the server is or more usually where the server is going to end up. This technique is really useful because it allows you to start building a centralized and configurable build system. Of course, it also requires a bit of knowledge on how to write web-based software, but even a basic PHP script can bring a lot to a kickstart file.

For example, here is a PHP snippet that sets an IP address based on the server's name:

```php
<?php

if $_GET['server_name'] == 'goliath' {

  $ip = "192.168.0.2"
}
else {

  $ip = "192.168.0.3"

}

// Back to the kickstart file
?>

network --bootproto=static --ip=<?php echo($ip);?>
```

This is just a snippet, but there is really no reason why you couldn't store the options for a given server in a database and then set up a script to pull that information back out on demand. This would allow you to control your kickstart configuration by updating a database rather than text files. Of course, you could use any source you like to determine what to put in the kickstart file as long as you ensure that it follows the correct file format and no required options are left out.

Installing CentOS over HTTP

Once you start moving to network-based kickstarts, you might decide that you want to run your installs this way too. There are several benefits in doing this. First, it means you can install CentOS by using the netinstall disc we discussed way back in Chapter 2. This file is only 7MB in size, so it's quick to download and can be burned on a small CD or even one of the credit card–shaped discs. It also means that you can easily install more than one machine at once without needing DVDs for each machine you want to build. This isn't such a problem when you're building one or two machines, but it can become a pain if you want to install a whole classroom full. It also makes it easier when installing onto blade servers and VMware instances. It is far easier to remotely mount a small 7MB ISO image (say if you're working from home or from a different office) and then pull the files over the local LAN than it is to mount a 3.7GB DVD image and try to install from that! Last of all, it comes in handy when doing Xen-based virtual machine installs. Xen is able to use an HTTP-based copy of the CentOS install media, so you can install guests without needing any physical media.

Setting this up is actually really easy to do. All you have to do is copy the content from the DVD onto your web server. If you wanted to use the web server we set up in Chapter 5, we could place the content under /var/www/html/centos/. One way to do this would be (as root) as follows:

```
mkdir /tmp/centos
mount /dev/cdrom /tmp/centos/
cp -rfa /tmp/centos/ /var/www/html/centos/
umount /dev/cdrom
rmdir /tmp/centos
```

That's it! You'll now have the entire CentOS install tree on your web server. To view it, you can visit your web site with http://<yourip>/centos/.

It is possible to install via HTTP without using a kickstart file, so we will show this method first. When you've booted from your CentOS DVD and are at the initial install screen, you should enter the following:

```
linux method=http://192.168.0.1/centos/
```

Obviously you'll need to replace 192.168.0.1 with your own IP address, but other than that, this is all you'll need to do. If you are using static addressing, however (that is, your network doesn't support DHCP), then you should follow the instructions for setting your IP address manually in the kickstart section.

Updating Your Kickstart File to Install CentOS via HTTP

Once you're happy that your server is able to install via HTTP (see the previous section), then you can update your kickstart file to also use it as an install method. This is easy to do and requires only a simple change. You need to replace cdrom with the following:

```
url --url http://192.168.0.1/centos/
```

Once you've saved your changes, you can then use that kickstart file, and it will automatically use content from your web server. You don't need to specify it in addition to your kickstart. Once you've reached this stage, you can then install from the netinstall image provided on the CentOS web site.

Summary

This chapter covered the basics of doing a core build, specifically what they are and why you'd want one. We looked at Anaconda kickstart files and also covered the basic options available to you and how you can change them. We talked about how to build your package lists, things to watch out for, and how to create your list as painlessly as possible. We took a brief look at writing %pre and %post scripts and where and how you might want to use them. We then got a little bit more advanced and covered how to use kickstart files that are hosted on the network and then how to use the network to host both the kickstart file and the CentOS package information.

In the next chapter, we'll give you a look at a high-availability solution that can help ensure that even if a server fails, you can keep your vital services up and running.

CHAPTER 12
■ ■ ■

Using High Availability

High availability (HA) may look simple on the surface but is actually pretty hard to do correctly. It would be possible to devote a complete book to the subject alone. In this chapter, we will cover the basics just to give you a flavor of how HA works. If you get hungry for more, we are sure that you will find what you are looking for in other sources. First we'll go over some of the general theories about HA. Then we'll discuss the two HA suites you can use with CentOS. Finally, we will detail how to use these suites to set up a simple two-node HA cluster.

But before we start with all that, first answer this question: why do you need, or think you need, HA? From a distance, the basic idea seems very appealing. Having something to take over when something else breaks—sounds great, right? But this also means that you need to double a lot of things. And this violates the basic rule of "the simpler, the better." Stated differently, adding more complexity increases the chance of something breaking. That is why you need to make sure that an HA setup will actually solve the problem you are trying to solve.

One final rule you must know before starting with HA is that if you are going to implement HA, you really need to test everything. This means not only making sure your setup works when everything is normal but also that it keeps working as expected when things go wrong, such as when a component of your HA setup fails. So, you need to test your setup for all things that could potentially break.

Clustering and High Availability

Although *clustering* and *HA* are sometimes used as synonyms, the two are not the same. Therefore, we'll explain the relationship between clustering and high availability in this section.

In a general IT sense, a *cluster* is a set of devices working together in some way. The functions that the set of devices are performing doesn't matter. In most cases, the device is a computer or, more specifically, a server. But it can be other things as well, such as storage units, routers, and switches.

Basically, you can divide clusters into four types (although some in-between forms of clustering probably exist). These four types are high-availability clusters, load-balancing clusters, storage clusters, and high-performance computing (HPC) clusters.

This chapter deals with *high-availability clusters*. A simple way to define this type of cluster is that there is a set of devices, and each device performs a specific action. In the case of a problem, however, one of the other devices in the cluster can take over that action. In short, each machine in a cluster is a backup for another machine in the cluster.

Load-balancing clusters are used to handle a higher load than a single machine can deal with. Here there is a set of machines that will perform the same task. In front of these machines there is usually a device, called a *director*, that distributes the incoming traffic between all the machines. So, each machine performs only a certain portion of the total load received. Web servers are one of the most load-balanced applications.

Storage clusters are sets of devices working together to give you access to data stored on them. A storage cluster makes sure that the failure of one device does not hamper the access to your data, and usually all working devices divide the incoming load between them. There are different ways to build storage clusters; it can be done in the hardware, with software, or with a combination of both.

Finally, there are the *high-performance computing clusters*, which are sets of machines that work together to perform a single set of calculations. This is also called *parallel computing* or *supercomputing*. Instead of having a computer working 10,000 hours on a problem, you let 10,000 computers work on the same problem for an hour. In the end, the same amount of work is done, but the total processing time is much smaller. HPC clusters are used a lot these days for any form of calculation that can be broken down in pieces and then put together again to get the final result. Examples are weather predictions, nuclear reactions, and the flow of liquids.

As you can see, clustering is a pretty big field with a lot of different areas. So, it is wise to study the area of clustering you are going to use before implementing it in production.

Theory of HA

Before going into detail on the practical aspects of HA clustering, first we'll deal with some theoretical aspects. For reasons of simplicity, in the rest of this chapter we presume that you are working with a two-node cluster; let's call the nodes node1 and node2. The two HA software suites we will be using can handle larger clusters, but adding more nodes makes everything a bit more complex, so we will stick to just two nodes.

One of the basic requirements in an HA cluster is that both nodes need to be able to know the status of the other node at every moment. This is because if there is something wrong with node1, node2 needs to react and perform the necessary steps to make sure all the provided services of the cluster keep on working. To know the status of the other node, an HA cluster uses a heartbeat between the nodes; that is, node1 sends a constant stream of data over the network to node2, and vice versa. As soon as a node does not see this message coming in, it presumes that the other node is no longer available and needs to start the services running on the failed node. In its simplest form, this heartbeating is just a single message saying, "OK, I'm still here." But usually the heartbeat messages contain more information, such as the status of the different services running on each node.

The nodes use these heartbeat messages to construct an in-memory overview on the status of the cluster and make decisions based on the overview. These heartbeat messages are thus crucial for the cluster to work correctly and therefore need to be made as redundant as possible. In other words, all possible heartbeat paths that are available should be used.

The most commonly used heartbeat path is the network. Each HA software suite probably implements it in its own way, but just make sure to use each available network connection between the nodes for heartbeating. If there is only one network connection, you are strongly advised to add at least one more so that at least two network paths are available. Most cluster suites even recommend setting up a private network between all nodes solely for heartbeat traffic.

Other heartbeat paths are serial connections, Fibre Channel connections, InfiniBand, or any link that exists between the two nodes. But the basic rule is always the same. Make sure you have at least two paths between the nodes that can be used for heartbeating and preferably a mix of technologies (for example, network and serial). If you don't do this, you could end up with a split brain.

Split Brain and Fencing

A *split brain* in HA cluster terminology refers to the situation in which the two nodes in the cluster are still operational but both think that the other node is dead. This situation occurs when all heartbeat paths between the nodes are down and the nodes do not receive heartbeat messages from each other. In the case of a split brain, each node will start locally all the services that were running on the other node. In the best-case scenario, you would just have the web server running on both nodes and nothing breaks. In the worst-case scenario, you would lose data because both nodes would try to access the same storage at the same time. Of course, you definitely want to avoid that. Therefore, you must make sure that the cluster is in a consistent state at all times.

To prevent split brains, HA clusters use a technology called *fencing*. Fencing makes sure that when a node thinks the other node is unavailable, the other node is unavailable. You can make sure the other node is dead usually by pulling the plug on the other node. Physically powering off a node is the only way to make sure it is really down.

In short, fencing is important as soon as you start using some form of shared data because you will want to avoid losing data at any price.

Resources

Now that you know how an HA cluster keeps track of the status of the other node and how it prevents a split brain, we can talk about a final component in an HA cluster: resources. A *resource* is something that is managed by the HA cluster. This means that resources include the actual service(s) that you would like to be highly available. But usually these services have dependencies on other things. So, these things also need to be managed by the HA cluster and therefore also get defined as resources in the HA cluster.

Common examples of resources are an IP address, a daemon (web server, mail server, file server, and so on), a storage device, a filesystem, and so on. Most HA cluster suites use standardized, simple shell scripts to manage these resources. This is to make the suite less complex, to allow these scripts to be adjusted easily, or to allow you to add your own scripts. Most suites also come with a set of ready-made scripts so that you don't need to create them all on your own.

Usually these resource scripts look like extended init.d scripts (the scripts that are used to start and stop services at boot and at shutdown). These scripts just have more arguments that they accept to be able to tell the script what resource you want managed by the script, such as the IP address to enable or disable that points to the clustered service.

Service or Virtual IP Address

Any service that needs to be available on a network needs to have an IP address that is used to access that service. For normal (nonclustered) services, this usually is the IP address of the machine on which the service is running. However, this method does not work anymore when you operate this service using an HA cluster.

In an HA cluster, the service can run on both nodes of the cluster. So, you cannot use the IP address of the machine to connect to the service since you can't know on which of the two nodes the service is running at a certain moment in time. And if you could, you would need to tell people to use the IP address of the other machine when the service gets moved from one node to the other. So, you need something that will always point to the service, no matter where it is running.

This something is what is called a *service IP address* (SIP) or *virtual IP address* (VIP). It is an additional IP address (next to the normal IP addresses of the machines) that is managed by the HA cluster itself and that is always present on the node where the daemon is running for the service that you want to be HA.

This means that a very basic HA cluster will at least have two resources defined: one resource that controls a daemon like Apache and one resource that controls the clustered IP address used to talk to the daemon. This also means that you need to configure the daemon itself to accept incoming connections from the clustered IP address. Most daemons will listen by default to all IP addresses active on a machine, but some don't.

For the rest of this chapter, we will use the term SIP to refer to a clustered IP address.

HA Cluster Suite Components

Now that we have gone over the basics of HA clustering and introduced some terminology, we are almost ready to start talking about the practical side of things. There is just one final thing that we need to cover, and that is how all the things we talked about present themselves in the software of the HA cluster suite.

It is almost impossible to write a single big piece of code that does all the different aspects that are needed for a working cluster. Therefore, an HA cluster suite is usually a set of daemons, programs, and scripts working together. Sometimes a single daemon does more than one task, but that is then accomplished using different threads inside the daemon. Let's go over the most important components of an HA cluster suite.

The basis for every cluster is the daemon that keeps track of all the members of a cluster. It is this daemon that does the actual heartbeating between all the nodes. It also informs all the other daemons of the cluster suite if there are any changes in the membership of the cluster.

A second important aspect of any cluster is its configuration. This needs to be available on all nodes and needs to always be up-to-date on all nodes so that if a node dies, the other node still knows the current configuration of the cluster. To this end, a daemon is responsible for managing the cluster configuration and making sure that all changes are propagated to all the nodes that are part of the cluster.

Now that the status of the cluster nodes is managed and the configuration of the cluster is managed, you can have a third daemon that will manage the different resources of the cluster. This daemon reads the configuration, and using the current state of the cluster, it will determine where (on which node) to start certain services. This daemon also can monitor the state of these resources themselves and put this information into the configuration so all nodes will know this. Also, when there is a node that appears or disappears, this daemon will check whether there are services that need to be moved to other nodes and does this if needed.

Then there are the different scripts that are used to start and stop the individual resources. These we already mentioned earlier.

Besides this core set of daemons, there is usually some additional software present in an HA cluster suite. Some suites have a daemon specifically for fencing; other suites see fencing as a special resource and let the resource manager do the fencing. Some suites have a special logging daemon that is used by all other components. Sometimes there is also a daemon that checks whether the cluster nodes can access certain network components outside their own network to verify that Internet connectivity is still working, for example. This information can then be used by the resource manager to determine where to run a resource. And then there usually is a set of tools to manage the cluster (change the configuration, report the status, manage resources, and so on).

HA Clustering with CentOS

Now that we have gone over all the basics of HA clustering, it is time to introduce the two clustering suites we will use in this chapter.

The first suite is the Cluster Suite, which is delivered with CentOS. Created and developed by Red Hat, Cluster Suite consists of elements Red Hat has created or that came from companies that Red Hat acquired. You can use the complete suite for three types of clustering, namely, HA clustering, load-balancing clustering, and storage clustering. As you can imagine, the suite is pretty big and consists of a lot of different components. You can find the complete documentation of the Cluster Suite at `http://www.centos.org/docs/5/`. We recommend that you read this documentation when using the Cluster Suite. For the rest of this chapter, we will call this suite CCS (for CentOS Cluster Suite).

The other suite that we will use is the Heartbeat/Pacemaker Suite. These packages are not available from CentOS but can be installed from a third-party repository. The Heartbeat/Pacemaker Suite consists of two separate projects. First, the Heartbeat project has been around for quite a while and is used frequently. In this suite it is used as the cluster membership layer, since, as the name indicates, it does the heartbeating between the nodes. You can find more information about Heartbeat at `http://linux-ha.org`. The other project is Pacemaker, which is pretty new and which grew from the Heartbeat project but is now independent. Pacemaker manages the configuration and the resources in the cluster. For more information for Pacemaker, take a look at `http://www.clusterlabs.org/wiki/Main_Page`. For the rest of this chapter, we will call this suite HPS (for Heartbeat/Pacemaker Suite).

Preparing Your Cluster

Before we continue with the practical part of this chapter, you first need to set up the two nodes that you will use. We will presume that these two nodes are installed with CentOS 5 and are fully up-to-date. Call the nodes `node1` and `node2`. Both nodes should be connected to the Internet because you need to download the HPS suite. We also presume that each node has two network interfaces and that both these interfaces are configured and connected to a network device. Both nodes need to be able to ping each other over both network interfaces.

When you install both nodes, you do not need to install any graphical environment like Gnome or KDE.

For setting up and testing the cluster, disable the firewall and put SELinux in permissive mode so that neither will interfere with the testing. When you are finished with testing and plan on putting the cluster in production mode, we advise you to reenable both the firewall and SELinux to protect your setup.

Installing CCS

Installing CCS is very simple. To install CCS, run the following command:

```
# yum groupinstall "Clustering"
```

Here Yum uses a group called Clustering to do the install. This group consists of all packages that are required to install CCS. And you simply perform this command on both nodes of your cluster.

Installing HPS

Installing HPS is a bit more work since it doesn't come with CentOS. There are different places where you can download HPS. In this chapter, we will use the OpenSUSE build service HA-Clustering repository to get the HPS packages from. To configure Yum to use this repository, run this command:

```
# cd /etc/yum.repos.d/
# wget http://download.opensuse.org/repositories/➥
server:/ha-clustering/RHEL_5/server:ha-clustering.repo
```

This will download a Yum configuration file that will allow Yum to use this repository. Now you can use Yum to download and install HPS using this command:

```
# yum install pacemaker
```

This will install Pacemaker, Heartbeat, and all the necessary dependencies. You will need to perform this installation on both nodes.

Configuring CCS

You can set up CCS in three different ways. First, there are a set of command-line tools that you can use to set up the cluster. Second, there is a GUI tool called *system-config-cluster* to create a cluster configuration. Finally, there is a web-based management tool called Conga. It consists of two daemons. The first one is called `ricci`. This is a daemon that runs on every cluster node. The second one is called `luci`. This daemon is run on one machine (which needs to be part of the cluster), which provides a web interface that can be used to manage the cluster. The `luci` daemon will use the `ricci` daemons running on each node to execute all the actions done inside the web interface. For the rest of this chapter, we will use the Conga environment to configure the cluster.

The central configuration file of CCS is called `/etc/cluster/cluster.conf`. All of the tools mentioned work with this file to configure CCS. As a form of backup, this file will

also be present on every node of the cluster. This is done by CCS itself and does not need
to be done manually.

When you installed CCS, the two Conga daemons were part of the Clustering group.
The ricci daemon is automatically configured to start at boot during this installation. To
start ricci, you can therefore either reboot or run the following command:

```
# service ricci start
Starting ricci:                                              [  OK  ]
```

For the luci daemon, you need to choose one host that will run the daemon. We have
selected to run it on node1. Before you can start luci, you need to configure it. You can do
this using the luci_admin init command, like this:

```
# luci_admin init
Initializing the luci server


Creating the 'admin' user

Enter password:
Confirm password:

Please wait...
The admin password has been successfully set.
Generating SSL certificates...
The luci server has been successfully initialized


You must restart the luci server for changes to take effect.

Run "service luci restart" to do so
```

This command asks you for a password for the admin user. This is the user who
you will use later to log into the web interface. When the command has finished, luci is
ready to start, but first you need to make sure that luci will start at boot, and then you
can start it:

```
# chkconfig luci on
# service luci start
Starting luci: Generating https SSL certificates...  done
                                                             [  OK  ]


Point your web browser to https://node1:8084 to access luci
```

If you get the messages, as mentioned earlier, then `luci` has been started successfully. Then you can surf to the URL as mentioned to test whether `luci` is indeed working. `luci` assumes that DNS is configured properly for all your nodes. If that isn't the case, now is a good time to fix that before continuing with this chapter. Also, when surfing to that URL, a modern browser will give an error on the SSL certificate used by `luci` since it is self-signed. In this case, you can ignore the warning and accept the `luci` certificate. If all is working, you then end up with a login prompt. In the next section, you will log in and make a basic configuration.

Configuring HPS

The configuration of HPS works in layers because HPS consists of two separate applications that work together. It is not a fully integrated suite like CCS is. The first layer is the Heartbeat application. The second layer is the `pacemaker` daemon. You can find all the configuration files of Heartbeat in the directory `/etc/ha.d/`. In that directory, you need to create two files. The first is `ha.cf`, which is the main configuration file for Heartbeat. This is the file used in the following example:

```
# Logging
debug                           0
use_logd                        true

# Misc Options
traditional_compression         off
compression                     bz2
coredumps                       true

# Communications
udpport                         694
bcast                           eth0
bcast                           eth1
autojoin                        any

# Thresholds (in seconds)
keepalive                       1
warntime                        6
deadtime                        10
initdead                        60

# Enable pacemaker
crm                             yes
```

The first section, `Logging`, specifies how Heartbeat does logging. Here you tell Heartbeat to use a separate daemon (called `logd`) and not to log any debug information.

The second section, `Misc Options`, contains some miscellaneous options. The first two enable compression of the messages that are sent in the heartbeat packets between the nodes. You can also let Heartbeat create a core dump if it crashes (they are useful for debugging).

The next section, `Communications`, tells what network paths are used to send heartbeat packets over. The port used by Heartbeat for the heartbeat traffic is 694 (Heartbeat always uses UDP). For the heartbeating, it uses the interfaces `eth0` and `eth1`. In this case, the heartbeat traffic is transmitted using the broadcast address, meaning that everything on the network receives them. Heartbeat also supports using multicast and unicast to transmit the heartbeat traffic. Also specified is that you allow all nodes on the network that use the same parameters.

In the `Thresholds` section, you'll find a set of options that specifies how long Heartbeat will wait with certain activities or actions. The `keepalive` option is the interval between heartbeat messages. The `warntime` and `deadtime` options specify how long Heartbeat will wait to report a change in the state of a node. The `initdead` is a timeout during the startup of Heartbeat to allow all nodes to start up before Heartbeat starts checking the status of the other nodes.

The last section, `Enable pacemaker`, is to tell Heartbeat to use Pacemaker as a resource manager. Heartbeat will then also start Pacemaker as part of its own startup process.

The second configuration file of Heartbeat is `authkeys`. It is used to encrypt the heartbeat messages so that only nodes that have the same key configured can read each other's messages. This is a security feature to prevent an external source from sending heartbeat messages to the nodes of the cluster and making the cluster do things that you don't want. This is the `authkeys` file we used:

```
auth 1
1 sha1 somerandomstring
```

The first tells Heartbeat to use the key with index 1. The second line defines a key with index 1 that uses the SHA1 hash method and `somerandomstring` as the key. In your own cluster, you should change the key to another string. When you create this file, you need to allow only root to read and write the file. If not, Heartbeat will refuse to start. You can do this using this command:

```
# chmod 600 /etc/ha.d/authkeys
```

Now Heartbeat is configured and ready for use so that you can start it. By default Heartbeat isn't configured to start at boot. You therefore first configure Heartbeat to start at boot, and then you start it:

```
# chkconfig heartbeat on
# service heartbeat start
Starting High-Availability services:
                                                    [  OK  ]
```

You can follow the startup of Heartbeat in the log file /var/log/messages. Heartbeat and Pacemaker are now up and running; in the next section, you will create a basic configuration for the cluster.

Building Clusters Using CCS

In the following sections, you will make cluster configurations using CCS.

Creating a Basic Cluster with CCS

In this section, you will create a simple cluster with CCS. As mentioned earlier, you will use the luci web interface to do this. So, surf to the URL luci gave you when you started it, and log in with the admin username and the password you entered. When you have logged in, click the Cluster tab, and then click Create a New Cluster. Fill in a name for your cluster, and fill in the hostname of both nodes and their root passwords. Select Use Locally Installed Packages (you already installed everything needed), and deselect the Enable Shared Storage Support check box. The result should look like Figure 12-1.

Then click the Submit button. Not much seems to have happened. But the open lock symbols behind each node should be closed now. This means that luci succeeded in contacting the ricci daemon on both nodes. Now click Submit again to start with the creation of the cluster. This can take a while, and in our case we got an error back from luci. But that was only because the cluster wasn't started completely. Check /var/log/messages to follow the startup progress, and when everything is ready, click the Cluster tab again. You should see something like Figure 12-2.

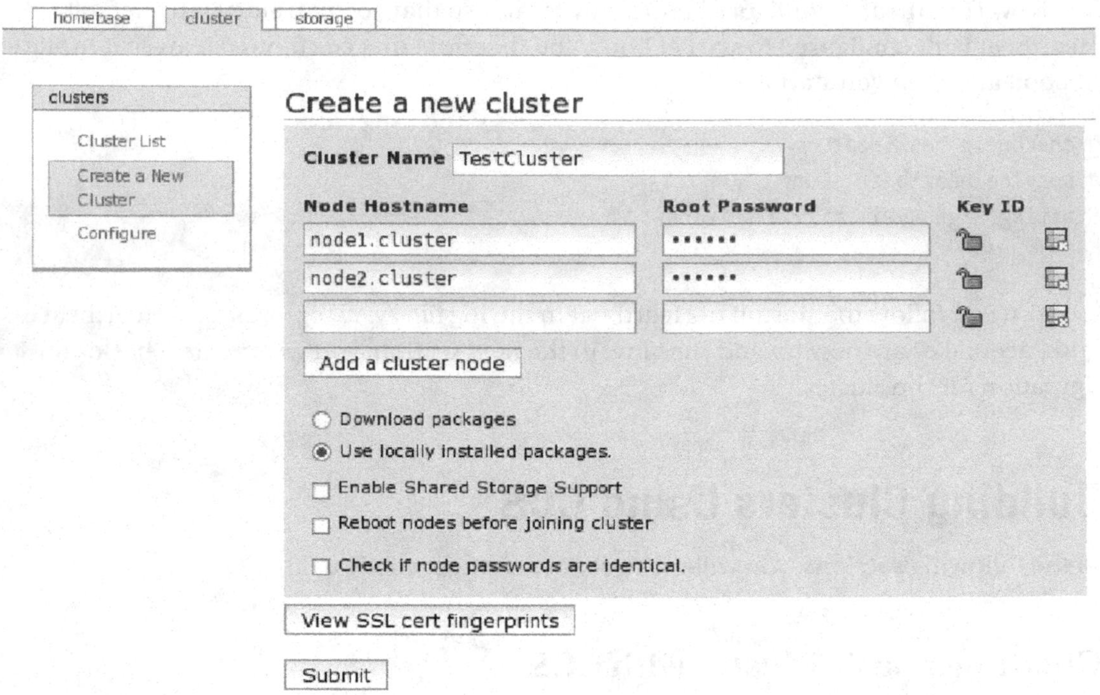

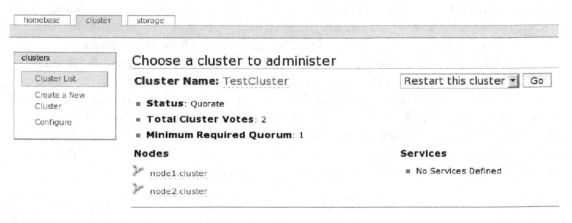

Figure 12-1. *Creating a new cluster using* luci

Figure 12-2. *List of available clusters in* luci

Here you can see the cluster you have just created, including the nodes that are part of it, the status of the cluster, and what services are defined in the cluster (none for the moment). This means that the cluster is up and running and ready for use. This also means that the file /etc/cluster/cluster.conf has been created on both nodes.

To continue configuring the cluster, click the cluster name (all green, underlined pieces of text are links that you can click). You should then end up with Figure 12-3.

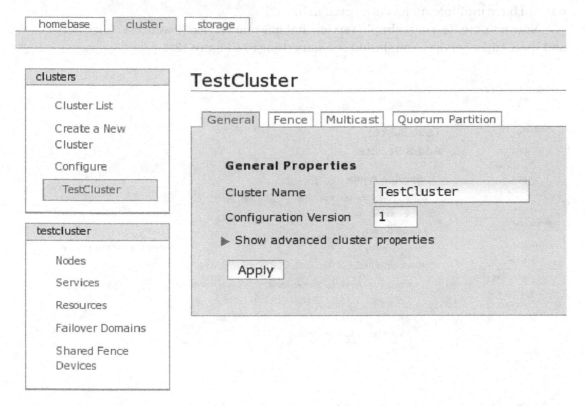

Figure 12-3. *Overview of a cluster in* luci

With the tabs in the center, you can configure the behavior of the cluster. Normally there should be little need to change something there. In the bottom menu on the left, you can see all the different objects you can configure in a cluster. The Nodes item speaks for itself. This can be used to configure, add, or remove nodes. The Service item is an object that contains one or more resources that together form a certain service and that is managed by the cluster. The Resources item is a specific instance of a resource script that is configured with certain parameters. For example, it can be the IP address resource script with a specific service IP address for a certain service. Failover Domains is used to limit where services are run. If you don't specify a failover domain for a service, it can be moved to any node inside the cluster. With failover domains, you can control on which nodes a service can run. Shared Fence Devices includes devices that are used to fence nodes but that are not node specific, such as a power distribution bar of which the sockets can be switched on or off remotely over the network. This kind of power distribution bar can have multiple nodes connected to it.

Now let's create a very simple service that has one service IP address. Click Services and then Add a Service. You should see something like Figure 12-4.

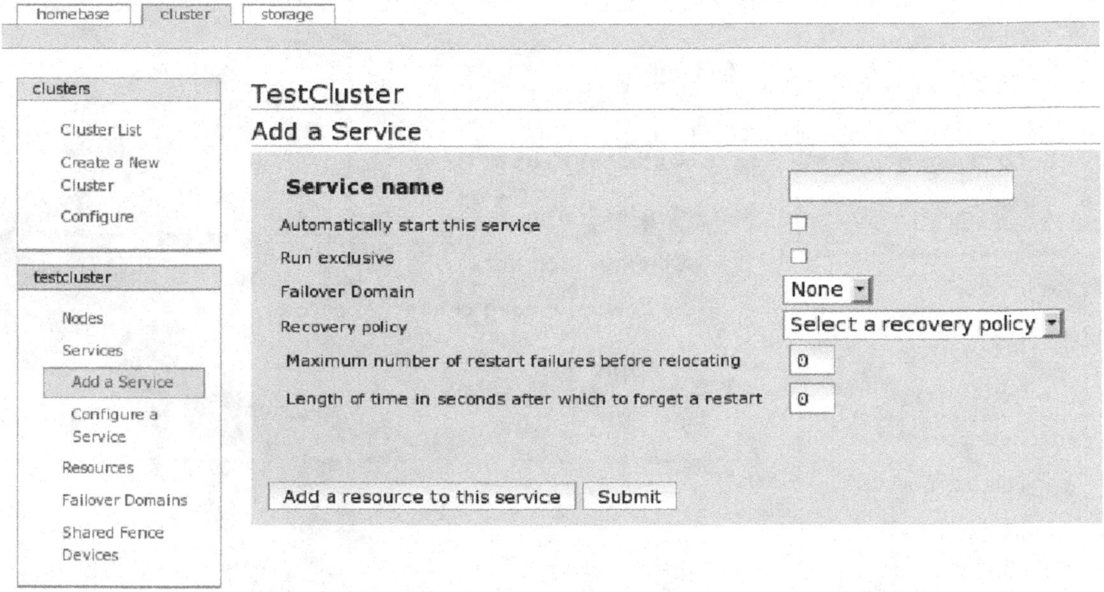

Figure 12-4. *Adding a service using* `luci`

Fill in a name for the service, and choose whether you'd like the service to be started when the cluster is started. Choose a recovery action, and depending on which recovery action you chose, fill in the parameters for the failover action. Then click "Add a resource to this service." You should get Figure 12-5.

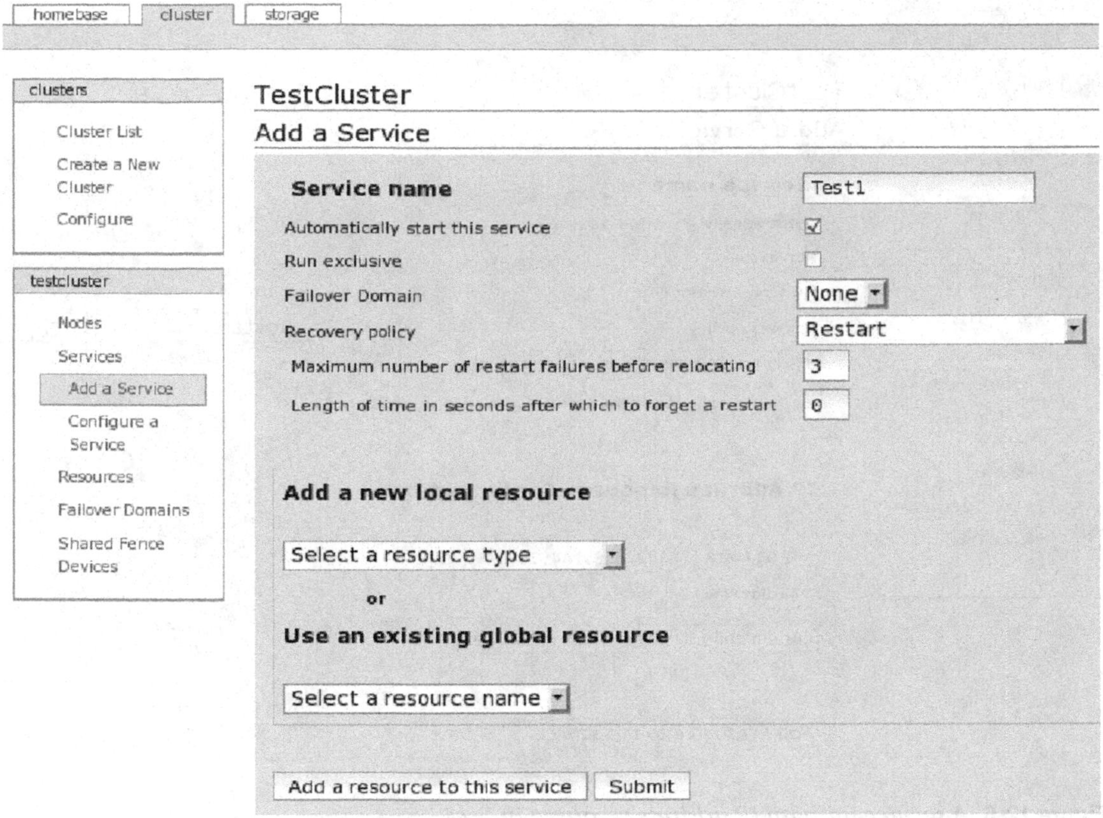

homebase | cluster | storage

clusters

Cluster List

Create a New
Cluster

Configure

testcluster

Nodes

Services

Add a Service

Configure a
Service

Resources

Failover Domains

Shared Fence
Devices

TestCluster
Add a Service

Service name	Test1
Automatically start this service	☑
Run exclusive	☐
Failover Domain	None ▼
Recovery policy	Restart ▼
Maximum number of restart failures before relocating	3
Length of time in seconds after which to forget a restart	0

Add a new local resource

Select a resource type ▼

or

Use an existing global resource

Select a resource name ▼

Add a resource to this service | Submit

Figure 12-5. *Adding a resource to a service using* luci

From the "Add a new local resource" drop-down box, select IP Address. You can configure the resource. Enter an IP address for this service, and select whether the interface link should be monitored. Remember, this IP address should be different from the IP addresses of the nodes. The result should look like Figure 12-6.

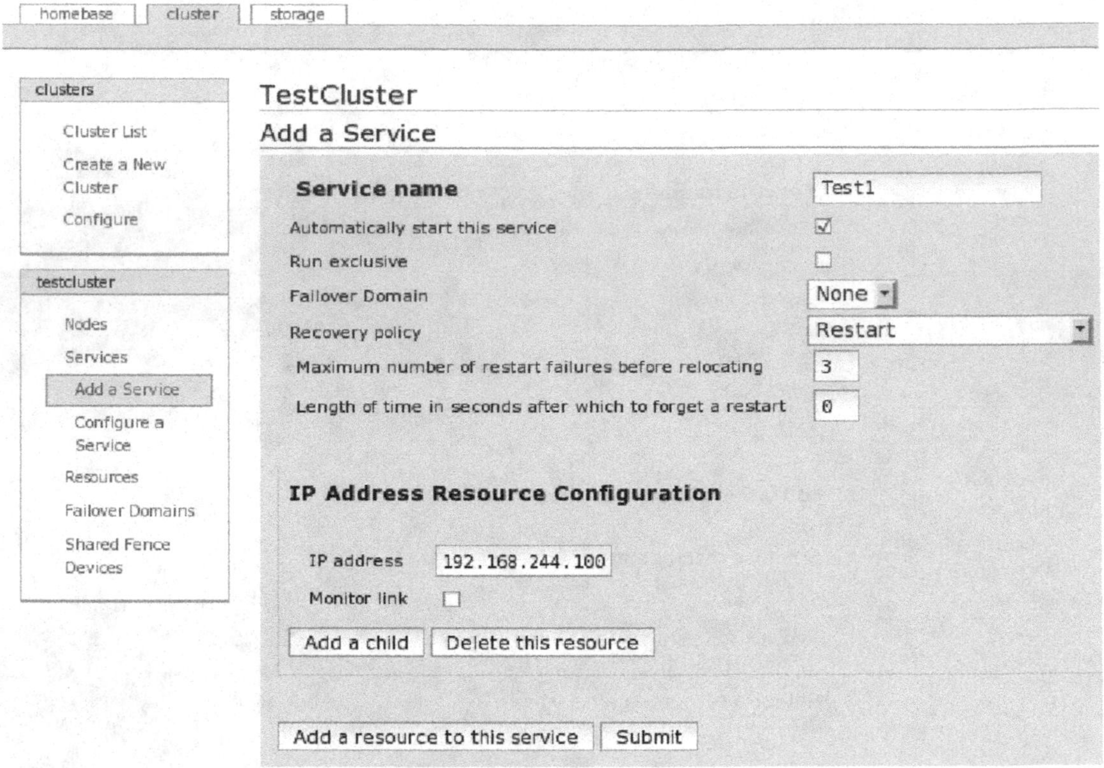

Figure 12-6. *A service with an IP address resource in* `luci`

To finish, click the Submit button, and confirm that you want to create this service. The cluster will now be reconfigured, and the service will be started. When this is ready, click the Services entry in the testcluster menu on the left. You should then see the state of the service and on which node it is running if it was started. You should now also be able to ping the service IP address that you configured.

To double-check the cluster configuration, you can check the content of the file /etc/cluster/cluster.conf, which contains the actual cluster configuration as used by the different daemons.

Advanced Configurations Using CCS

As you have seen, configuring a cluster with CCS is pretty simple using the `luci` web interface. So, now that you have the basics of how this works, let's explain a bit more how you can make certain configurations.

When you look back on how you created the service, you can see that you can add multiple resources to a service and that you can also add child resources to a service. This is used to determine the order in which resources are started and stopped.

A child resource will start only when its parent resource has been started successfully, and a child resource will need to be stopped before its parent resource can be stopped. This method is therefore used when a resource needs something from another resource to function, just like a filesystem needs a storage device present before it can function. So, you define the filesystem resource as a child of the storage device resource.

Multiple resources that are part of a service can be viewed as a group of resources. In this case, there is no explicit order in which the resources are started and stopped. The order of resources in the service usually does not matter. There is an exception to this rule: a set of resources have been predefined with a specific order inside the code of CCS. This order is as follows:

- lvm

- fs

- clusterfs

- netfs

- nfsexport

- nfsclient

- ip

- smb

- script

This means, for example, that an lvm resource is always started before an ip resource and that an smb resource is always stopped before an fs resource. But remember that the child-parent relationship mentioned earlier has precedence over this. You can force a filesystem to be stopped before a service IP address by making the filesystem resource a child of an IP address resource.

You can find more information about these relationships and ordering in Appendix D of the Cluster Administration Guide on the CentOS web site.

Another feature in CCS are the failover domains, but they make sense only if you have a cluster of more than two nodes. Failover domains allow you to limit on which nodes a certain service can run. You can also look at it as a group of nodes.

For example, you have a cluster of four nodes. Two of the nodes are to run a web server, the other a database. Then you create two failover domains: one for the web server that contains the two nodes that will have the web server installed and a second for the database that contains the two nodes that will run the database. And then when you create the services, you assign them to the proper failover domain so that the web server service will run only on the nodes that have a web server and the same for the database service.

Advanced Example with CCS

To finish up this chapter about HA, we'll show an example of CCS that uses some of the advanced options mentioned earlier. First we configured a failover domain as shown in Figure 12-7.

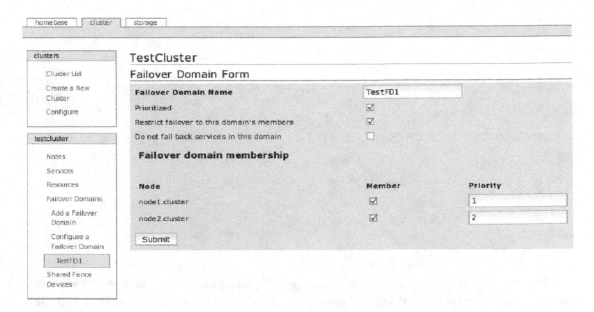

Figure 12-7. *Failover domain example using* `luci`

What you can see is that the failover domain is called TestFD1. The prioritization of nodes is enabled, meaning that you can indicate on which node the services using this failover domain will run by default. Also, failover is restricted to nodes that are part of the failover domain, meaning that services in the domain will never run on nodes not part of the domain. Then you see a list of all nodes in the cluster, if they are a member of the domain, and their priorities (a lower number is a higher priority). In this example, both nodes are members of the domain, and `node1` has the highest priority.

Then we created a service that uses the failover domain shown earlier. Its configuration looks like Figure 12-8.

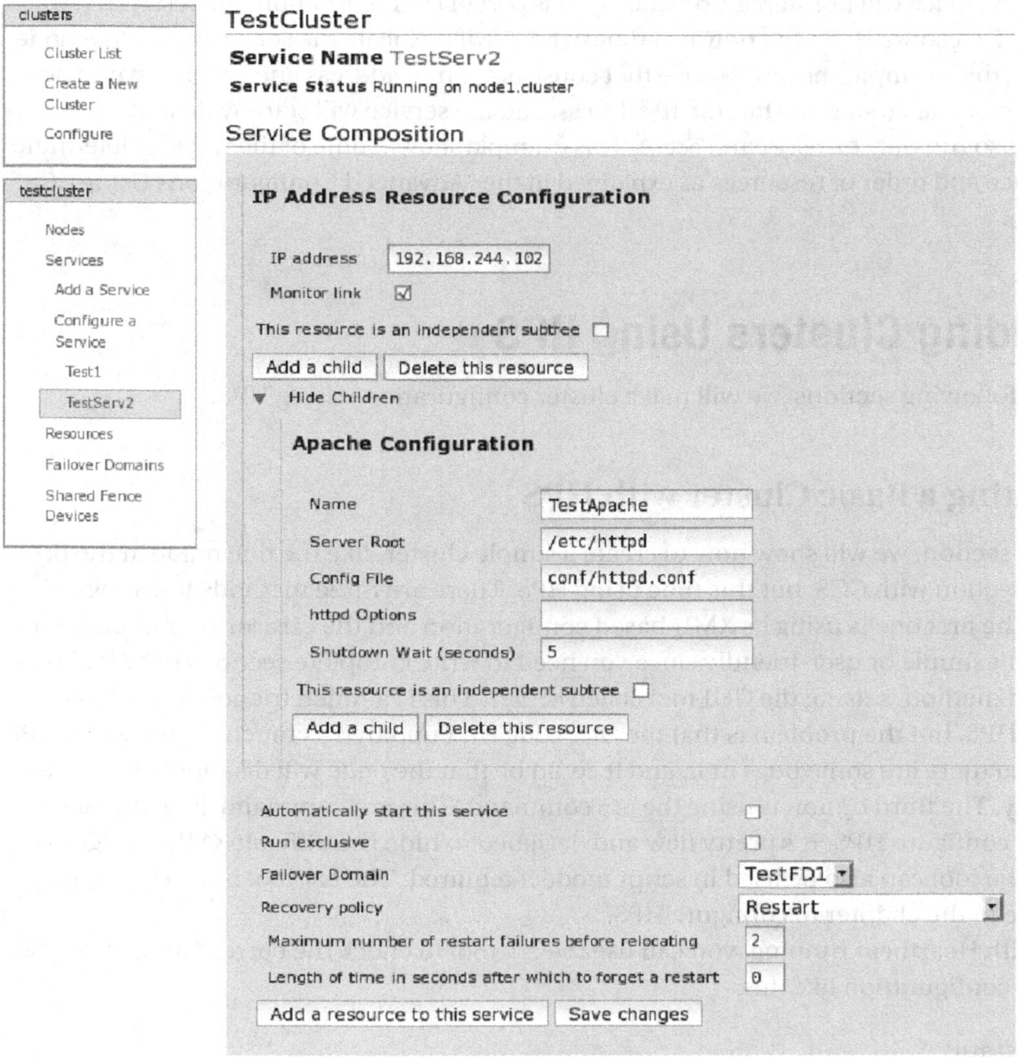

TestCluster

Service Name TestServ2

Service Status Running on node1.cluster

Service Composition

IP Address Resource Configuration

IP address   192.168.244.102

Monitor link   ☑

This resource is an independent subtree ☐

Add a child | Delete this resource

▼ Hide Children

Apache Configuration

Name   TestApache

Server Root   /etc/httpd

Config File   conf/httpd.conf

httpd Options

Shutdown Wait (seconds)   5

This resource is an independent subtree ☐

Add a child | Delete this resource

Automatically start this service   ☐

Run exclusive   ☐

Failover Domain   TestFD1 ▾

Recovery policy   Restart ▾

Maximum number of restart failures before relocating   2

Length of time in seconds after which to forget a restart   0

Add a resource to this service | Save changes

Left navigation:

clusters
- Cluster List
- Create a New Cluster
- Configure

testcluster
- Nodes
- Services
- Add a Service
- Configure a Service
- Test1
- TestServ2
- Resources
- Failover Domains
- Shared Fence Devices

Figure 12-8. *Advanced service example using* luci

This service is called TestServ2 and has two resources. The first resource is an IP address (192.168.244.102), and the link state of the interface running this IP address will be monitored. The second resource is a child of the IP address resource, meaning that it will be started only if the IP address is active, and it needs to be stopped before the IP address can be removed. The second resource is an Apache web server resource named TestApache; the server root is located in /etc/httpd, and the config file of Apache is conf/httpd.conf (the path is relative to the server root). We also specify that when stopping Apache, the resource will wait five seconds after it has stopped the Apache daemon itself before continuing.

The service will not start automatically. It is part of the failover domain TestFD1. It will restart if a resource fails, but only two times; then it will relocate the service to another node.

So, this example shows a service that consists of an IP address and a web server. The web server will be started after the IP address, and the service will start by default on node1. It will also run only on node1 and node2. This example shows some of the ways to determine the place and order of resources as explained in the "Advanced Configurations Using CCS" section.

Building Clusters Using HPS

In the following sections, we will make cluster configurations using HPS.

Creating a Basic Cluster with HPS

In this section, we will show how to create a simple cluster, like the one made in the previous section with CCS, but this time using HPS. There are three methods to configure HPS. The first one is using its XML-based configuration and the cibadmin command. But this isn't simple or user-friendly since you need to write complete sections of XML. The second method is using the GUI tool called hb_gui. This is a much friendlier way to configure HPS, but the problem is that the GUI code isn't updated as much as the rest of HPS code, so there are some bugs in it, and it could be that the code will disappear from HPS entirely. The third option is using the crm command. This is a command-line interactive tool to configure HPS. It's pretty new and designed to hide the difficult XML configuration. The tool can also be used in script mode if required. The crm tool is also what you will use in the chapter to configure HPS.

With Heartbeat running, you can use the crm tool to check the current and, of course, empty configuration like this:

```
# crm status
```

```
============
Last updated: Wed Apr  1 21:29:19 2009
Current DC: node2 (f75fc6cb-6aba-4fd5-a5ee-532d53ebd6c7)
Version: 1.0.2-c02b459053bfa44d509a2a0e0247b291d93662b7
2 Nodes configured.
0 Resources configured.
============

Node: node1 (1e71963e-412a-4359-89a4-c9cb69e1c336): online
Node: node2 (f75fc6cb-6aba-4fd5-a5ee-532d53ebd6c7): online
```

Here you use the crm tool in script mode by directly giving it a command to execute. You can see that Heartbeat has detected both nodes and they are "online." But for the rest, there is no configuration. Let's change that. You will, like in the previous chapter, create a simple cluster with only an IP address. To do this, execute the crm command without any parameters. You should get the following prompt:

```
# crm
crm(live)#
```

You are now at the prompt of the crm tool. The (live) part of the prompt means that you are configuring the current running configuration of HPS. This is then how to configure a service IP address:

```
crm(live)# configure
crm(live)configure# primitive testip IPaddr2 params ip=192.168.244.101
crm(live)configure# end
There are changes pending. Do you want to commit them? y
crm(live)# status

============
Last updated: Wed Apr  1 21:43:48 2009
Current DC: node2 (f75fc6cb-6aba-4fd5-a5ee-532d53ebd6c7)
Version: 1.0.2-c02b459053bfa44d509a2a0e0247b291d93662b7
2 Nodes configured.
1 Resources configured.
============

Node: node1 (1e71963e-412a-4359-89a4-c9cb69e1c336): online
Node: node2 (f75fc6cb-6aba-4fd5-a5ee-532d53ebd6c7): online

testip  (ocf::heartbeat:IPaddr2):      Started node1
crm(live)# quit
bye
```

The first command, configure, enabled the configuration mode in which you can make changes to the configuration of the cluster. Then you configure a primitive, which is HPS-speak for a resource using a "primitive" statement. Then you exit the configuration mode using the end command. The crm tool then asks if you want to save the changes made to the configuration. Then you're asked again for the status of the cluster, where you can see that the newly created resource testip has been started and is running on node1. Finally, you end the crm session using the quit command.

The most important line here is the `primitive`, so we'll explain it. The first option is the name for the resource (in this case `testip`).

The second option specifies the type of resource. This is done by giving the name of the script that will be used to manage the resource (in this case IPaddr2). You can find all resource scripts that are included with HPS in the directory `/usr/lib/ocf/resource.d/heartbeat/`. If you check the content of that directory, you will see that there are a lot of premade scripts included.

The third option is called `params` and means that the following options are parameters for the resource script used for this resource. The only parameter defined here is `ip`, and it is given a value of 192.168.244.101.

You can find more information on how to use the `crm` tool at `http://clusterlabs.org/wiki/Documentation`. On that page, follow the links "CRM command line interface" and "Example Configurations (with the CRM shell)."

Advanced Configurations Using HPS

You can also group and order services/resources in HPS. For this, HPS has more flexible and more powerful methods, but they are also more complex.

Without any additional configuration, defined resources in the HPS cluster will run wherever HPS would like to run them, and HPS will also start and stop the resources in the order HPS prefers. To limit this behavior, HPS uses a concept of constraints. These are rules that specify where to run or where to not run a certain resource. The placement of resources can be based on nodes or other resources. This means that you can specify on which nodes a certain resource should or shouldn't run on. You can also specify whether a resource can or should be run together with another resource or whether a resource cannot run together with another resource.

Constraints can also be used to determine in which order the resources should be started and stopped. This can be specified resource per resource, but this can also be done in what is called *resource sets*. These resource sets are a simpler notation of normal order constraints, which is useful if you have a larger set of resources that need to be started and stopped in order.

Using these three constraint mechanisms (constraining based on node, constraining based on resource, and constraining based on start order), you should be able to make resources do what you want them to do. However, you should probably take some time to think through what exactly you want your resources to do and how to implement these inside HPS using these mechanisms.

Besides the constraints, HPS offers a couple of special resource types with special features or ways to simplify common constraint configurations. These special types are groups, clones, and multistate.

A *group* is just what the name implies; it is a set of resources that belong together. Resources that are in groups will always be run on the same node. And the resources in a group will always be started and stopped in the order of how they are defined in the group. A group is basically a simpler way of using resources and start order constraints.

A *clone* is a resource that is run multiple times and usually with one clone instance per node. It was originally made to run an IP address on multiple nodes at the same time (for load-balancing purposes) but can be used for anything where it seems like it'd be a handy feature. When you create a clone, you can specify how many copies of the clone should run in the cluster and how many copies of a clone can run per node. Inside a clone, you can define one normal resource (a.k.a. *primitive*) or one group resource.

A *multistate* is a special version of a clone. With a normal clone, each instance of the clone is similar to the other instances. With a multistate resource, a clone instance can be either in a *master* or in a *slave* state. These states are just names and can mean whatever you would like them to mean. For a multistate resource, you can specify, besides the normal clone parameters, how many master instances can be in a cluster and in a node. Multistate resources are, for example, used for replicated setups (database, filesystem, and so on). The master instance sends its data to the slave instance.

Advanced Setup with HPS

In this section, we will show how to create an advanced setup with HPS using some of the advanced configuration options available for HPS. Here is the example that was created using the `crm` tool:

```
crm(live)# configure
crm(live)configure# erase
crm(live)configure# primitive ip1 IPaddr2 params ip=192.168.244.101 op monitor \
 interval=60s timeout=10s
crm(live)configure# primitive apache1 apache params /
configfile=/etc/httpd/conf/httpd.conf /
op monitor interval=60s timeout=30s
crm(live)configure# primitive pingd pingd params name=pingd multiplier=100 \
dampen=5s host_list="192.168.244.1"
crm(live)configure# group webserver ip1 apache1
crm(live)configure# clone conn pingd meta globally-unique=false clone-max=2 \
clone-node-max=1
crm(live)configure# location node_pref webserver rule 50: #uname eq node1 \
rule pingd: defined pingd
crm(live)configure# end
There are changes pending. Do you want to commit them? y
crm(live)#
```

Let's go over this line by line. The first two lines enable the configuration mode and erase the configuration so that you can start with an empty cluster. Then you define three resources (called *primitives* by HPS). The first is an IP address resource with the name ip1 that uses the IPaddr2 script to manage the resource, that uses 192.168.244.101 as the IP address, and that will be monitored (checked if it is still running) every minute with a timeout of ten seconds.

The second resource is an Apache resource called apache1. It uses the apache resource script, it will start Apache with /etc/httpd/conf/httpd.conf as the configuration file, and it will be monitored every minute with a 30-second timeout.

The third resource is a ping daemon. It checks whether hosts are available and sets an attribute in the cluster configuration with the result. It is called pingd and uses the pingd resource script. The attribute that the ping daemon will set is called pingd and will have the value 100 if it can reach all the nodes listed. It will change the attribute only if the availability is the same for at least five seconds (this is to prevent a single missed ping from making a resource move), and the host that it will ping is 192.168.244.1 (multiple hosts are separated by spaces).

Then a group called webserver is created that has ip1 and apache1 as members. So, these two resources will always be run on the same node and started in the order as specified.

Then a clone resource is made that has conn as the name and pingd as the resource. The globally unique parameter tells HPS that the clone behaves the same on all nodes, and there will be a maximum of two clones active in the cluster with a limit of one clone per node. The clone is used to run the ping daemon on all nodes of the cluster because we want to test the connectivity of each node.

Then a location constraint is created called node_pref for the group webserver. The constraint has two rules, the first rule has a value of 50 if true, and the rule is #uname eq node1, meaning that hostname equals node1. This rule makes the group webserver run by default on node1 since the default score for a node is 0, but node1 will get a score of 50. The second rule will have the value of the attribute pingd if true, and the rule is defined pingd, meaning true if attribute pingd exists. This rule makes the group web server run only on nodes that can reach the host(s) specified in the ping daemon configuration. If no nodes can reach the host(s) specified, then nothing changes.

Then to finish, the configuration mode is exited, and the changes are applied and committed. The new configuration is live from that moment.

To conclude, this example behaves almost exactly as the example using CCS. The only difference is that here the network connectivity is checked using a ping, while with CCS only the physical state of the interface is checked.

Summary

In this chapter, we introduced you to clustering and explained the purpose of HA clusters. We reviewed the basic theories of how an HA cluster works and how it looks. Then we introduced you to two HA suites that can be used with CentOS, namely, the CentOS Cluster Suite and the Heartbeat/Pacemaker Suite. We then showed how to set up a simple cluster with both suites to give you a feel for how to configure each suite. Then we explained some of the more advanced configuration options for both HA suites. Finally, we showed you an advanced example of a cluster using both suites.

For more in-depth knowledge about both cluster suites and more information on how to configure them, you can refer to the documentation of both suites.

CHAPTER 13

Monitoring Your Network Using Nagios

The concept of network monitoring and the need for it should not be that hard to understand. When you have machines providing services and they are somehow critical to you, you will want to know their state and be alerted if a service is no longer available or is producing some sort of error. That is where monitoring comes into play.

Generally speaking, there are two types of monitoring. First, *system monitoring* is where you check statistics about things local to a computer system (CPU usage, available memory, filesystems, process load, the presence of certain processes, and so on). These are all things that help monitor the "health" of a computer system. For this to work, you need a daemon to run locally on each machine that is going to be monitored. The SNMP protocol provides a common way to get information from other systems and devices. On Linux systems, you can use the Net-SNMP project to be both an SNMP client and an SNMP server. But next to SNMP, a lot of monitoring tools provide their own specialized daemons to get local information from a system. In general, this type of daemon is called a *monitoring agent*.

The second type of monitoring is *network monitoring*. This is where a central machine checks the status of services available on the network. Does the web server still return pages? Does the mail server still accept mails? Can files still be retrieved from the file server? This central monitoring server acts like a special client that speaks to the different services on the network and returns the status to the monitoring server.

Nagios started initially as a network monitoring tool, and system monitoring was added later. The current version of Nagios (3.0) is capable of monitoring large networks, and it can do both system monitoring and network monitoring.

How Nagios Works

The Nagios project consists of the Nagios daemon that does all the actual checks and the web interface that can be used to view the status of everything that is monitored. Then there is the separate Nagios plug-in project that consists of a large collection of scripts that can be used to check specific things (such as HTTP, SMTP, FTP, and so on). So, to have a functional Nagios setup, you need to have both the Nagios daemon and the Nagios plug-ins installed on your system.

The Nagios daemon behaves like a scheduler that runs certain scripts at certain moments. It stores the results of those scripts and will run other scripts if these results change. All these scripts are, of course, the scripts from the Nagios plug-in project or are scripts that you have created.

The web interface will visualize the state of all the things it monitors. It can also change certain runtime aspects of how/when the daemon will do the checks. The web interface cannot be used to actually change the configuration of Nagios, but there are third-party projects that do provide a web interface to manage the Nagios configuration.

You can configure Nagios by defining objects (hosts, services, contacts, commands, and so on) that are linked together. The two most important objects inside Nagios are hosts and services. A *host object* is simply the mapping between an IP address and a name. This name will be used internally in Nagios and will be shown in the web interface. Usually, the DNS name that is linked to the IP address will be used as the name.

A *service object* specifies a certain service that is running on a host that Nagios needs to check. A service object has a link to one host object, and the IP address of this host will be used as the target for the check. The service object also has one link to a command object, which contains the actual script that will be executed to perform the check.

When Nagios needs to send an alert, it uses a *contact object* that is attached to a service or a host. This contact object contains information on how to reach that contact and defines a method for alerting the contact.

Nagios also allows you to put the host, service, and contact objects into groups. These groups can be used to put related objects together and to simplify the Nagios configuration.

Finally, *time periods* are used by Nagios to specify when a check must or must not be done and when contacts will receive notifications.

There are also a couple of object extensions that are used to add extra information to an object or to specify certain relations between objects.

So, to summarize, configuring Nagios consists of mapping your network and all its components to Nagios objects. Nagios will then check all the service objects that exist in your configuration.

Installing Nagios

As always, the recommended way to install packages in CentOS is to use the yum command. The CentOS repositories do not contain any Nagios packages, but luckily there are third-party repositories that have prebuilt Nagios packages for CentOS that you can use. One of those repositories is RPMforge. Before you enable the RPMforge repository, you first need to set up the yum-priorities plug-in. yum-priorities makes sure that third-party repositories do not replace packages that are also in the CentOS repositories. To enable this plug-in, first you need to install it:

```
# yum -y install yum-priorities
```

Then you enable the RPMforge repository by downloading and installing the rpmforge-release package, which contains all the needed configuration files. You can find the correct rpmforge-release package for your system at https://rpmrepo.org/RPMforge/ Using. We used the following:

```
# rpm -ivh http://packages.sw.be/rpmforge-release/\
rpmforge-release-0.3.6-1.el5.rf.i386.rpm
```

Then you need to give each repository a priority. To do this, edit each file that ends with .repo in the directory /etc/yum.repos.d by adding a line like priority=1. The smaller the number, the higher the priority of that repository. We advise you to give all CentOS repositories a priority of 1 (these are all present in the CentOS-Base.repo file). For the RPMforge repository, we used priority 10. This is how the RPMforge repository config file (called rpmforge.repo) should look:

```
# Name: RPMforge RPM Repository for Red Hat Enterprise 5 - dag
# URL: http://rpmforge.net/
[rpmforge]
name = Red Hat Enterprise $releasever - RPMforge.net - dag
#baseurl = http://apt.sw.be/redhat/el5/en/$basearch/dag
mirrorlist = http://apt.sw.be/redhat/el5/en/mirrors-rpmforge
#mirrorlist = file:///etc/yum.repos.d/mirrors-rpmforge
enabled = 1
protect = 0
gpgkey = file:///etc/pki/rpm-gpg/RPM-GPG-KEY-rpmforge-dag
gpgcheck = 1
priority=10
```

Now the system is ready to install Nagios. Use this yum command:

```
# yum install nagios nagios-plug-ins httpd
```

This will install Nagios, the Nagios plug-ins, and the Apache web server (so you can use the web interface). After installation, you will find all the Nagios configuration files in the directory /etc/nagios. The main configuration file is called nagios.cfg, and all the files in the /etc/nagios/objects directory contain all the different object definitions. The file /etc/httpd/conf.d/nagios.conf contains the Nagios configuration for the Apache web server. In the directory /usr/lib/nagios/cgi you'll find CGI scripts that form the Nagios web interface. The /usr/lib/nagios/plugins directory contains all the scripts that Nagios uses to do the checks and to send out alerts. The directory /usr/share/nagios contains the static part of the web interface. All the Nagios log files are located in /var/log/nagios, and the directory /var/nagios contains all the runtime information from Nagios, such as the current status of all defined hosts and services.

Initial Setup of Nagios

The packages used to install Nagios contain a basic configuration of Nagios that is almost ready to start using immediately. There are just a couple of things that still need to be done before you can start Nagios.

The first step is to edit the file contacts.cfg in the directory /etc/nagios/objects/. In that file you will find a definition of a contact object. Replace the current e-mail address nagios@localhost with the e-mail address to which all alerts from Nagios should be sent. Later you'll learn how to add contacts and how to control what alerts are sent out.

Next you create a user that is allowed to log in to the web interface (it is password protected by default). To do this, run the following command:

```
# htpasswd -c /etc/nagios/htpasswd.users nagiosadmin
New password:
Re-type new password:
Adding password for user nagiosadmin
```

The nagiosadmin name is the same username as the one in the contact definition in the previous step. The file /etc/nagios/htpasswd.users is used by the Apache web server and contains the user's name and an encrypted password. Remember the password you use, because you will need it to log in to the web interface.

Now you can start the Nagios daemon and configure it to always start at boot:

```
# chkconfig nagios on
# service nagios start
Starting nagios: done.
```

As a final step, start the Apache web server and also configure it to start at boot:

```
# chkconfig httpd on
# service httpd start
Starting httpd: httpd: Could not reliably determine the server's fully qualified
domain name, using 127.0.0.1 for ServerName
                                                    [  OK  ]
```

If you get the same warning about Apache not being able to get the server's name, you can ignore it for the moment. Apache (and Nagios) will work fine. When you plan to put Nagios into production, check Chapter 5 for how to get rid of this warning.

Now that Nagios and Apache are running, you can surf to `http://<hostname>/nagios/` (replacing `<hostname>` with the actual hostname or IP address of the host where you installed Nagios). Then you will get a request for a username and password. Use `nagiosadmin` as the user, and use the password you entered previously. You then should see the Nagios start page. Next, click the Service Detail link in the Monitoring section of the menu on the left. You then will see a host called localhost with a couple of services that are selected (Current Load, HTTP, SSH, Swap Usage, and so on). These services will normally be in the OK state (green background), and the timestamp for the Last Check field should be fairly recent. If this is the case, then Nagios is running correctly and is actively checking the defined services.

Nagios Configuration Overview

Now that you have your Nagios setup running, you will probably want to expand what is being monitored. Before going into detail on how exactly to add hosts and services to Nagios, we will go over how the configuration of Nagios works, and we'll introduce some of the general concepts that are used in the Nagios configuration files.

The main Nagios configuration file is `/etc/nagios/nagios.cfg`. This is read by the Nagios daemon when it starts. This file contains the options that relate to the operation of the Nagios daemon and contains references to other files that contain specific information.

The web interface of Nagios is based on CGI scripts, as shown earlier, and these CGI scripts use the file `/etc/nagios/cgi.cfg` as the main configuration file. It has options specific to the operation of the web interface and has a reference to the main Nagios configuration file so that it can find the rest of the Nagios configuration.

The list of options on the main Nagios configuration file and in the CGI configuration file is pretty long. We won't go over each option here. Once you have used Nagios for a while and have a better feeling for how it works, we suggest you go over these files again, read the comments for each option, and also read the Nagios documentation included and on the web site. The default settings in these files are OK in most cases.

There are only three options that we want to talk about, and they are all present in the main Nagios configuration file (`nagios.cfg`). The first one is `resource_file`. This resource file is used to configure user-defined macros. A *macro* is Nagios-speak for a variable; macros look like `$<macro name>$` and are used a lot in Nagios, mostly with configuration checks or alert commands. There are 32 user-defined macros available in Nagios, named `$USER1$` through `$USER32$`. In the configuration that comes with the Nagios packages used here, the `$USER1$` macro is used to point to the directory where the plug-ins are installed. All the other user-defined macros are still available. For more information about macros and a complete list of all the available macros, refer to `http://nagios.sourceforge.net/docs/3_0/macros.html`.

The other two options are `cfg_file` and `cfg_dir`. Both are used to point to configuration files that contain object definitions. You could put all these definitions inside the main configuration file, but that would result in one big configuration with no overview and no structure. Therefore, we advise you to put all your object definitions in separate files and to put group definitions into logical groups.

There is no general structure on how to do this; it all depends on your specific situation. A common situation is that all object definitions except those for hosts and services are in one file based on the type of object (commands, contacts, time periods, and so on). The host and service object definitions are usually grouped either in a file based on the environment (production, testing, Linux, Windows, and so on), using the `cfg_file` option, or in a directory where each file in that directory represents one host, using the `cfig_dir` option.

Like for many other configuration files in Linux, the # character is used to indicate comments.

Objects and Templates

You already know that Nagios uses objects to define what to check, and you also learned about the files where you put these object definitions. Now you will see exactly how these object definitions work.

A good way to learn how to define objects is to take a look at the `localhost.cfg` file in the `/etc/nagios/objects` directory. This file contains the host and service definition for localhost, a.k.a. the Nagios server, which you have already seen in the Nagios web interface.

This file starts with the definition of a host object with localhost as the name and 127.0.0.1 as the IP address. Then it defines a host group called `linux-servers` that has localhost as a member. Then it defines eight services, such as the service named `PING` that is tied to localhost and that uses the `check_ping` command to do the actual check.

You may notice that all these definitions are pretty short. This is because Nagios provides a template system in which you can create a template of how a host or service should look and then use these templates for real hosts and services by just filling in the specific details for that host or service.

If you look back at the `localhost.cfg` file, you will see that all host and service definitions there have the `use` keyword. This keyword is used to point to a template. For example, the localhost definition uses template `linux-server`.

In the included example configuration, all templates are defined in the file `templates.cfg`. If you will look in that file, you will see that it contains template definitions for contact, host, and service objects. Let's use the localhost object as an example of how this process works. This is the definition of the localhost object:

```
define host{
        use                     linux-server
        host_name               localhost
        alias                   localhost
        address                 127.0.0.1
        }
```

This object uses the template linux-server and defines the host_name, alias, and
address options. This is then what the linux-server template looks like:

```
define host{
        name                    linux-server
        use                     generic-host
        check_period            24x7
        check_interval          5
        retry_interval          1
        max_check_attempts      10
        check_command           check-host-alive
        notification_period     workhours
        notification_interval   120
        notification_options    d,u,r
        contact_groups          admins
        register                0
        }
```

As you can see, this definition looks a lot like the localhost definition, but what makes
this a template is the register option, which is set to 0 here. This tells Nagios that this
object is not a real object but is usable only as a template. You can also see that, besides
other normal options, this template used another template called generic-host. This template looks like this:

```
define host{
        name                         generic-host
        notifications_enabled        1
        event_handler_enabled        1
        flap_detection_enabled       1
        failure_prediction_enabled   1
        process_perf_data            1
        retain_status_information    1
        retain_nonstatus_information 1
        notification_period          24x7
        register                     0
        }
```

This template does not use another template, so the template chain stops here. When Nagios starts, it will follow the template chain for each object and put all the defined options together. In this case, that would look like this:

```
define host{
        host_name                   localhost
        alias                       localhost
        address                     127.0.0.1
        check_period                    24x7
        check_interval                  5
        retry_interval                  1
        max_check_attempts              10
        check_command                   check-host-alive
        notification_period             workhours
        notification_interval           120
        notification_options            d,u,r
        contact_groups                  admins
        notifications_enabled           1
        event_handler_enabled           1
        flap_detection_enabled          1
        failure_prediction_enabled      1
        process_perf_data               1
        retain_status_information       1
        retain_nonstatus_information    1
        notification_period             24x7
        }
```

As you can see, using templates makes defining objects a lot simpler and shorter and means you need to make changes in only one place instead of having to edit each object separately.

One question you will undoubtedly have is, what happens when an option is defined in multiple places? The basic rule is that locally defined options replace the ones defined in the template. So, an option defined in the localhost object will override any others if that option is present in both the linux-server and generic-host templates. If an option is defined in the linux-server and generic-host templates but not in the localhost object, then the value from the linux-server template is used.

You can find more information about this template system in the Nagios documentation and at http://nagios.sourceforge.net/docs/3_0/objectinheritance.html.

Basic Nagios Configuration

Now that you know how the configuration of Nagios works and how to use and create templates, it is time to put this into practice and define a couple of new hosts and services. In this example, we will show how to add the definitions to monitor a web server. But you can use this procedure for any type of service as long as there is a plug-in for it or you create one yourself.

The first step is to look to see whether a plug-in is available that can check the service you want to monitor. For this example, we want to do a ping to the web server to see whether it can be reached over the network, and we want to do an actual HTTP request to see whether the web server itself is still running and functioning normally.

The first place to look for plug-ins is in the directories /usr/lib/nagios/plug-ins/ and /usr/lib/nagios/plug-ins/contrib/. For our example, the check_ping and check_http commands are available. If you can't find what you need, the second place to look is at http://www.nagiosexchange.org/, where you will find a lot of contributed plug-ins.

Once you locate the plug-in you want to use, you need to find out exactly how it works. To do this, run the plug-in with the --help argument. This will show you all the available options for each plug-in.

Now that you have found a plug-in and know how it works, you can move to the next step. Define the check command inside Nagios. For this example, both the ping and http commands are already defined in the file commands.cfg. This is how they look:

```
# 'check_ping' command definition
define command{
        command_name    check_ping
        command_line    $USER1$/check_ping -H $HOSTADDRESS$ -w $ARG1$ -c $ARG2$ -p 5
        }


# 'check_http' command definition
define command{
        command_name    check_http
        command_line    $USER1$/check_http -I $HOSTADDRESS$ $ARG1$
        }
```

Defining a command is pretty simple, as you can see. It requires only two lines: the name of the command and the actual command that needs to be executed to run the check. It also shows an example of how to use macros inside Nagios. The $USER1$ macro is replaced by the directory where the plug-ins are installed (/usr/lib/nagios/plugins/). The $HOSTADDRESS$ macro is replaced by the value given for the address option of the host for which the check is run. This is normally the IP address of the host. The $ARG1$, $ARG2$, and so on, macros are replaced by arguments given to the check command in the service object definition. We will return to this when we show how to create the service objects.

The next step is to create a host object for the web server. To do this, create a new file in the directory /etc/nagios/objects called webserver.cfg with this content:

```
define host{
        use                     linux-server
        host_name               webserver
        alias                   Apache HTTP Server
        address                 192.168.0.11
        hostgroups              linux-servers
        }
```

This defines a host using the template linux-server called webserver with the alias Apache HTTP Server (the alias is shown in the web interface and can be used when sending out alerts). The address is 192.168.0.11, and it is part of the host group linux-servers. The template linux-server and the host group linux-servers are already part of the example configuration included with the Nagios packages.

Moving on, the next step is where you create the service objects for the services you want to check. As mentioned, you want to do a ping check and an http check. To do this, add the following lines to the webserver.cfg file:

```
define service{
        use                     local-service
        host_name               webserver
        service_description     PING
        check_command           check_ping!100.0,20%!500.0,60%
        }

define service{
        use                     local-service
        host_name               webserver
        service_description     HTTP
        check_command           check_http!-u /index.html -t 5
        }
```

Both service objects use the local-service template and have webserver as the host. service_description is a name for the specific service and has to be unique per host. Finally, the command to use to do the service check is defined. You can also see how the arguments are given to the command. These arguments come after the name of the command to use and are separated by the ! character. In the case of the ping check, two arguments are given to the command. If you put these arguments together with the command definition, the following is the actual command executed to perform the check of the service:

```
/usr/lib/nagios/plugins/check_ping -H 192.168.0.11 -w 100.0,20% -c 500.0,60% -p 5
```

The same process is done for the http check, but it has only one argument.

Now that you've created all the necessary configurations, the next step is to tell Nagios to use your newly created configuration file webserver.cfg. To do this, edit the main Nagios configuration file (nagios.cfg), and add this line to it (preferably in the same place as the other cfg_file options):

```
cfg_file=/etc/nagios/objects/webserver.cfg
```

This will tell Nagios to also read the webserver.cfg file and use all of the object definitions that it contains.

The next step is to check the updated Nagios configuration. The Nagios daemon can run a syntax check on the configuration so you can check whether everything is OK before you tell Nagios to actually start using it so that you don't break Nagios. To do this, run the following command:

```
# nagios -v /etc/nagios/nagios.cfg

Nagios 3.0.6
Copyright (c) 1999-2008 Ethan Galstad (http://www.nagios.org)
Last Modified: 12-01-2008
License: GPL

Reading configuration data...

Running pre-flight check on configuration data...

Checking services...
        Checked 10 services.
Checking hosts...
        Checked 2 hosts.
Checking host groups...
        Checked 1 host groups.
Checking service groups...
        Checked 0 service groups.
```

```
Checking contacts...
        Checked 1 contacts.
Checking contact groups...
        Checked 1 contact groups.
Checking service escalations...
        Checked 0 service escalations.
Checking service dependencies...
        Checked 0 service dependencies.
Checking host escalations...
        Checked 0 host escalations.
Checking host dependencies...
        Checked 0 host dependencies.
Checking commands...
        Checked 24 commands.
Checking time periods...
        Checked 5 time periods.
Checking for circular paths between hosts...
Checking for circular host and service dependencies...
Checking global event handlers...
Checking obsessive compulsive processor commands...
Checking misc settings...

Total Warnings: 0
Total Errors:   0

Things look okay - No serious problems were detected during the pre-flight check
```

If the last line of the output says that everything is OK, you can proceed. If not, look at all the warnings and all the errors shown in the output and fix them before continuing.

The last step is where you tell Nagios to use your updated and checked configuration. You can do this using the following command:

```
# service nagios reload
Running configuration check...done.
Reloading nagios configuration...done
```

Now the new configuration is active, and you should be able to see the new host and its services in the web interface. It could be that Nagios does not execute the new service checks immediately. Until it does the checks, you will see PENDING as the status.

You can use this procedure to add checks for any service and host that you want, as long as there is a plug-in that can check the service.

Contacts and Notifications

Now that you know how to set up Nagios to check your network, you probably want to be informed if there are any changes in the state of the things that are being checked. Nagios does that using *notifications*. A notification will be sent out if the state of a service or host changes.

To whom Nagios sends these notifications depends on who is a member of the contact group that is attached to the service for which a notification will be sent out. In the examples used in this chapter, you can see that all the templates have defined a contact group called admins, meaning that every contact that is a member of the group admins will receive the notifications.

If you look in the file /etc/nagios/objects/contacts.cfg, you will see that the contact nagiosadmin is the only member of the admins group. In the same file, you can also see that the default e-mail address specified for that user is nagios@localhost. Feel free to change this if you want notifications to be sent to another e-mail address.

In the example configuration, all notifications will be sent out using e-mail. You can check that in the templates.cfg file (also present in /etc/nagios/objects) in the generic-contact template. service_notification_commands and host_notification_commands both use a command that uses the mail program to send the notifications. But because these notification commands work like any other command (see the file commands.cfg), you can send out alerts for anything you can write a script for. Other commonly used notification methods are SMS messages and pagers, but you can find a lot of other examples on the Internet.

Now that you know to whom notifications are sent, you still need to know when these will be sent. This is controlled using the notification_period options present in the host, service, and contact object definitions. In the example configuration used, these are all defined in the templates. With this option, a time period is specified that says during which periods notifications can be sent out. These time periods are defined in the file timeperiods.cfg.

This time period has to be set both for a host/service and for a contact. The time period for both the host/service causing the notification and for the contact receiving the notification must allow the notification to be sent out. This allows you to control when notifications are sent on two levels. One level is that of the services and hosts being checked, and the other is that of the contacts being alerted. If the time when the notification needs to be sent falls outside of either one (or both) of the time periods, no notification will be sent out about this host/service to this contact.

You can find more information about how notifications work in Nagios at this URL: http://nagios.sourceforge.net/docs/3_0/notifications.html.

Advanced Nagios Configuration

In this chapter, we used the example configuration that comes with the Nagios package to show how to create checks for networked services. With these examples, you can start setting up Nagios for your own environment. But we have covered only the basics of what Nagios can do and what features it has. So, in this section, we'll give you a couple of pointers on what else is possible and where to find more information.

In the examples shown, we have checked services only over the network (except for those checks about the Nagios server itself). But Nagios can also be used to check things locally on systems (disk space, memory usage, CPU usage, and so on). For this, Nagios uses a special daemon running on each system or SNMP. You can find more details on how to do this for another Linux system at http://nagios.sourceforge.net/docs/3_0/monitoring-linux.html, for Windows systems at http://nagios.sourceforge.net/docs/3_0/monitoring-windows.html, and for systems that provide SNMP access at http://nagios.sourceforge.net/docs/3_0/monitoring-routers.html.

Nagios can, besides performing checks of services, also accept results for checks from external sources. These types are called *passive checks* in Nagios. This feature is used to forward SNMP traps to Nagios, for example, or to set up distributed monitoring where multiple Nagios servers send the check results to a central Nagios server. You can find more information about this at http://nagios.sourceforge.net/docs/3_0/passivechecks.html.

Another very nice feature of Nagios is the ability to express relations between hosts and between services. For hosts, there are two kinds of relations that you can specify. *Parent-child relations* are used to tell Nagios how all the hosts that it knows about are connected. This creates a kind of tree structure of the network, and Nagios can use this to see whether a host is really down or whether it is just unreachable because another host is down and the network traffic passes through that other host. This is explained in more detail at http://nagios.sourceforge.net/docs/3_0/networkreachability.html.

A second kind of relationship that you can specify for hosts, as well as for services, is called a *dependency* in Nagios. For example, you can use a dependency to express that a web application needs a database server that is running in order to function. You can then use this relation to filter alerts, such as not sending an alert about the web application when the database is down but sending an alert from the web server hosting that web application when the database is down.

To conclude, we suggest that you go over the Nagios documentation at http://nagios.sourceforge.net/docs/3_0/toc.html since it explains everything in great detail.

Summary

In this chapter, you were introduced to Nagios and how to use it to monitor your network. We explained how Nagios works and then showed how to install it from the RPMforge repository. Using the example configuration included in the Nagios package, we showed how to set up Nagios and start it, and then we explained the basics of how to configure Nagios. Then we set up a basic example where we let Nagios check some network services. Finally, we explained how contacts are used to send out notifications from Nagios, and we reviewed some more advanced options available in Nagios and where to find documentation about them.

With this chapter, you have reached the end of this book. In the first part, you were introduced to CentOS, and you got to know the basics about the distribution. In the second part, you learned how to set up the different production services that come with CentOS like the Apache web server and the Samba file server. In the final part, you learned how to set up different enterprise features with CentOS such as high availability and monitoring.

Index

You Need the Companion eBook

Your purchase of this book entitles you to buy the companion PDF-version eBook for only $10. Take the weightless companion with you anywhere.

We believe this Apress title will prove so indispensable that you'll want to carry it with you everywhere, which is why we are offering the companion eBook (in PDF format) for $10 to customers who purchase this book now. Convenient and fully searchable, the PDF version of any content-rich, page-heavy Apress book makes a valuable addition to your programming library. You can easily find and copy code—or perform examples by quickly toggling between instructions and the application. Even simultaneously tackling a donut, diet soda, and complex code becomes simplified with hands-free eBooks!

Once you purchase your book, getting the $10 companion eBook is simple:

❶ Visit **www.apress.com/promo/tendollars/**.

❷ Complete a basic registration form to receive a randomly generated question about this title.

❸ Answer the question correctly in 60 seconds, and you will receive a promotional code to redeem for the $10.00 eBook.

2855 TELEGRAPH AVENUE | SUITE 600 | BERKELEY, CA 94705